22·99

Vocational A-level
Information and Communication Technology

Vocational A-level Information and Communication Technology

Maggie Banks, Peter Bradshaw, Bob Crooks, Alison Duff, Alan Jarvis and Julia Wright

Series Editor: Jenny Lawson

Pearson Education Limited
Edinburgh Gate
Harlow
Essex CM20 2JE, England
and Associated Companies throughout the world

ISBN 0 582 35709–8

British Library Cataloguing-in-Publication Data

A catalogue record for this book is available from the British Library.

Set by 3 in Humanist, Rotis Serif, Caslon
Produced by Pearson Education Limited
Printed by Henry Ling Ltd, at the Dorset Press, Dorchester, Dorset

Contents

About the Authors

The authors responsible for writing the seven chapters of this book have, between them, more than 100 years of valuable experience of ICT – in the computing industry; as teachers delivering GNVQ courses; as examiners, preparing course specifications, devising student assessment material, marking examinations and verifying students' portfolios; and as IT consultants working for government organisations such as QCA and FEDA. They have all worked for the GNVQ awarding bodies and several are still active in the preparation of examination materials, with in-depth knowledge of the specifications and assessment methods. They are all totally committed to the GNVQ qualification and, as examiners, know exactly what is expected of students on a Vocational A-level course.

Maggie Banks BSc Physics (1969); PGCE Physics (1981); Diploma in Computer Education (1989)

Maggie is an independent Education and IT Consultant, specialising in the development of ICT-based qualifications and assessments. As Chief Examiner and Chief Standards Moderator for ICT for the GNVQ new model pilot, she has been responsible for the standardisation of marking and moderation across all awarding bodies. She has also been involved in the development of the new units and assessments at all Foundation, Intermediate and Advanced level GNVQs. Maggie has been an External Verifier for City and Guilds for the past five years. She taught for ten years, latterly as Head of IT at Cornwallis School, Maidstone, and was then an IT advisory teacher in Kent for three and a half years. Her writing has been supported by her partner, Rod Banks, who has worked in the computer industry for 30 years, including selling systems to local government and major UK companies.

Peter Bradshaw BSc (Joint Hons) Mathematics and Physics with Computing and Education (1978); PGCE Secondary (1979)

Peter has worked in IT education for 20 years. He has been a teacher, IT co-ordinator, advisory teacher, programme leader for BTEC National IT and GNVQ co-ordinator. Involved in GNVQ since the 1992 pilot, Peter has written and edited tests and unit specifications and is Chief Examiner for GNVQ IT Part One. He has also examined at GCSE and GCE A-level Computing and helped to write the new OCR ICT A/AS-level specifications. Seconded to the DfEE, his most recent appointment is as a facilitator to the Online Community of School Leaders, part of the government's newly established National College of School Leadership. This followed on from an appointment as a Tesco SchoolNet 2000 advisory teacher in which he has worked with schools and on an Internet-based project for the Millennium Experience. He has published material for Foundation GNVQ IT and has worked in all phases of education from first school to further education. Outside of education, he co-ordinates a folk festival, is a morris dancer and qualified signalman, croquet coach and coach driver!

Bob Crooks BSc (Hons) Physics (1969); PGCE (1970)

Bob has over 20 years' computer industry experience as a software specialist on mainframe, minicomputer and microprocessor systems. He has worked in further education since 1993 and is currently Programme Manager for GNVQ ICT, A-level Computing and A-level ICT at Richmond-upon-Thames College. He has also worked as an examiner for OCR and AQA examination boards.

Alison Duff BEng Manufacturing Systems Engineering (1994); PGCE Information Technology & Games (1995)

Alison Duff worked for Ford Motor Company during her degree course studying design and engineering systems and has worked in IT since completing her PGCE course. She teaches at the City Technology College Kingshurst, co-ordinates the GNVQ ICT courses and internally verifies work across Levels 2 and 3; she also delivers Key Skills. Alison was involved in the writing of the specifications for RSA/C&G optional units, and also works for OCR writing Full and Part One award GNVQ question papers. She has more recently been involved with contributing to the TTA numerical question paper project. She works for FEDA as a consultant for Key Skills and has been involved with the writing of the new Keys Skills IT Level 1 and 2 papers. Outside of education, Alison is a keen scuba diver and skier and, whenever possible, follows these pursuits abroad.

Alan Jarvis BSc (1979); Cert. Ed. (FE) (1997); MSc Business Information Technology (1999)

Alan spent 15 years in the commercial IT industry working in programming, user support and training. For the past five years, Alan has been working at Southgate College in North London as an IT lecturer and course manager on GNVQ and HNC courses. He was involved in the writing of the unit specifications for OCR/AQA optional units for Intermediate and Advanced IT. Along with his partner, Neela, who also works at Southgate College, he has recently been involved in setting up the School of IT website and ILT pilot project. Neela also worked closely with Alan on the *Systems Analysis* chapter.

Julia Wright BSc Management Sciences (1981); PGCE Business Studies & Economics (1984)

Julia is a GNVQ External Verifier for OCR Examinations Board and a Key Skills Trainer for FEDA. She has also worked as an IT Scrutineer for QCA (1997) and as Lead Reviewer for the Part One GNVQ Controlled Assignment. Julia has been involved in GNVQ delivery since 1994. She was involved in the writing of the unit specifications for OCR/AQA optional units, and test specifications for the new GNVQ award. Julia has also been involved in unit test writing for both new and old GNVQ specifications. She has taught Business and IT in Bradford schools for 16 years and is currently GNVQ co-ordinator at Fulneck School in Pudsey.

Jenny Lawson BSc (Hons) Mathematics (1973)

Jenny has worked in a computing/IT environment for over 30 years, as a programmer, systems analyst, director of a software house, a trainer in IT, a teacher and an examiner. She taught in schools and colleges for ten years, including five years as Head of Computing at Woking Sixth Form College. As Chief Examiner and Vocational Adviser to the RSA, for many years Jenny worked on the IT GNVQ qualification almost since its inception, being involved in all aspects of syllabus writing, test specification writing, examination paper production, marking and awarding, plus the training of other examiners. Her educational consultancy work continues and has included projects on IT Key Skills, and A/AS-level ICT and Computing.

For the last ten years, Jenny has been director of a publishing company, First Class Publishing, which utilises IT to the full. She is author of the previous *Foundation GNVQ ICT* book published by Addison Wesley Longman (Pearson Education). Alongside this Vocational A-level ICT book, Jenny has written a book for Intermediate GNVQ ICT, and, as series editor, has overseen the preparation of books to support the optional units at Intermediate GNVQ and Vocational A-level ICT.

Introduction

This book is written for students of the Vocational A-level Information and Communication Technology (ICT) course and covers the six mandatory units as specified by the Qualifications and Curriculum Authority (QCA), plus one optional unit which is externally assessed – *Impact of ICT on Society*. Other books in the series cover the remaining optional units offered by the various awarding bodies: OCR, AQA and Edexcel.

What is Vocational A-level ICT?

Advanced GNVQs were first introduced in 1993 and were designed to offer students a vocational alternative to A-levels, each Full Award GNVQ being broadly equivalent to two A-levels. Since then, the GNVQ award has been restyled to offer flexibility and even more choice to students, and three awards are now available:

- ✪ A 3-unit award – in a limited number of subjects, including Information and Communication Technology – broadly equivalent to GCE AS-level award.
- ✪ A 6-unit award, sometimes called the single award – equivalent to a single GCE A-level.
- ✪ A 12-unit award – equivalent to two GCE A-levels.

GNVQs are now referred to as the Vocational A-levels, because they are related to broad areas of the world of work, such as ICT. A Vocational A-level qualification in Information and Communication Technology (ICT) helps you to develop an understanding of ICT and introduces you to some of the skills and knowledge you will need to go on to work or further study.

In Vocational A-level ICT, there are six **mandatory units**:

1   Presenting Information
2   ICT Serving Organisations
3   Spreadsheet Design
4   Systems Installation and Configuration
5   Systems Analysis
6   Database Design

These units cover all the material needed to understand how ICT is used at work. Each awarding body then offers more units, called **optional units**. These give you the opportunity to choose areas that you find particularly interesting, and to broaden your experience or to specialise in particular areas of ICT, whichever you prefer.

In ICT, a 3-unit award is also available. For this award, there is no choice – you study only the first three mandatory units.

How do you achieve an award in Vocational A-level ICT?

For Vocational A-level ICT, you must complete a minimum number of units:

✪   3 units for the 3-unit award – the first three mandatory units
✪   6 units for the 6-unit award – the first three mandatory units plus any three others chosen from the remaining mandatory units and the full range of optional units
✪   12 units for the 12-unit award – the six mandatory units, plus another six units selected from the full range of optional units

Depending on your timetable, you may have the opportunity to take some additional units. You will need to check exactly what units your school or college offers.

The assessment is designed to reward students for what they can do as well as what they know. Each unit is assessed *either* by portfolio assessment, *or* by an externally set assessment, *not* by both. The type of external assessment depends on the examination board and the unit being assessed: for any given unit, an awarding body may decide to rely on portfolio assessment, or, for external assessment, provide a written test, or set an assignment. Details of how each board assesses each unit is shown in the *Examination Guide* on page 361.

There is a minimum number of externally assessed units for Information and Communication Technology:

- ✪ 1 unit for the 3-unit award
- ✪ 1 (not 2) unit for the 6-unit award
- ✪ 3 (not 4) units for the 12-unit award

This means that most of your work will be assessed as you work through the course (continuous assessment). Tests and assignments are scheduled to take place at set times of the year (e.g. January or June), after you have worked on a particular unit (end testing). Details of each board's arrangements are shown in a table in the *Examination Guide* on page 361. Whichever award you are aiming for, you will need to refer to this grid and be sure to select at least the minimum number of externally assessed units.

Each unit, whether assessed by portfolio or external assessment, is individually graded on a scale A to E. Then, a single grade of A to E is decided on a points basis, to reflect your performance over all your units; this single grade is then your 'final' grade for the Vocational A-level award (as with GCE A/AS-levels) and can be used for entry to higher education on the usual points basis.

While studying for your Vocational A-level, you will have the opportunity to gain the Key Skills qualifications. As far as possible, evidence of Key Skills may be seen within your portfolio of work, and your teacher will advise you on how you can build evidence of Key Skills into your assignments. The *Key Skills Guide* on page 355 also provides useful information about Key Skills.

What is a unit?

A unit covers one area of study. For example, Unit 5 of Vocational A-level ICT concentrates on 'Systems Analysis'.

Each unit specification then has four main headings:

- ✪ **About this unit**
- ✪ **What you need to learn**
- ✪ **Assessment evidence**
- ✪ **Essential information for teachers** (including teaching and assessment strategies, notes on resources and signposting for Key Skills)

The final section is written as guidance for teachers, but since your success on this course depends on you, not your teacher, you should find it very useful.

It explains how you can work hard to achieve a good grade for the unit, and what Key Skills you might achieve while doing the unit. With Vocational A-levels, you are expected to take responsibility for your own learning, so it is a good idea to read this section very carefully.

How to 'read' a unit

The title of the unit gives a broad description of what the unit covers. However, before deciding which units you might want to study, you need to read more, to discover exactly what the unit entails. Some units are quite theoretical; others are very practical. So, check the other sections, especially the Assessment Evidence section, to see what you will need to produce for a portfolio, or to see what you may be tested on.

In deciding which tested units to take, you should also look at some sample examination papers.

About this unit

This section provides an introduction to the unit. It explains what benefits you may expect from completing the unit, and describes what you will do. It also tells you about links between this unit and other units, so if you are interested in a particular topic, you could take two or more units on similar topics. Alternatively, you may prefer to choose units that are not linked, so that you have as broad a range of topics as possible.

What you need to learn

This section lists all the topics you should cover for this unit, though not necessarily in the same order you will learn about them.

Notice that this section is called 'What you need to learn' rather than 'What you will be taught'. This is because it is quite possible that your teacher will do very little traditional teaching! Vocational A-level students are expected to take control of their own learning, and it is your teacher's job to guide you towards this independent approach to learning, rather than just give you all the knowledge you need. At first, you may find this a strange and difficult experience, especially if your previous courses have been teacher-led rather than student-centred. You may find you have more freedom to decide what to do, but also that you need to make decisions for yourself. It is very important that you meet deadlines set, and put in the hours expected on your course. Otherwise, this will be reflected in poor assessment grades for your portfolio material. However, your teacher will help you to learn how to work responsibly. One of the objectives of Vocational A-levels is to prepare you for a job, and this teaching style is an important part of that process.

How will your understanding of the units be tested?

For some of the units, you will demonstrate your understanding by your portfolio material. For others, you will be externally assessed.

According to the unit, and your awarding body, you may be expected to do an assignment, or perhaps some preparatory work before sitting a written test. Details of the format of the external assessment are given in the *Examination Guide* on page 361.

The obvious way to learn about work is through your work experience placement or a part-time job. However, your course should also offer you the opportunity to try out a variety of work experiences:

- ✪ **Working on your own as well as with others in a team**
- ✪ **Doing short projects and completing long assignments**
- ✪ **Visiting local firms and businesses, and interviewing people such as the employers, their staff and their customers**
- ✪ **Designing products and services**
- ✪ **Organising events**

Assessment Evidence

In each unit specification the Assessment Evidence section is presented as a chart.

The top part of the chart explains what evidence you need to produce for this unit. Depending on the unit, this may be a single large piece of evidence, or a major task may be broken down into a number of smaller tasks for you to complete. You will need to have covered the unit and developed an understanding of the topics in the 'What you need to learn' section to produce your portfolio evidence, but it may not be necessary to have evidence for all the topics.

If you have to produce more than one of something (e.g. printouts), or in a different way, this top part tells you how many, and how things must be different. For example, in Unit 1: Presenting Information you have to produce 'six original documents', and they need to show a 'range of writing and presentational styles'.

The lower part of the chart has three columns. The first column explains what is expected for a Grade E pass. When producing your evidence, you should refer to this column to check that your work is at the required standard.

The second and third columns explain what is expected of a Grade C and Grade A student. To achieve a higher grade, you do not have to produce more work as such. However, you will have to produce work of a higher quality and this may mean you have to spend more time than a Grade E student, especially when checking your work, and doing research.

So, you should not think of the last two columns as lists of extra tasks for you to complete. Instead, they provide you with an excellent opportunity to demonstrate qualities that a prospective employer will want from you:

- **Managerial qualities:** being able to plan and organise your own work which may help you to plan and organise others.
- **Independence:** carrying out your work without a lot of help will mean you could be trusted to work without supervision.
- **Quality:** having a pride in what you produce and being able to present better quality work.
- **Knowledge:** showing a greater understanding of what you have learnt.

It is important that you read this Assessment Evidence chart very carefully. It will be your responsibility to produce evidence of what you can do. Check especially which items, if any, relate to your portfolio evidence.

The portfolio

Your portfolio contains all the evidence collected as you work through the units which are not to be externally assessed.

Mostly, this will be evidence of your work on a computer system and so will be printouts, annotated to explain what you have done. Some units may ask for a special form of evidence to be produced by you:

- Unit 1 asks for a portfolio of six original documents and a report.
- Unit 3 asks for a spreadsheet solution and user and technical documentation.
- Unit 4 asks for specifications of ICT systems and a record of set-up, installation, configuration and test activities.
- Unit 6 asks for a relational database together with design and analysis notes, a user guide and technical documentation.

▼ ▼ ▼ ▼ ▼ ▼ ▼ ▼ ▼

Report
This is a finished piece of work which brings together lots of ideas and information or some other documentation.

▲ ▲ ▲ ▲ ▲ ▲ ▲ ▲ ▲

Sometimes you will need to write a **report**.

For example Unit 1: Presenting Information asks for a 'report describing, comparing and evaluating two different standard documents used by each of three different organisations'. You will be expected to demonstrate your ICT skills in producing your portfolio, so all reports should be word processed, not handwritten.

Before handing in your work to your teacher for assessment, you should check exactly what is required for each unit, and make sure that your portfolio holds all this information in an easily accessible way. Hints on how to present your portfolio are given in the *Portfolio Guide* on page 349.

Grading

By the end of your course, your portfolio will contain a great deal of evidence. In deciding what grade to award, your teacher will consider many things:

- ✪ **Your approach to learning and how you tackled your work**
- ✪ **How much responsibility you took for planning your work**
- ✪ **How you decided what information you needed**
- ✪ **How well you reviewed and evaluated your own progress**
- ✪ **The quality of your evidence**

It is important, therefore, to aim high.

When you submit your portfolio, your teacher will mark each entry in each column of the assessment grid, so although you should have completed everything in the Grade E column to pass the Vocational A-level, work you have done (of a higher standard) in the second and third columns may be rewarded. For details about how your teacher is expected to assess your portfolio, you should refer to the Assessment Strategies section of *Essential Information for Teachers*.

During your course, you should receive feedback from your teacher giving you a clear picture of how you are doing, and how you might improve your performance.

The external assessment

When you have completed the work for a unit, you should be ready for the external assessment.

How and when you are assessed depends on your awarding body. Full details for each awarding body are given in the *Examination Guide* which starts on page 361.

How should you use this book?

This introductory chapter explains how Vocational A-levels work. The main part of this book is then divided into seven chapters, which match the six mandatory units in Vocational A-level ICT, plus one chapter for an optional unit – Impact of ICT on Society.

Included in each chapter, there are:

- ✪ **notes** on what you need to know, with plenty of diagrams and examples mostly based on case studies;
- ✪ **exercises** to check you have understood what you have been reading about;
- ✪ **activities** to test your understanding and to help you to produce portfolio evidence;
- ✪ a set of **revision questions**.

In this book you will find helpful icons showing which Key Skills the Activities can be used for:

 Communication

 Application of number

 Working with others

 Problem solving

 Improving own learning and performance

Towards the end of the book, there are three guides:

The *Good Working Practice Guide* provides useful information about health and safety issues and other good practice expected of you during your practical work.

The *Portfolio Guide* includes a checklist of what should appear in your portfolio plus some help in gaining higher grades.

The *Key Skills Guide* explains what you have to do to demonstrate your Key Skills in Communication and Application of Number. (Key Skills in IT are automatically covered within the Vocational A-level ICT course, although you will have to sit the external test.)

There is also a list of abbreviations and a comprehensive index. The index offers a complete list of all important words used in the book. Indexed words appear in **bold** within the text, or within headings. The index also includes cross references, to help you find what you are looking for.

What else do you need?

You need a copy of the unit specifications for Vocational A-level ICT, plus sample papers and past papers for the written examinations. All the information is available on the Internet and can be downloaded free of charge.

The seven unit specifications are available on the sites of the three awarding bodies. Access to these and other useful sites is available through Pearson Education's website: http://www.longman-fe.com.

You do need an Adobe Acrobat reader to download the PDF files, but the reader is also available to download free of charge. Your teacher will probably have already done this and the specifications may well be available on your school or college computer network already.

You are also recommended to visit the website of the British Computer Society (BCS) and to obtain a copy of the Glossary published by the BCS, which explains all the terms used for this Vocational A-level. There are two versions available:

A Glossary of Computing Terms, 380 pages, 0582–36967–3

IT Glossary for Schools, 215 pages, 0582–31255–8

Both books are published by Pearson Education on behalf of the BCS, and can be purchased on the Internet, and in all good bookshops.

Acknowledgements

This book has been written as a team effort. Each writer contributed new ideas, energy and enthusiasm, which we hope will help you to enjoy reading this text.

As a team, we are particularly grateful to all the companies and individuals who allowed us to base our case studies on them. As individuals, thanks are also due for the support received by each writer:

- ✪ To all our colleagues at our respective colleges and schools, and the examination boards for whom we work

- ✪ To the team at Pearson Education for their encouragement and expertise, especially Sonia Wilson, Irith Williams, Judith Ockenden and the team at First Class Publishing: Les, Chris, Suzanne, Lena and Brenda, Caroline and Andrew

- ✪ To our families and friends who have helped in so many ways, especially Rod, Lorraine, Garry, Neela, Geoff, Frankie and Dan.

We acknowledge permission to reproduce copyright material, and thank the copyright holders:

- ✪ John Allen, John Allen Hairdressing (Chapter 1)
- ✪ George Boneham (photograph for artwork in Figure 4.12 on page 170)
- ✪ Browns Transport Ltd, Ash, Nr Seven Oaks, Kent (Chapter 2)
- ✪ Tim Marcus at Hyperion-Media, http://hyperion-media.co.uk (Chapter 4)
- ✪ Abraham Moon and Sons Ltd (Chapter 1)
- ✪ Jim Robinson (web page on page 18)
- ✪ Swanage Folk Festival committee, http://come.to/swanage.folk.festival (Chapter 4)

Presenting Information

1

- Create original documents in styles that suit your readers

- Improve the accuracy, readability and presentational quality of documents that you create

- Understand some of the ways organisations present and gather information

- Understand why organisations use standard layouts for documents

- Choose and apply standard layouts

- Understand the needs for some standard ways of working

- Develop good practice in your use of ICT

Introduction

This chapter looks in detail at six topics:

- ✪ Organisations and their use of information
- ✪ Standard documents and their purpose
- ✪ Presentation techniques and combined information
- ✪ Long document presentation techniques
- ✪ Accuracy of information
- ✪ Suitability of prepared documents

This unit is assessed entirely through your portfolio. You will carry out an investigation and produce a major document, reporting on your investigation. You will also collect examples of standard documents from different organisations and produce a formal report that evaluates these documents. You will need to learn about presentation skills and be given opportunities to practise these before producing your portfolio work for final assessment.

Two case studies are used in this chapter: Abraham Moon & Sons Ltd and John Allen Hairdressing.

Abraham Moon & Sons Ltd

Abraham Moon & Sons Ltd are based in Guiseley, West Yorkshire. The company, which manufactures quality woollen cloth, was started in 1837. They also produce woollen accessories such as scarves, shawls and throws.

John Allen Hairdressing

John Allen and his wife, Katy, own a hairdressing salon in the Horsforth area of Leeds. They employ several stylists and like to play an active part in local fundraising. They take part in the Clothes Show every year and cut hair for 24 hours during Comic Relief. Katy's dad helps them to produce some of their publicity material. A public relations consultant is also used. The salon has a website on the Internet.

Organisations and their use of information

Presentation of information is of major importance in industry and commerce. Often, the first contact a business may have with its customers is through a document. Documents can be both paper-based and screen-based. Increasingly companies have websites on the Internet or may use slide show presentations to present the company to an audience. Initial impressions of a company are formed at this stage. Poorly presented information may influence a customer to go elsewhere, because it reflects on the whole company.

DTP
Desktop publishing

The development of IT is an important tool in helping businesses to improve their information presentation. Word processing and **DTP** packages are commonly used to enhance information presentation.

Some advanced word processing packages incorporate many desktop publishing features, reducing the need to buy two pieces of software.

It is useful to evaluate whether IT always provides the most effective way of presenting information. Sometimes, a personal drawing or a handwritten note can convey more meaning to the recipient, as the sender has probably taken more time and trouble to do it this way. Figure 1.1 shows an example of a very informal note.

Figure 1.1   *Handwritten note*

Standard documents and their purpose

Different documents serve different purposes.

- ✪ To gather accurate information
- ✪ To inform the reader
- ✪ To persuade the reader
- ✪ To create a good impression
- ✪ To summarise information

Therefore, they are presented in different ways.

Activity 1.1

List the main purpose of each document in Table 1.1. Then, consider six of these documents and decide what style and presentation you would use for each one.

> Consider the language, the lettering, the accuracy of information, and whether you would include pictures or graphs.

Table 1.1   *Examples of documents*

Document

(a) Passport application form

(b) Newspaper advertisement to sell something second-hand

(c) Letter to a potential employer

(d) Formal invitation to a party

(e) Single page advertisement for cosmetics

(f) Results of an opinion poll

(g) Agenda for a meeting

(h) Minutes of a meeting

(i) League table of results for a sporting activity

(j) Draft results of a survey

(k) E-mail to a company asking for product information

(l) Report to colleagues of a meeting that you attended on their behalf

(m) Essay plan

(n) Questionnaire

(o) Company's web page

(p) Curriculum vitae (CV)

Businesses tend to use a **house style** and **logo** to help develop the corporate image.

Most business documents have a particular purpose and style. They can be used to communicate **externally** or **internally**, and are in a **formal** or **informal** style. Examples are given in Table 1.2.

Table 1.2 *Formal and informal documents*

	Formal	Informal
Internal	Payslip	Memo or note
External	Quotation	*

* Informal external documents are not appropriate.

Business letters are usually laid out in a house style, based on a prepared template. Correct use of spelling, punctuation and grammar are paramount in these documents, because mistakes in a letter can reflect on the company.

Figure 1.2 shows an example of a **memo**. The heading on the memo shows who the memo is to and from, the date and the subject. It is not necessary to make the language in this document too formal, because it is only read by employees within an organisation.

These days electronic mail (**e-mail**) is replacing the memorandum as an internal form of communication. Messages are sent from one computer user to

Memorandum

From: Jim Baker

To: All holders of Policies Portfolio

Date: 8th December 1999

New Policy

Please insert the attached new policy and updated index sheets into your Policies Portfolio.
Thank you.

Figure 1.2 *Memorandum*

another on a computer network. It is not necessary for both users to access their computers at the same time, since messages are left in a mailbox. Electronic mail is also widely used as an external form of communication.

E-mail messages are often brief and have the added advantage of saving paper if the recipient chooses not to print a hard copy of the message. The message style is often informal. Some companies have introduced a protocol to ensure that the system is not used for inappropriate messages. Figure 1.3 shows an example of an e-mail.

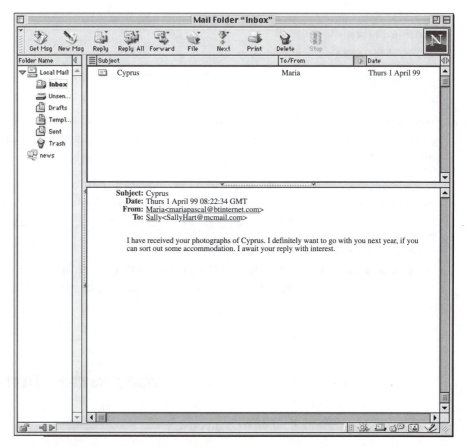

Figure 1.3 *E-mail message*

Orders are used by customers to place an order for goods or services. They can be produced either by the buyer (called a **purchase order**) or by the seller (called a **sales order**). They are legal documents forming a contract between the two parties: the buyer and the seller. Therefore, they must contain all the necessary information to ensure that the correct order is despatched. They are often identified by a unique number. This number is either pre-printed on the buyer's purchase order form, or allocated by the seller if the order has been placed by letter or 'phone. In this latter case, the sales order is often called a **confirmation of order**.

Abraham Moon & Sons Ltd

Abraham Moon & Sons Ltd won the Queen's Award for Export Achievement in 1996. Figure 1.4 shows an example of the confirmation of order document used by this company.

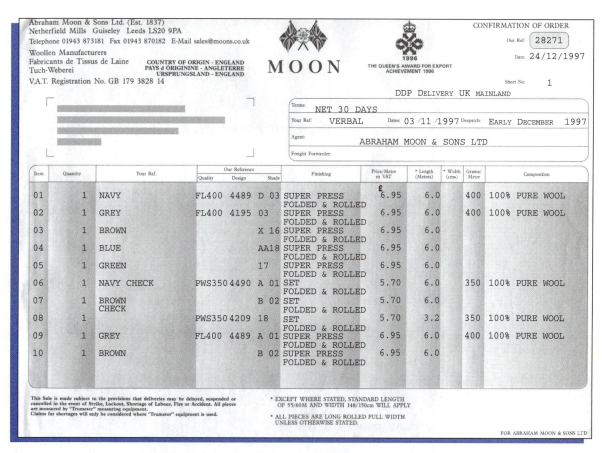

Figure 1.4 *Confirmation of order*

An **invoice** is a 'bill', sent by the seller to the buyer, showing the date of the invoice (called the **tax point**) and how much is owed for the goods or services provided. The invoice amount is usually broken down into the number of units and the cost per unit. Companies which are registered for VAT must include the VAT registration number and the amount of VAT charged on the invoice.

Invoices are legal documents and it is important to ensure that all relevant information is entered correctly. However, invoices often show the abbreviation 'E&OE' or 'Errors and Omissions Excepted'. This means that any mistakes made by the supplier are not binding. The invoice is identified by a unique number and includes the original order number. 'Terms' are also included, which show how many days before payment must be received. These also show if any discount is available for prompt payment.

Orders and invoices are often sent in **window envelopes**. They have a transparent space which allows the address on the document to show through. This saves the sender time, as the envelope does not have to be addressed separately. Figure 1.5 shows the importance of the positioning of the address details on the letter. The letter must be folded correctly and placed carefully inside the envelope; otherwise the address will not show through the window!

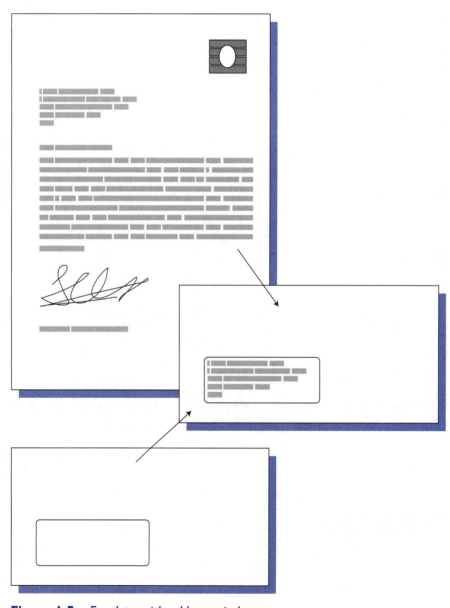

Figure 1.5 *Envelope with address window*

Abraham Moon & Sons Ltd

The design of the invoices used by Abraham Moon & Sons is similar to that used for their confirmation of order document. See Figure 1.6a.

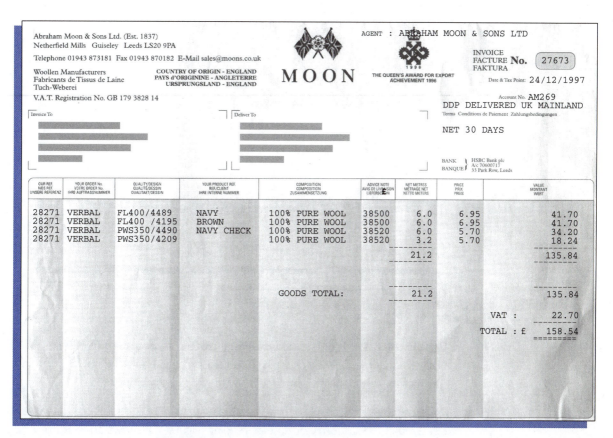

Figure 1.6a *Invoice example*

John Allen Hairdressing

John Allen Hairdressing do not produce invoices for their clients. Invoices are received from suppliers, though. See Figure 1.6b.

Invoice

```
John Allen Hairdressing
83, New Road Side,                                  01/01/00
Horsforth,
Leeds,
LS18 4QD                                            D001A

              DETAILS                           NETT PRICE

       Services 01.07.99-14.12.99                  12.88
```

SERVICE CHARGE
Service Charge relates to a 6 month period, for general cleaning and maintenance
of external areas including drains and common areas.
Transport costs and materials inclusive.

The charges have been pro-rated and relate to the proportion of the property
of which you have a leasehold interest.

```
----- AS INVOICED -----
```

Figure 1.6b   *Invoice example*

Credit notes, **price lists** and **delivery notes** are examples of other business documents which require excellent presentation skills. You might find some of these when studying Unit 2: *IT Serving Organisations*.

An **itinerary** gives details of travel, including dates, times and places. It is often displayed in tabular form for ease of reading. Figure 1.7 shows an example of an itinerary. Accuracy is very important to prevent some people missing the coach, or the journey being delayed in waiting for latecomers. People who travel on business often use an itinerary.

An **agenda** lists the date, time and place of a forthcoming meeting. The topics for discussion are also itemised. The last items on an agenda are always AOB (any other business) and the date and time of the next meeting. Figure 1.8 shows the agenda for a Neighbourhood Watch Committee.

Minutes are a record of what has been said at a meeting. Action minutes state who has been allocated a task to do as a result of the meeting. Figure 1.9 shows the minutes from a Neighbourhood Watch meeting.

ITINERARY - SIGHTSEEING TRIP TO LONDON

9.00	Meeting at Village car park
9.15	Coach departs
10.45	Arrive Buckingham Palace
11.30	Changing of the Guard
12.30	Picnic lunch in St James Park
1.30	Coach tour with guide: Houses of Parliament, Tower of London
3.30	Visit to Madame Tussauds
4.30	Meet coach and depart
6.30	Arrive at Village car park

Figure 1.7 *Itinerary*

Meeting of the Neighbourhood Watch Committee on Tuesday
April 21st at 14 Drysdale Avenue, starting at 8pm

AGENDA
Minutes of the last meeting
Matters arising
Chairman's report
Treasurer's report
Secretary's report
Newsletter editor's report
Any other business
Date of the next meeting

Figure 1.8 *Agenda*

Activity 1.2

You are required to plan a day trip for your class. You have been asked to hold a meeting to discuss this.

Working in small groups, plan an agenda for the meeting and print one copy for each group member. Appoint a chairperson and secretary, and hold the meeting. Remember to take notes during the meeting. Afterwards, word process the minutes of the meeting.

★ Keep the discussion focused on its purpose.
★ Judge when to contribute and how much to say.
★ Show that you are listening.
★ Make helpful and sensitive comments.
★ Encourage people to contribute.

Minutes of the meeting of the Neighbourhood Watch Committee held on Tuesday April 21st at 14 Drysdale Avenue, starting at 8pm.

Present: Joan Blackwell (Chairman)
John MacDonald (Secretary)
Nigel Lawson (Treasurer)
Reece Jones (Newsletter editor)
Penny Lane
Mark Lawrence

Apologies for absence were received from Gwen Thomas and Igor Spasky.

The minutes of the last meeting were read and agreed.

Matters arising:
The infra-red marker has been traced. It is now with Mrs Davies at 22 Drysdale Avenue.

Chairman's report
The Chairman advised the committee that, in total, 87 residents had attended the talk given by the local police liaison officer on 'Beating the Burglar'. The next talk, on alarm systems, is scheduled to take place on June 3rd.

Treasurer's report
The Treasurer reported a credit balance of £442.13. It was agreed that a further two infra-red markers be purchased.

Secretary's report
John MacDonald advised the meeting that his house move had now been confirmed; he would be moving out of the district at the end of May. He expressed thanks to the committee, and he was thanked for all his hard work in keeping the minutes for the last two years.

Newsletter editor's report
Reece Jones reported that the Summer newsletter was almost ready for printing. It was agreed to add an advertisement for a replacement secretary.

Any other business
Mark Lawrence reported that the new family at 11 Drysdale Avenue had now moved in, and that he has introduced himself to the new residents, a Mr and Mrs Cockerill. Mr Cockerill is an ex-police officer and may be willing to stand on the committee. John MacDonald agreed to contact him.
Date of the next meeting: Tuesday 23rd June, 8pm at 32 Drysdale Avenue.

Figure 1.9 *Minutes*

A **fax cover sheet** is the first page of a fax (facsimile) transmission and shows the company name and logo, the sender, the recipient, the date and the number of sheets sent. See Figure 1.10.

Abraham Moon & Sons Ltd

Abraham Moon & Sons' fax cover sheet includes their logo and fax number, plus other essential information at the top of the page. At the foot of the page, the Queen's Award for Export Achievement and statutory information about the company is included (Figure 1.10). Notice that the fax number shown suggests that the company receives faxes from overseas.

MOON

FAX 00 44 1943 870182

Ref. No. .... Page .... of .... Date ....

To .... From ....

Attention ....

creating the cloth

Abraham Moon & Sons Ltd. (Est. 1837)
Netherfield Mills Guiseley Leeds LS20 9PA Telephone 01943 873181 Fax 01943 870182 Reg. No. 163364 (England)
Directors: A.J.P. Walsh (Chairman), J.P.T. Walsh, D.R.W. Spence, G.G. Lockwood, M. Aveyard.

1996
THE QUEEN'S AWARD
FOR EXPORT
ACHIEVEMENT

Figure 1.10 *Fax cover sheet*

Newsletters are used to inform people about past and future events in a club or organisation. Schools, Neighbourhood Watch groups and Examination Boards all make use of newsletters. Figure 1.11 shows a newsletter produced by the Neighbourhood Watch Committee.

Newsletters are often desktop published, so that a more complex page layout, such as 3 columns, can be used.

Publicity flyers are designed to sell a product or a service. Mailshots are

Drysdale Avenue Neighbourhood Watch Newsletter

Beat the burglar

John MacDonald

H

K

Alarm systems

Figure 1.11   *Newsletter*

John Allen Hairdressing

John Allen Hairdressing use publicity flyers to advertise its services (Figure 1.12).

John Allen has been trading for more than six years and his cool, smart salon is favoured by celebrities and models. They visit for the warm, friendly atmosphere and the creativity of the staff.

The salon has worked with KMS at the Clothes Show Live and their photographic work appears regularly in national hair magazines, including Hairflair.

Cut and blowdry	£19.50
Perms	£31.65
Highlights	£24 - £55
Colour	£12 - £25

Figure 1.12 *Publicity flyer*

publicity flyers delivered to people's homes. They are eye-catching and often include illustrations. Pizza delivery firms often distribute publicity fliers.

Business cards are small wallet-sized cards that are used to remind potential customers of a company's name, address and telephone number. They often incorporate the company logo, and the name and title of the person representing the company. See the case studies on page 16.

Websites are a collection of pages published on the World Wide Web. Anybody can develop a website with **hot links** that allow the reader to access

John Allen Hairdressing

John Allen Hairdressing provides business cards for its salon consultants.

Telephone 0113 - 239 0299

HAIRDRESSING

83 New Road Side
Horsforth
Leeds LS18 4QD

KATY ALLEN
(Salon Consultant)

Figures 1.13a and 1.13b   *Business card examples*

Abraham Moon & Sons Ltd

The Managing Director of Abraham Moon & Sons needs business cards to give to potential clients he meets when on business trips abroad.

M O O N

J O H N P. T. W A L S H
managing director

creating the cloth

Abraham Moon & Sons Ltd
Netherfield Mills Guiseley
Leeds LS20 9PA
Telephone (44) 01943 873181
Fax (44) 01943 870182

Working in groups, each collect six different examples of publicity flyers or business cards. Write down why you have collected these particular documents. In your group, discuss how each of your examples could be improved.

> Ask your assessor to keep a record of your group discussion.

Activity

1.4

Make summary notes on:

★ the effectiveness of presentation in at least three of the documents collected during Activity 1.3;

★ recommendations for improvements.

> Identify accurately, and compare, the lines of reasoning and main points from texts and images.
>
> Present the key information in a form that is relevant to your purpose.

John Allen Hairdressing

John Allen Hairdressing have a website which was designed by one of their clients. The draft home page is shown in Figure 1.14.

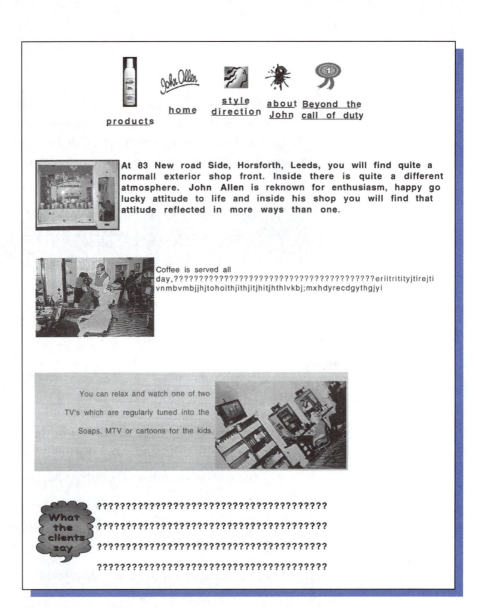

Figure 1.14   *Web page*

related information. Most websites open with a home page which shows the contents of the site.

Technical specifications are used within manufacturing companies for design specifications of products. They consist of a line drawing with dimensions and tolerances shown. Figure 1.15 shows a drawing of a cooker.

Technical specifications are often produced using vector-based graphics software because the image can be scaled up or down without any loss of resolution. It is necessary to produce them with a high degree of accuracy so that the resulting product is built according to specifications.

Many documents are produced in rough first, and gradually improved after research and consultation. Each version is called a **draft**, and is usually printed

Draft
is a document in the process of preparation

Activity 1.5

Using Figure 1.14 as your starting point, make improvements to the content and style of the draft home page. Show your version to a friend and ask for their opinion.

Ask your assessor to keep a record of your discussion.

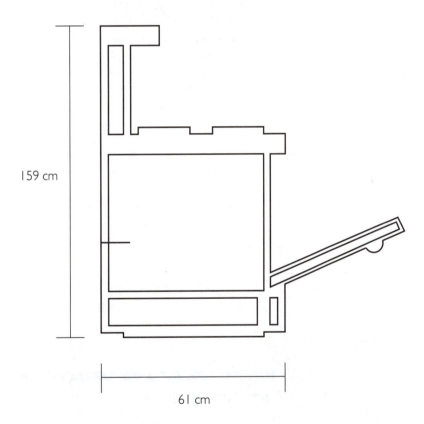

159 cm

61 cm

Figure 1.15 *A technical drawing*

with double line spacing to allow the editor room to make corrections. Figure 1.16 shows a draft version of a section from a textbook.

Word processing packages allow the writer to correct errors quickly without the necessity to re-type everything. It is essential that each version is labelled with the date and draft number, so that the reader is aware of which is the most recent draft. It is not necessary for draft documents to be presented to a high standard, although the final version should always be error free.

Printer

Printers are used to produce **hardcopy** of data as a permanent record. There are two main types of printer in use nowadays: character printers and page printers.

Character printers print one character at a time. Examples of character printers are dot matrix printers, daisy wheel printers and ink jet printers. Dot matrix printers and daisy wheel printers are both **impact printers**; they involve a printhead hitting the paper through an inked tape. Impact printers are noisy and slow.

Dot matrix printers form each character from a grid of pins. The more pins that are used, the greater the resolution and therefore the quality of printing. Most dot matrix printers also offer two modes: draft and 'near letter quality' (NLQ). NLQ printing involves printing the same character twice, close to each other; this gives a better printed effect, but takes twice as long.

Daisy wheel printers have their print characters on a wheel which spins before printing each character. This makes it very slow. However, the quality is very good, and different fonts are available (although you do have to change the daisy wheel each time).

Ink jet printers 'squirt' ink at the page and so they are much quieter. The paper must be a good quality otherwise the printing may 'bleed' and the end result can be poor. Colour printing is possible which offers good opportunities to produce excellent artwork and designs. Ink jet printers are inexpensive but they are still slow, so a page printer is of more use to most businesses.

Page printers print one page at a time. The most common form is the **laser** which works on the same kind of principles as a photocopier. A laser beam is used to 'draw' the shape onto a light-sensitive electrostatically charged drum. This drum then rotates over a source of toner - powdered ink - which sticks to the parts of the drum that have been affected by the laser beam. Finally, the drum rotates over a sheet of paper and the image is transferred from the drum to the paper. The paper is heated as the drum rotates and this makes the toner stick to the paper as it passes.

Most laser printers offer good resolution - about 300 dpi (dots per inch) - but they are expensive to buy and to run. Toner cartridges need replacing frequently, and the running costs are higher than for dot matrix printers or daisy wheel printers.

page 64

Figure 1.16 *Draft text*

A **questionnaire** is a form used to collect information from people. Designing a good questionnaire is very difficult and it is always a good idea to pilot your questions first. It is important that you consider whether you or the interviewee are going to complete the questionnaire. You must also ensure that you leave enough space for people to write answers to open-ended questions. Closed questions usually require a box for ticking (Figure 1.17).

A **report** is a formal document, often written to summarise research findings. You will need to produce a report as part of your assessment evidence for this unit. The heading on the report shows the subject matter and often shows

HOTEL GUEST QUESTIONNAIRE

I would be grateful if you could complete these questions to help me gain a better understanding of the hotel's strengths and weaknesses and help us improve our service in future. All responses are anonymous.
Thank you for your help.

1 PERSONAL DETAILS

Please tick the appropriate box

a Sex Male ☐ Female ☐

b Age category 18-25 ☐ 26-35 ☐ 36-45 ☐ 46-55 ☐ 56-65 ☐ over 65 ☐

c Purpose of visit to hotel Business ☐ Leisure ☐

2 RECEPTION

For each of the statements tick the box that best represents your answer

	Strongly Agree	Neither agree nor disagree	Disagree	Agree	Strongly Disagree
a The reception staff are friendly	☐	☐	☐	☐	☐
b Booking in was fast and efficient	☐	☐	☐	☐	☐
c Reception staff are smart in appearance	☐	☐	☐	☐	☐
d The reception area was clean and tidy	☐	☐	☐	☐	☐

3 ACCOMMODATION

For each of the statements tick the box that best represents your answer

	Strongly Agree	Neither agree nor disagree	Disagree	Agree	Strongly Disagree
a Rooms are clean and tidy	☐	☐	☐	☐	☐
b Tea and coffee facilities were good	☐	☐	☐	☐	☐
c Decor was pleasant	☐	☐	☐	☐	☐

4 RESTAURANT

If you did not use the restaurant facility, please give a reason why below and move on to question 5.

For each of the statements tick the box that best represents your answer

	Strongly Agree	Neither agree nor disagree	Disagree	Agree	Strongly Disagree
a Restaurant staff are friendly	☐	☐	☐	☐	☐
b The quality of the food was high	☐	☐	☐	☐	☐
c The menu was varied	☐	☐	☐	☐	☐

5 VALUE FOR MONEY

For each of the statements tick the box that best represents your answer

	Yes (Y)	No (N)
a The price paid was good value for money	☐	☐
b I am likely to return to the hotel	☐	☐

6 IMPROVEMENTS

What suggestions would you make for improvements?

Figure 1.17 Questionnaire example

who the report was written by and who it is to. The report should start with an introduction, include major findings and end with a conclusion and recommendations. It is helpful to include a contents page at the beginning and an alphabetical index at the end. Appendices that are referred to in the text should be numbered and placed at the end of the report.

A **bibliography** is often put at the end of a report to show what sources were used in the research for the report. These may be from books, newspapers or the Internet. Figure 1.18 shows an example of an entry from the bibliography section of a textbook.

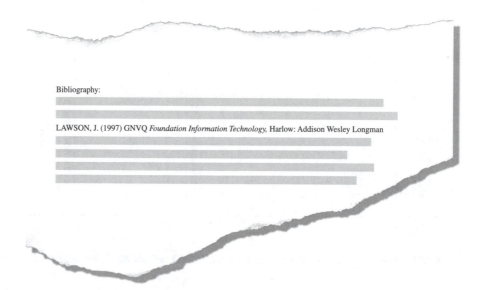

Bibliography:

LAWSON, J. (1997) GNVQ *Foundation Information Technology,* Harlow: Addison Wesley Longman

Figure 1.18 *Sample bibliography*

✪ Books should be referenced by author (surname, forename), date of publication, title, place and publisher. If a book has more than one edition, this should also be stated. The reader must have enough information to be able to locate the book if necessary.

✪ Articles from newspapers and magazines should be referenced by the title of the article and the newspaper/magazine, the date it was published and the page number on which the article appears. If the article was written by a particular journalist, the journalist should also be acknowledged.

✪ Internet material should include the **URL** and any other details needed to locate the website. If the website shows acknowledgement of sources of information, these should be repeated.

▼▼▼▼▼▼▼▼▼▼
URL
Uniform Resource Locator or a unique Internet address
▲▲▲▲▲▲▲▲▲▲

Activity
1.6

Produce a bibliography of at least five books to which you have access for your Vocational A-level ICT course.

- ★ Include enough information.
- ★ Use standard conventions of spelling and grammar accurately.
- ★ Use varied punctuation correctly.
- ★ Proof-read your bibliography.

Did You Know?

Appendices is the plural of appendix.

A **contents** page is found at the beginning of a report or book and lists the chapters or tasks in order of page number. An **index** is found at the end of a long document or book. It lists key words alphabetically, enabling the reader to look up a topic quickly and easily. **Appendices** are documents that are added to the back of a report. They are referred to in the main text as Appendix I, II, III, etc. It is often a good idea to include one example of any questionnaire you have used in an appendix.

Activity
1.7

When you have completed all the evidence requirements for this unit, you need to produce a contents page and include any relevant material in appendices.

At this stage, plan the content of your portfolio and produce a draft contents list. Remember that you will need to number your pages.

Organise relevant information clearly and coherently, using specialist vocabulary when appropriate.

Presentation techniques and combined information

Information should be presented in the most effective way. Consistency is very important since it helps to unify a document.

Many word processing packages contain standard templates for letters, reports, etc. These documents have already been formatted with certain fonts, margins and borders. They can be very time-saving. It is possible to edit these templates to create your own style. Companies often produce their own standard templates that reinforce the company's corporate image. Figure 1.19 shows one example of a standard template and Figure 1.20 shows a letter demonstrating a standard house style.

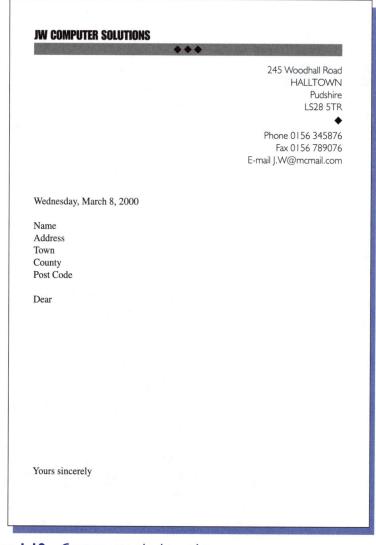

Figure 1.19 *Company standard template*

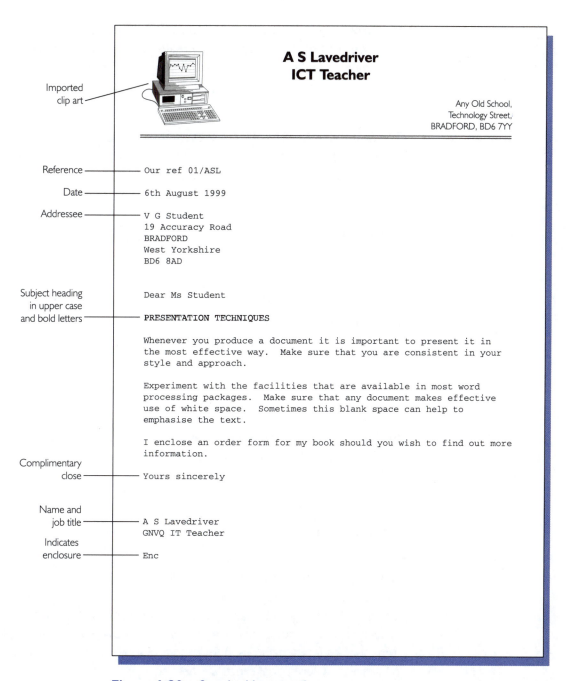

Figure 1.20 *Standard house style*

Presentation techniques can be divided into character format, paragraph format, edit tools and combined information.

Character format

A **font** describes the style (typeface) and size (point size) of the type. Fonts can be chosen to create a suitable impact on the reader.

- ✪ **Serif** fonts have small strokes attached to the upper and lower end of characters. These create the impression of being joined up and encourage the reader to move from letter to letter.
- ✪ **Sans serif** fonts are 'without' serifs and are best used for headings.

The **point size** can also be altered as appropriate. For example, a smaller point size can be used in footnotes, while larger ones are more suitable for headings. Figure 1.21 shows some examples.

Serif fonts	Sans serif fonts
6pt Century Schoolbook	6pt Arial, Century Gothic
8pt Century Schoolbook	8pt Arial, Century Gothic
10pt Century Schoolbook	10pt Arial, Century Gothic
12pt Century Schoolbook	12pt Arial, Century Gothic
14pt Century Schoolbook	14pt Arial, Century Gothic

Figure 1.21 *Examples of type sizes*

Bold highlights: Words and titles can be emboldened to make them stand out on the page. This is often used for important words.

Italics are sloping letters that are used to give emphasis or distinction to words.

Underlining is sometimes used to distinguish headings or sub-headings, but is more common in written work.

Subscript and **superscript**: Occasionally, it is necessary to incorporate special characters into the text. Subscript characters are those that occupy the bottom half of the line (e.g. $_2$) and superscript occupy the top half (e.g. ^{2}). Most software packages incorporate special facilities to allow you to insert these symbols. This facility is also used to move text above or below the usual printing line, when special effects are needed.

Titles and **headings** can be enhanced by using different fonts and features such as bold, case (upper or lower) or underline. A style sheet allows you to set a standard style for titles, sub-headings and paragraph headings. It is important to remain consistent when presenting headings.

Paragraph format

Justification describes how the text is arranged on the page. Figure 1.22 shows some examples.

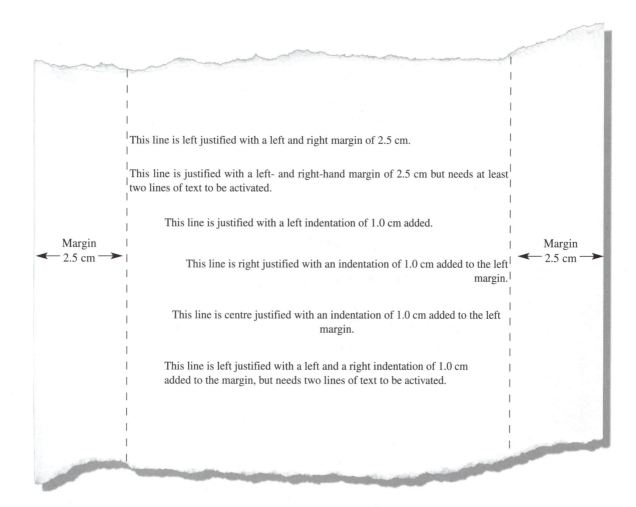

Figure 1.22 *Justification styles*

- ✪ **Left alignment** is with a straight left-hand margin.

- ✪ **Right alignment** is with a straight right-hand margin. This is often used where graphics are placed on the left-hand side, for example in a letterhead.

- ✪ **Full justification** is where both the right and left margins are straight and proportional spacing is automatically introduced between the words.

The spaces keyed in by the writer are **hard spaces** and those inserted by the software are **soft spaces**.

Centred is where the text is placed exactly in the middle of each line.

Indents refer to the distance between the margin and the start of the text. With **hanging indents,** only the first line starts at the left-hand margin. An example is shown in Figure 1.23. A hanging indent is usually used for list items that extend to more than one line.

- This is an example of the use of hanging indents and bullets. These can be particularly useful in the presentation of reports and documents.
- The left indentation has been set at 0.8 cm which is shown by the position of the bullet. The hanging indent is the start and leftmost edge of the paragraphs which follow. It is set at 0.3 cm.

Figure 1.23   *Hanging indents*

Tabulation (tabs) can be used to create a column effect. If the tab key is pressed the cursor jumps to the next tab position. Figure 1.24 shows how an indented list can be produced from setting tab positions.

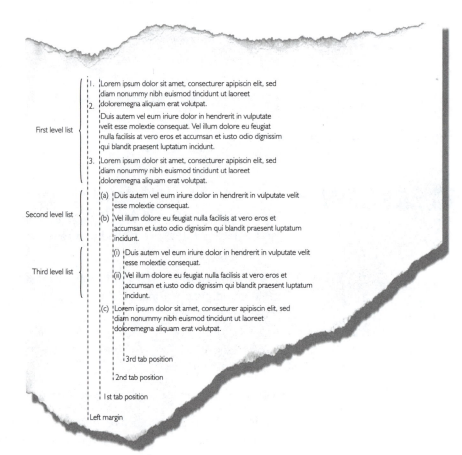

Figure 1.24   *Use of tabs*

Numbered lists can be used where the order is important, e.g. in following a recipe. Some WP packages provide the facility for automatic numbering of lists and sub-lists.

Bullet points are used for lists which you do not want to number. A circle or some other symbol is used at the start of each point instead of the numbers 1, 2, 3, etc. Items listed in this way should be of the same grammatical type. Figure 1.25 shows some examples.

Borders can be used to surround pictures and text, and thereby enhance them. These can be of different thickness and DTP packages will allow you to use decorative borders. Borders may also be shaded to give added impact.

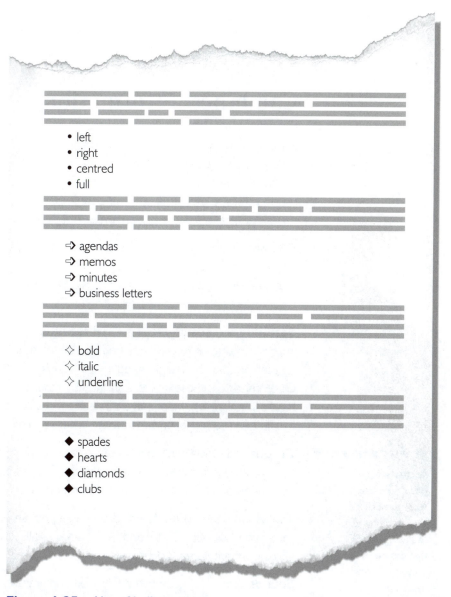

- left
- right
- centred
- full

⇨ agendas
⇨ memos
⇨ minutes
⇨ business letters

◇ bold
◇ italic
◇ underline

◆ spades
◆ hearts
◆ diamonds
◆ clubs

Figure 1.25   *Use of bullet points*

Shading can be used effectively in tables. It can be used to enhance important columns of text or to highlight headings.

Edit tools

Cut and **paste** allows you to cut out sections of the text and paste them elsewhere in the document, thus minimising the need for retyping. It is often useful to re-order items, so that they make more sense to the reader. You can use existing information to save time and effort.

Find and **replace** (or search and replace) allows you to scan a document for particular sequences of characters, and then to replace them with an alternative sequence. This can speed up editing. For example, for text that will appear in a fully justified format, it is better to have only a single space after a full stop, not the two spaces that used to be considered 'good practice'. Using find and replace, you can replace all double spaces with single spaces very quickly.

Combined information

It is possible to import **pictures** and **drawings** into a document. There are many picture libraries (e.g. clip art) which allow you to do this. Alternatively, you may create your own pictures and drawings, using a separate graphics package. It is usual to create a **picture frame** prior to importing a picture. Desktop publishing (DTP) packages also have **text frames** for inserting text into a document.

Clip art is a library of professionally drawn illustrations which can easily enhance the presentation of many documents. The pictures are stored in categories to allow easy access. Most clipart is copyright-free, provided you have a licence for the software package.

Scanning and **scaling** images: DTP packages and some WP packages allow images and drawings to be scanned into a document. This can be done using a digitiser or scanner. The scanned image is usually converted to a bitmap file. Once imported, these images can then be resized by using the resizing handles. Scaling a bitmap image can lead to loss of clarity, so vector graphics should be used for technical drawings where scaling is important.

Graphs and **charts** that have been created using a separate spreadsheet package can be imported into a document. These help to enhance the document, particularly if it is one that is reporting on figures.

Tables can be imported to word-processed documents from a separate spreadsheet file. Some WP and DTP packages allow you to create your own tables from within the document.

Sounds can also be combined with text and graphics in a **slideshow presentation**.

▼▼▼▼▼▼▼▼▼

Slideshow presentation
A series of slides, incorporating text, sound and graphics that can be used to present information by computer.

▲▲▲▲▲▲▲▲▲

Long document presentation techniques

Longer documents, e.g. reports, require the application of additional presentation techniques. In particular, you must be aware of those techniques relating to the page set-up.

Page set-up

Deciding page set-up involves making decisions on how each page in the whole document is laid out. When considering layout, it is worthwhile to look at **white space**.

Unless you are trying to economise on paper, it is not necessary to cram everything into a single page. White space has the advantage of adding contrast to ensure that other items stand out and draw the attention of the reader.

Activity 1.8

Figure 1.26 (pages 32 and 33) shows some examples of the use of white space. Find some more examples and decide whether the use of white space is good or poor. Make notes on your findings.

★ Identify accurately, and compare, the lines of reasoning and main points from texts and images.

★ Present the key information in a form that is relevant to your purpose.

Landscape and **portrait** refer to the **orientation** of the text on the paper. Figure 1.27 (on page 34) shows examples of both orientations.

Sometimes it is necessary to change the orientation to suit the type of document you are printing. For example, a calendar page may show the month name as a banner on the left-hand side (landscape), with the days in a table format (portrait).

Figure 1.26a   *Poor use of white space*

Margins and spacing All word-processing packages allow you the facility to change the default margin settings. You may wish to consider a wider left-hand margin for a document that needs binding, this can be done by adding **gutter margins**. Line spacing can also be altered from single line spacing. Larger line spacing is often required in documents that will require editing.

Widows and orphans These terms are used to describe the first line of a paragraph left at the bottom of a page (widow) and the last line of a paragraph left at the top of a page (orphan). Some word processing packages have an automatic control which ensures that there are no widows or orphans in the document. In packages without this facility, they can be avoided by inserting a page break or extra returns in the document.

Headers and footers These features are used for labelling purposes, e.g. for the title of a report, the author's name, and file name. In a multi-page document, the same information would appear on each page. Some packages allow you the facility to insert variable information, such as the date. This will automatically change each time you open and edit the document.

Page numbering It is good practice to number pages of all multi-page documents. This serves as useful information referencing and allows for use of an index and contents list. Word processing and DTP packages often have the facility for automatic page numbering within the header and footer facility.

Pagination Pagination is automatic and depends on the paper size, the font size and the size of the top and bottom margins. Documents can be paginated manually by inserting a page break to ensure that there are no widows and

A good haircut is not merely external.
It is also internal.

A haircut should work in equilibrium with your outer self:
your hair type, the shape of your face and your body.
And it should balance your inner self:
your spirit and your character.

At John Allen, we treat your hair
as part of your whole.

We always consult your wishes before beginning,
and if cutting half an inch is all that is necessary,
that is all we do.

We do not impose a style upon you,
you are our inspiration.

83 New Road Side
Horsforth, Leeds
LS18 4QD

Telephone 0113 - 2390 299

A 365 SALON

Figure 1.26b *Good use of white space*

orphans. Certain items such as tables should not be split over two pages, unless they are very long. New chapters usually start on a new page.

Styles These are groups of paragraph and character formats that are usually identified by name, e.g. List Bullet. They can be applied to longer documents by using preset document templates or creating your own template. Figure 1.28 (on page 35) shows an example of a choice of styles.

Master documents These are created using a template with styles defined. Sub-documents or sections can be incorporated within a master document. Some software packages allow the user to automatically produce indexes and contents lists from the master document.

Landscape

Figure 1.27 *Landscape and portrait orientations*

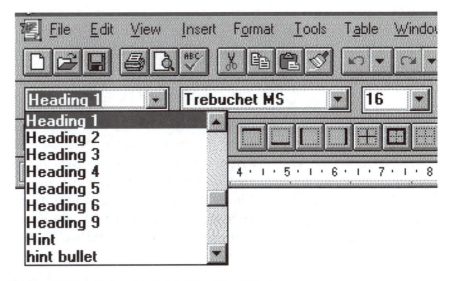

Figure 1.28 *Example of style box from Word*

Activity 1.9

Working in a group, produce a slide show presentation to use with a year group of students who are considering their options for the next year. Try to use as many presentation techniques as possible. Show your presentation to an audience and include an oral explanation.

★ Speak clearly and adapt your style of presentation to suit your purpose, subject, audience and situation.

★ Structure what you say so that the sequence of information and ideas may be easily followed.

★ Use a range of techniques to engage the audience, including effective use of images.

Accuracy of information

Incorrect use of grammar and punctuation, and mis-spellings give a bad impression of a company.

Exercise 1.1

Spot the spelling and keying mistakes in this e-mail:

Subject: Cyprus
Date: Thurs 1 April 99 08:22:34 GMT
From: Maria<mariapascal@btinternet.com>
To: Sally<SallyHart@mcmail.com>
I have received your photographs of Cyprus. I definately want to go with you next year, if you can sort out some accomodation. I awaityour rely with intrest.

Compare your answer with the e-mail shown in Figure 1.3.

★ Use standard conventions of spelling and grammar.

★ Use a variety of punctuation marks correctly.

Spellings

It is very easy to mis-key or mis-use a word without realising it.

Some software packages have an automatic correction facility that fixes common keying errors. You can add your own mis-spellings to the list.

Table 1.3 *Common words mis-used, mis-keyed and mis-spelt*

Common words mis-used	Common words mis-keyed	Words commonly mis-spelt
there/their	adn (and)	accommodation
its/it's	studnet (student)	advertisement
we're/were/where	teh (the)	business
to/too/two		confidential
weather/whether		definite
your/you're		liaison
		receive
		representation
		separate

Spell-checkers will query unfamiliar spellings and detect repeated words, giving you the opportunity to correct or delete them.

Grammar

Grammar is a set of rules that should be followed so that sentences have a meaning.

Verbs and nouns confused

Look at the examples of verbs and nouns that are often confused in Table 1.4. What do you notice about the verbs? What do you notice about the nouns?

Table 1.4 *Verbs and nouns*

Verb	Noun
to practise	the practice
to advise	the advice
to devise	the device
to license	the licence

The verb or 'doing' word ends with 'se', and the noun or 'object' ends with 'ce'.

Exercise 1.2

Complete these sentences using the correct noun or verb.

Choose from:
ADVICE/ADVISE
PRACTISE/PRACTICE
LICENCE/LICENSE
DEVICE/DEVISE

1   She took her cat to the vet for some .... on how to get rid of fleas.
2   .... what you preach.
3   The driver was caught speeding and had 3 points put on her driving ....
4   The incendiary .... kept ticking until it exploded.

Agreement of subject and verb

The subject of the sentence (what/who) and the verb (doing/being) should match. For example:

- ✪ *I like apples. She likes bananas. (I/like, She/likes)*

- ✪ *The manager wants three reports. (manager/wants, he/wants)*

In longer sentences the subject and the verb can be quite far apart. Be careful to make the verb agree with the subject, not with a different part of the sentence. For example:

- ✪ *The use of computers in homes has increased in recent years. (subject = The use, verb = has increased)*

It would be wrong to write: The use of computers in homes have increased in recent years.

> ### The subject is usually at the beginning of the sentence.

Active and passive voice

Formal documents such as reports should be written in the passive voice (action attributed to where it is directed), rather than the active voice (action attributed to where it came from). In the passive voice, you avoid using 'I' and 'we'. The majority of other documents can be written in the active voice.

- ✪ **Passive**: The computers were purchased through a Mail Order company.
- ✪ **Active**: We purchased the computers through a Mail Order company.

Punctuation

Punctuation can help to provide the reader with a better understanding of the tone and meaning of the written words. Punctuation includes the full stops at the ends of sentences, commas which break up a sentence, question marks and exclamations marks.

Consider these two sentences; both use the same words.

- ✪ *The wine which is from France should be served chilled.*

- ✪ *The wine, which is from France, should be served chilled.*

The first sentence means: Only *the French wine should be served chilled.*

By the insertion of commas in the second one, this sentence has a different meaning: All *the wine is from France.*

Exercise 1.3

Add punctuation and capital letters to this text.

trip to france this trip will start at eleven o'clock it will be important for everyone to arrive on time we plan to travel by coach through the channel tunnel arriving at our hotel in time for dinner so don't be late or we'll leave without you also don't forget your passport

Compare your text with someone else. Did they use punctuation in the same places as you?

> Use varied punctuation correctly, e.g. semi-colons and brackets.

▼▼▼▼▼▼▼▼▼▼

Addressee
The person to whom a letter is addressed.

▲▲▲▲▲▲▲▲▲▲

An 'open' style of punctuation is often used in business letters. This is where no commas or full stops are used in the date, **addressee**, salutation (e.g. Dear Sir) or complimentary close (e.g. Yours faithfully). The 'house style' should be followed.

John Allen Hairdressing

John Allen Hairdressing use a style which is fully displayed and fully punctuated. See Figure 1.29.

> John Allen Hairdressing,
> 83 New Road Side,
> Horsforth,
> LEEDS,
> LS18 4QD

Our ref. JA/KA11   18th January, 1998

Mrs Julia Wright,
11 Thornhill Street,
Calverley,
LEEDS,
LS28 7JD

Dear Julia,

COMIC RELIEF

We are keen to raise some money for Comic Relief. After some very animated discussion, I got my way and we are going to stage a 24 hour 'cut-in'.

We will be open between 8.30 am on Saturday 8th March, until 8.30 am on Sunday 9th March. There are still some appointments available if you would like to make a booking!

From 7.00 pm, ALL products will carry a 20% discount.

We look forward to seeing you in the salon.

Your sincerely,

John Allen

Figure 1.29   *Example of fully displayed and fully punctuated layout*

Full stops, commas and semi-colons

Sentences should always begin with a capital letter and end with a full stop. Commas should be used to show a natural pause in a sentence and to separate different items. A good way to test whether commas are in the right place is to take out the middle clause from a sentence, separated by commas, to see if the sentence still makes sense. (Try it with the sentence you have just read.) Semi-colons are used where a longer pause than a comma is required.

Activity 1.10

Re-type the John Allen letter shown in Figure 1.29, using blocked style and open punctuation.

★ Organise relevant information clearly and coherently.

★ Ensure your spelling grammar and punctuation are accurate.

★ Proof-read your document before printing out the final copy.

Use of the apostrophe

An apostrophe can be used in two different circumstances:

✪ **To indicate belonging**
✪ **To indicate one or more letters are missing**

When indicating belonging, the apostrophe is always placed at the end of the noun to which the object belongs. Turn the sentence around to work out where to put the apostrophe:

✪ **The school belonging to the girls – the girls' school.**
✪ **The book belonging to the girl – the girl's book.**

Many commonly abbreviated words and phrases make use of an apostrophe. See Table 1.5.

Table 1.5 *Use of apostrophe in abbreviated words*

Abbreviation	Full form
can't	cannot
don't	do not
I'm	I am
'phone	telephone
rock 'n' roll	rock and roll

Spacing between words

When using text processing software, it is usual to include one space between each word, and either one or two at the end of a sentence after a full stop. There should be no spaces *before* any punctuation mark.

Spell-checkers and grammar-checkers

Spell-checkers and grammar-checkers assist the writer in checking accuracy. They do *not* replace proof-reading.

Spell-checkers are included in many software packages. When selected they will check the words in a current document against those stored in the dictionary. The user may choose to correct or ignore the word highlighted as possibly mis-spelt. In some cases, an American dictionary is used so it is wise to check the word before changing it. A spell-checker will *not* detect correctly spelt words used in the incorrect place (e.g. were and where). Some spell-checkers have the facility to allow you to customise the dictionary, by adding frequently used words or initials, such as your own name or ICT.

Grammar-checkers allow the writer to see where grammar errors may have been made. You may choose to correct or ignore the sentence highlighted by the grammar-checker.

This example shows why it is unwise to be over-dependent on the computer's spelling and grammar checkers.

Original text:
I waived to the buoy on teh beech. Knee lucked at me butt died knot now who eye whose. I touted berry lowed, 'Eye ham yore lector!'

After spell-checking:
I waived to the buoy on the beech. Knee lucked at me butt died knot now who eye whose. I touted berry lowed, 'Eye ham yore lector!'

After grammar-checking:
I waived to the buoy on the beech. Knee lucked at me butt died knot now who eye who is. I touted berry lowed, 'Eye ham yore lector!'

Intended text:
I waved to the boy on the beach. He looked at me but did not know who I was. I shouted very loudly, 'I am your lecturer!'

Proof-reading documents using standard symbols

It is good practice to proof-read your own work before submitting it. In businesses, people often proof-read each other's work and use standard symbols to show corrections.

Manuscript correction signs are used to edit work and are usually placed in the margin adjacent to the line where a correction is needed. It is important to understand their meaning. Some of the most commonly used ones are listed in Table 1.6.

Table 1.6 *Common proof-reading marks*

Margin mark	Text mark	Meaning
≠	(ICT)	replace upper case letters indicated with lower case
≡	ıc̲t̲	replace lower case letters indicated with upper case
⊘	I̲C̲T̲	stet (let it stand) do not change the words that are crossed out
⋂	ITC -	transpose or reverse the letters or words indicated
[	[ICT	indent
⌠	ıICT	start new paragraph
⌒	ICT2	do not begin a new paragraph (run on)
Y	ICTIteacher	insert a space between words
c∕	ı∧T	insert
⑨	ICTⱦ	delete

Exercise 1.4

Retype the article in Figure 1.30 using the standard symbols to help you.

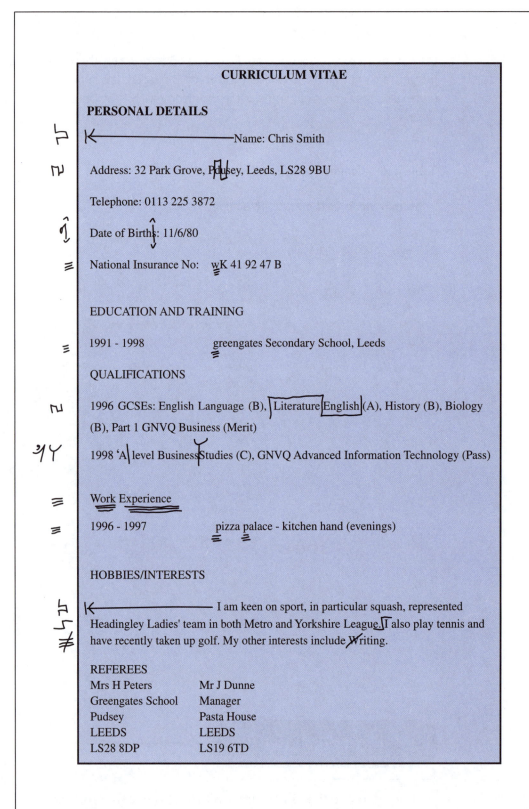

CURRICULUM VITAE

PERSONAL DETAILS

Name: Chris Smith

Address: 32 Park Grove, Pudsey, Leeds, LS28 9BU

Telephone: 0113 225 3872

Date of Births: 11/6/80

National Insurance No: wK 41 92 47 B

EDUCATION AND TRAINING

1991 - 1998   greengates Secondary School, Leeds

QUALIFICATIONS

1996 GCSEs: English Language (B), Literature English (A), History (B), Biology (B), Part 1 GNVQ Business (Merit)

1998 'A level Business Studies (C), GNVQ Advanced Information Technology (Pass)

Work Experience

1996 - 1997   pizza palace - kitchen hand (evenings)

HOBBIES/INTERESTS

I am keen on sport, in particular squash, represented Headingley Ladies' team in both Metro and Yorkshire League. I also play tennis and have recently taken up golf. My other interests include Writing.

REFEREES

Mrs H Peters	Mr J Dunne
Greengates School	Manager
Pudsey	Pasta House
LEEDS	LEEDS
LS28 8DP	LS19 6TD

Figure 1.30 *Proof-reading exercise*

Suitability of prepared documents

Every document should be produced with the **potential reader** in mind. How you word your **message** is important, because it is essential that the language used is accessible to the reader. For example, a story book written for pre-school children will use different words from those used in a magazine article aimed at fishing enthusiasts.

The **occasion** should also be considered – less formal documents require less formal language.

Figure 1.31 shows two invitation card styles, illustrating how different fonts can convey a different tone, and reach a different audience.

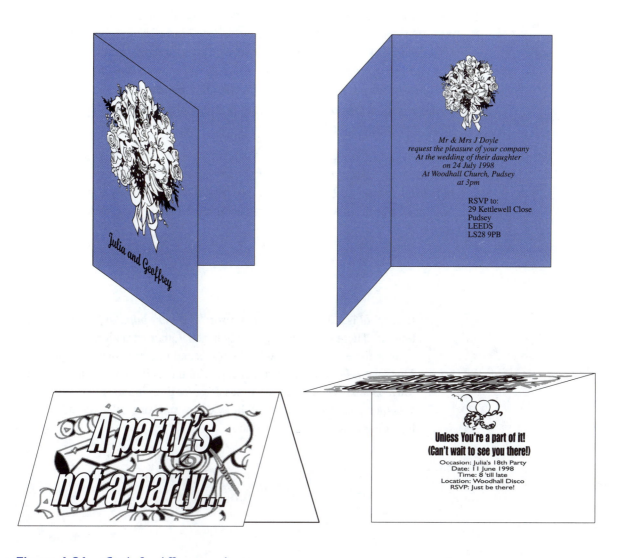

Figure 1.31 *Cards for different audiences*

Careful use of **colour** can also enhance a document by breaking up sections of black and white text and encouraging the reader to focus on a specific area of the page. Colour can also create meaning, e.g. yellow shading might indicate happiness. Using yellow as a font colour, however, makes the text difficult to read. Effective use can be made of contrasting colours, e.g. blue and yellow, as well as similar colours, e.g. purple and pink. Colour is best used sparingly but consistently. Consideration should also be given to the extra costs involved in producing full-colour documents.

Decisions also need to be made about whether to include pictures or tables. A carefully chosen graphic can speak volumes: 'a picture paints a thousand words'.

The reader

It is important to be aware of the potential audience, whether it is a potential customer or a current employee. Consider the level of language that they will understand and appreciate. Five-year-olds will have limited reading skills, but they will recognise symbols and pictures. Adults are more likely to understand complicated text. Ensure that the document has '**readability**'. Some software packages report on reading level based on the number of words per sentence and the syllables per word.

The readability statistics can be a useful facility, but there are other aspects that contribute to a document's readability. Sometimes, the choice of words can be improved. Figure 1.32 shows a text which uses the word 'very' many times, and other adjectives which do not really describe Blackpool as well as they might.

Blackpool is a *very nice* seaside resort. It is *very popular* with tourists. There is a *very long* sandy beach. Other attractions include the *well-known* tower, the trams and the three piers. There are *a large number of* pubs, restaurants and hotels in the town. Blackpool also has six miles of *great* illuminations. Whether you want an active holiday or a *restful* one, Blackpool has something to *offer* everyone.

Figure 1.32   *Poorly written paragraph*

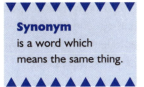

Synonym
is a word which
means the same thing.

A **thesaurus** can be used to modify the language used by finding **synonyms**.

Here are two sentences using the same word 'train' in different contexts.

✪ I want to *train* to be a nurse.

✪ I need to book two seats on the 9.30 a.m. *train*.

If you look up the word 'train' in the thesaurus, to start with there are different meanings it could have, depending on whether the word is being used as a noun or a verb. As a verb, train could mean 'instruct' or 'exercise'. As a noun, train could mean 'ordered sequence' (as in train of thought) or 'railroad'. When you have selected the meaning which is closest to what you want the sentence to say, the thesaurus offers synonyms which you can choose from. If you are not sure what the words offered by the thesaurus mean, you should look them up in a dictionary before replacing words in your original text. Not all the suggestions will make sense, or improve the readability of your text.

Activity
1.11

Copy the text in Figure 1.32, replacing each of the highlighted words and phrases with an alternative word or phrase. Use your computer thesaurus to help you.

Use standard conventions of spelling, punctuation and grammar accurately.

Setting the scene

The style of language should match the occasion or set the scene.

A party invitation may be very informal and say:

PARTY TONIGHT!! Bring a bottle . . . 8 till late . . . Student common room, B Block

A more formal invitation may begin more formally:

Lord and Lady Fordingham request the pleasure of the company of . . .

See Figure 1.31 for other examples. Most business documents will use functional language. This language is characterised by its good organisation, lack of description and its concentration on presenting facts. Layout and text fonts can also be used to create a special tone to the document. Text fonts can also be used to target a certain market. Figure 1.33 shows some examples.

Grove House Day Nursery

Harewood Country Hotel

HONG KONG TAKEAWAY

Figure 1.33   *Different fonts and tones*

Activity
1.12

Design a business card for a business that you would like to run. Your aim is to use the minimum number of words in the space available. However, you must include all essential information, so that customers may contact you.

★ Include just enough information to convey what you do and how you can be contacted.

★ Choose, produce and place images to suit your purpose.

Message

Before you start preparing a document, ask yourself what message you want to convey. Write down the main factors you want to include. For example, an **e-mail** message about a meeting must include the date, the time and the venue.

A publicity **flyer** that is designed to sell something will require a different style and presentation to a formal report. In some documents, you are very limited by space and a conscious decision should be made about what needs including and what can be omitted.

Good practice

Whether you are using IT for personal or business reasons, it is important to use it in the most effective way. You should apply this good practice to every unit. More details on good practice are given in the Good Working Practice Guide on page 335.

Log of IT problems

When learning to use IT, it is often helpful to keep a record of things that went wrong and how the problem was solved. This can serve as a useful reminder next time it happens! These can include equipment faults, system faults or software faults. In some cases, the log may form part of an overall reporting system and be used in major decision-making such as training requirements, purchasing policies, and computer efficiency comparisons.

> Keeping a log is important for all IT users. It should be a part of everyday activities, since it can provide a record of what has happened, especially what has gone wrong.

Editing and saving

Work should be saved regularly. This allows you to recall your work and edit it easily. In the event of a power failure you will only be able to recall your last saved version. Some software packages have an autosave facility that automatically saves your file on a regular basis.

Storing work

Work should be stored in appropriately named directories. It is often appropriate to backup work on to a separate storage medium such as a floppy disk. Ensure that all backup copies are dated.

Use of file names

File names should be sensible and convey information about the content of the file. This allows you, and others, to find the file easily at a later date.

Macros

A macro is a sequence of regularly used instructions which is defined by one or two keys. The macro can be recalled using the identifier. Macros can be written in most software packages. Chapter 3 looks in detail at macros within spreadsheets.

Activity 1.13

Work through the demonstration of macro writing provided on your software. Make notes if you feel it is very complicated. Then create your own macro. Choose from this list, or decide on your own macro.

★ Assigning a style to the current paragraph

★ Inserting a special character, e.g. a multiplication sign

★ Emboldening and centering highlighted text at the same time

★ Printing the current page

★ Saving and closing the current document

Document your macro. Your software may allow you to record a description of your macro.

In most word processing software, macros can be created and then run automatically. You can action a macro from a menu, but if you use the macro frequently you may prefer to assign a key on a toolbar, or some special key selection.

Combining information

It is possible to combine different types of information, such as text, sounds, graphics and numbers. This involves, for instance, importing a graphics file into a word processed document. Spreadsheet or database information could also be imported into a word processed document. Some information may have been input using a different input device such as a scanner. In some cases, the file format may be different and will need converting.

Judge standard software

Consider the effectiveness of the software in performing the task required. Find out what other software packages offer, and consider whether another package would have been more effective.

Security procedures

It is important to ensure that data is not lost, accidentally or deliberately, and that unauthorised access to information is prevented.

Making backup copies

A backup copy is a copy of a file that is stored in a different location to the original file. Backup copies are often made on different media such as floppy disks. Backup should not be confused with autosave, in which work is automatically saved at regular intervals in some software packages.

Data loss and corruption

It is necessary to follow some security procedures to ensure data is not lost, destroyed or disclosed to inappropriate persons. Passwords are an effective method of protection, but it is essential to remember them and to change them periodically. Corruption of data can also occur as a result of electrical interference or faulty equipment.

Virus protection

Viruses can be detected and removed using virus protection software. This software needs updating regularly as new viruses are continually introduced.

Confidentiality

The Data Protection Act (1988) stipulates that personal data held on individuals shall be accurate and not disclosed to others. An individual has the right to see the data held and to have any inaccuracies corrected or out of date material deleted. For more details see the *Good Working Practice Guide* on page 335.

Copyright laws

Software is subject to the same copyright as books. The Copyright, Designs and Patents Act (1988) makes it illegal to use software that has been copied from someone else and is not licensed to you. Network software may also be illegal if it has not been licensed for multi-users.

▼▼▼▼▼▼▼▼▼

Secondary research

Data you use that has already been collected by someone else. You look it up in books, magazines and on the Internet. With **primary research**, you collect new data through observation, completing questionnaires and interviewing.

▲▲▲▲▲▲▲▲▲

> Any information that has been collected using **secondary research** should be checked for **validity** and cross-referenced with other books to ensure that it is correct.

Revision questions

1 Explain what you understand by the term 'corporate image'.

2 What is the difference between an internal and external document?

3 What document would be produced to request payment from a purchaser?

4 Who might need an itinerary?

5 What document might you be sent in advance of a meeting?

6 What type of drawings often use vector-based graphics?

7 What is a bibliography?

8 Explain why it is always useful to include a contents page in long documents.

9 What are the advantages of using a slideshow presentation over other methods?

10 What methods can you use to make text more prominent to the reader?

11 When are bullet lists useful?

12 How can shading be used effectively?

13 What is white space?

14 What is the difference between landscape and portrait orientation?

15 When might you create a gutter margin?

16 What is the difference between pagination and page numbering?

17 What type of mis-spelling is not detected by a spell-checker?

18 When would you use a semi-colon rather than a comma?

19 Explain how colour can be used effectively in presenting information?

ICT Serving Organisations

2

- Understand how organisations are structured
- Understand how organisations use and exchange information
- Evaluate how well ICT can and does help organisations
- Consider how ICT supports many different activities in organisations
- See how ICT offers new opportunities

The assessment of this unit is based on an external assessment. A case study and related tasks will be released before this assessment. You need to analyse the case study and complete the tasks, before taking them into the assessment with you. In the test, you will be questioned on what you have produced, and on other aspects that you have studied.

Three case studies similar to the one that you will analyse are used to illustrate concepts in this chapter.

- ✪ The Media Direct Group
- ✪ Browns Transport Ltd
- ✪ I-Spy Security

These are only examples and it is important that you understand the different ways that ICT can be used to help different kinds of organisations, and that you can apply this to the one that you study.

You also need to understand the material covered in Unit 1: Presenting Information and Unit 3: Spreadsheet Design. It will also be useful to study Unit 5: Systems Analysis and Unit 6: Database Design. All of these offer invaluable supporting skills and are closely linked to the material covered in this chapter.

This chapter looks in detail at four topics:

- ✪ Types of organisation
- ✪ Functions within organisations
- ✪ Information and its use
- ✪ Management information systems (MIS)

Types of organisation

Introduction

Organisations can comprise any number of people who group together to use their own skills and other resources to make a product or provide some form of service. As such, organisations can vary in size from just a few people to the thousands employed by huge multinational conglomerates. The essential fact about all successful organisations is that all the people in it understand, and are working towards, the same business objectives. This is true whether the organisation is a small local shop or a national supermarket chain, a chemist, a farm, a doctor's surgery or a hospital, a craft pottery or a car manufacturer.

The introductions to the three case studies that follow illustrate the differences between organisations.

▼▼▼▼▼▼▼▼▼
Direct marketing
is using marketing and advertising services to gain a direct response from potential customers, e.g. by sending mailshots.
▲▲▲▲▲▲▲▲▲

Media Direct

The Media Direct Group is a large **direct marketing** agency based in the UK. It provides a wide range of direct marketing services, including mailshots, door drops, press inserts, and press and TV advertising, to a number of major organisations in the UK.

The group operates three agencies in the UK as separate companies, based in the north-west, Northern Ireland and London, together with a number of other marketing service companies. This case study relates to the London operation of the group, known as Media Direct. The Media Direct operation alone employs over 200 people, based in two locations in central London.

Browns Transport Ltd/Browns Tankers International Ltd/Redvers Brown

Browns is a family-run business that specialises in transporting freight between England and the Continent. The business consists of three separate companies in the UK and a French subsidiary company. Redvers Brown is the administrative company and is not described here. Browns Transport Ltd and Browns Tankers International Ltd are closely linked and, for the purposes of this case study, are treated as one company (referred to as Browns Transport) except where specific differences occur.

Browns employ a total of 41 people in the three UK companies. The organisation's main office and yard is in Kent, and it also has offices in Calais, France.

I-Spy Security

I-Spy Security is a small business that specialises in the provision, installation and maintenance of CCTV (closed circuit television) security systems. The business operates from a single small office in south-east London. I-Spy employs nine people, three of whom are part-time office staff.

Historically, I-Spy has been very successful in the retail marketplace, supplying systems for all the branches of a number of major store chains. Its business objectives are to not only maintain and grow its share of this retail market, but also to expand into other growing markets, one of which is education.

Activity 2.1

Perhaps operating as a group, find out how many people work for your college or school.

★ What services are offered?

★ What are the objectives of the organisation?

★ Where does the organisation operate?

> Some schools and colleges are now being run effectively as businesses, and may have objectives in addition to providing education.

Communicating information

All organisations, no matter what size, must handle information. This information can be generated internally, i.e. within the organisation, or can be passed on externally by suppliers, customers, statutory and legal bodies and any other organisations that support the business. Even in a small organisation, huge amounts of information are available. To run the organisation efficiently, it is critical that the volume of information communicated internally and externally is monitored and controlled.

Many successful organisations have recognised that information is a key business resource. It can be just as important to have the right information available as to have the right materials to manufacture a product or to have the right number of people available to provide a service. The right information being accessible to each level of management is critical to making correct decisions. The right information is generally:

- on time
- accurate and complete
- pertinent to the decisions to be made
- presented in an appropriate way

Did You Know?

In the 1960s, there were two major airlines operating in the USA. One airline decided to implement an on-line seat reservation system. By the 1970s, the company who did not implement the system had gone out of business. The other company is now one of the most successful, airlines in the world.

Discuss the effects of information not being on time. What if information is inaccurate or incomplete?

Think of situations where the consequences of poor information can cost lives.

Some organisations have become even more successful by using information available to them to gain an advantage over their competitors.

Over the years, many organisations have been established whose sole purpose is to provide information as a resource to other organisations. Such **information providers** vary from long-established press organisations (like Reuters) who supply international news information, through companies who provide lists of potential customers for direct mail advertising, to the more recent type of organisations who provide information via the Internet.

Activity 2.2

Find out whether your college or school uses any information providers, and, if so, which ones, and for what purposes.

The awarding bodies provide the specifications for Vocational A-levels and other qualifications, as well as other information on their websites.

Types of information

All organisations must communicate the right information to the right people, both internally and externally. The different types of information that are communicated externally are shown in Table 2.1 and those that are communicated internally are shown in Table 2.2.

The way in which information is communicated is also very important. Information can be passed on verbally, on paper or electronically. This is particularly important when you are considering the information flow within an organisation.

The larger the volume of information of any given type, the more likely it is to be stored in some form of **database** system.

Table 2.1 *Types of information that are communicated externally*

RECEIVED FROM customers and clients, wholesalers and retailers	★ Orders for the procurement of products or services
SENT TO customers and clients, wholesalers and retailers	★ Invoices for the supply of products or services
RECEIVED FROM distributors	★ Delivery confirmations for the shipment of goods to customers, retailers or wholesalers ★ Invoices for the delivery of goods
SENT TO distributors	★ Delivery notes for the shipment of goods to customers, retailers or wholesalers
RECEIVED FROM suppliers	★ Invoices for the provision of products or services
SENT TO suppliers	★ Purchase orders for the supply of products or services
RECEIVED FROM manufacturers	★ Invoices for the provision of products or services
SENT TO manufacturers	★ Advance orders for the manufacture of products ★ Changes to the specification of products ★ Specifications of new products ★ Purchase orders for the supply of products or services

Table 2.2 *Types of information that are communicated internally*

Managers and employees	All organisations will communicate large amounts of internal information to their managers and employees. The type of information will vary from organisation to organisation. You will need to understand about all types of information that are referred to in all the other sections of this chapter.
Products	★ Product specifications ★ Product pricing and discount structures ★ Stock levels ★ Design **briefs**

▼ ▼ ▼ ▼ ▼ ▼ ▼ ▼ ▼

Brief
This term is used in many contexts within different organisations. It is used to describe a summary of the specification of a product or service.

▲ ▲ ▲ ▲ ▲ ▲ ▲ ▲ ▲

Look in the Yellow Pages or on the Internet to find organisations that provide information.

Think of the information a business might need and who would provide it?

Functions within organisations

The various functions are described here. Typical information systems used by these job functions are listed in 'Information flow' (p. 93).

Job functions and departments

Generally, within any organisation groups of people are given the responsibility of performing a specific task, or set of tasks, for that organisation. These different job functions may be called departments, teams, shifts or offices. It is important to understand how these job functions or departments affect the flow of information. The way that these job functions or departments relate to one another will determine the overall structure of the organisation.

As you establish the structure of the organisation you are investigating, you need to go into further detail before you can fully understand and describe the different job functions or departments and how they inter-relate. A typical organisation probably includes administration, finance, human resources, sales, purchasing and ICT services departments. You may also find marketing, distribution, research and development (R&D), design and production functions within your selected organisation. A structure diagram for an organisation that includes all these departments is shown in Figure 2.1.

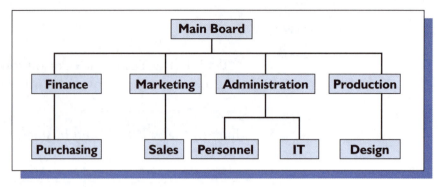

Figure 2.1 *Typical organisational structure*

Activity 2.4

Identify the functions or departments within your school or college.

You are unlikely to find all of the departments listed and you might find some functions are combined.

Did You Know?

In addition to their well-known role in ports and airports, Customs and Excise is the government department responsible for the collection of **VAT** in the UK.

Accounts or finance

The **finance** function in an organisation is responsible for all aspects of the money that comes in to and goes out of an organisation. This function communicates externally with organisations that are associated with money, such as banks, finance houses, Customs and Excise and the Inland Revenue.

Activity 2.5

Find out who is responsible for the finance function at your school or college.

Finance handles all financial information relating to the organisation:

- ✪ Profit and loss information
- ✪ Cash flow forecasts
- ✪ Expense analyses
- ✪ Payroll costs, etc.

Internally, information passes to and from this function to most other functions in the organisation, e.g. marketing and sales and personnel.

Activity 2.6

Your school or college may not have a separate purchasing department, but find out who is responsible for this function.

Purchasing is often part of the finance function and deals specifically with money that goes out of the organisation to purchase goods and services. It communicates primarily with suppliers externally, and with all functions internally that need to buy products or services from suppliers. Purchasing handles all information relating to the buying of goods and services, such as purchase orders and supplier invoices.

The **sales order processing** function, or just SOP, again is often a part of finance. This function is responsible for the administration of an organisation's financial transactions with its customers. As such it generally only deals externally with them. The information that this function normally handles includes contracts and sales orders, and sales invoices. Internally, this function communicates information to and from the sales department, the warehouse or stock room and production.

Human resources

The **human resources (HR)** department is the part of the organisation responsible for its dealings with employees. This department is sometimes called the personnel department.

For the HR department to function effectively, it must be in regular communication with all other parts of the organisation. HR receives information from external agencies, such as tax code notices from the Inland Revenue. It also communicates with external organisations, such as employment agencies (to assist in staff recruitment) and with hotel chains that have special arrangements with the organisation.

The information that this function deals with relates primarily to employees, including personal information, employment history, payroll and training records, etc.

Marketing and sales

In most organisations, **marketing** has responsibility for the planning of future sales and monitoring of the relationships with customers and potential customers. The marketing department needs to be supplied with information from all parts of the organisation, but particularly from sales, HR, finance, R&D and design.

Much of the information that this function creates is used for management decision-making, but information is also passed to sales and design. Externally, marketing will mainly communicate with groups of customers and potential customers to establish their longer-term needs, and with external information providers for financial and market forecast information. Primarily, this function handles information on forecasts for sales, products, HR needs, etc., but it also produces considerable amounts of information on future products and services, to be distributed externally.

The **sales** function in any organisation is responsible for its day-to-day contacts with individual customers. Clearly, this function has close links internally with marketing and SOP, but often has direct links to any other part of the organisation that deals with products or services, such as the warehouse or stock room and production. Information that the sales function needs includes product or service costs and prices and all customer information, but may also include prospective customer lists and information on competitors' products or services (e.g. from an external information provider).

Distribution

The **distribution** function within an organisation is responsible for the physical delivery of products to customers, retailers or wholesalers. The means by which this is achieved varies, but may include mail and couriers, rail and air freight, independent hauliers and fleets of vans or trucks.

Within any organisation, the responsibility of this department is to ensure that the right products reach the right place at the right time.

Distribution may need to communicate information with SOP, production and the department responsible for holding stocks within an organisation. This function may also communicate directly with sales and marketing. The type of information this department handles is primarily delivery documentation, but it may also be concerned with invoices.

Research and development (R&D)

You are most likely to find a **research and development (R&D)** department in an organisation that manufactures a product, but some service organisations also include one.

As the name implies, this department investigates new techniques, technologies or materials and their applicability to the products or services supplied by an organisation. After such research, the development function may produce a prototype of the product or service using the new technique, technology or material.

R&D, particularly in modern high-tech industries, is very expensive, so the R&D department needs to work very closely with the marketing department to ensure that any products or services under development closely match the long-term needs of the organisation's customers. For the same reason, R&D also needs to interact extensively with the production and design departments.

Design

After R&D have finished a prototype and the organisation has decided to take the product or service to the market, the **design** department then becomes involved. The design department is responsible for accepting a prototype and improving it into the final product or service that will be supplied to customers. This may vary from a relatively simple process of changing the prototype so that it meets the organisation's **house style** to a lengthy and complex process of totally redeveloping the product or service prototype.

A good example of house style is the range of computers produced by Apple, which started with the iMac, and has been continued with the iMac G3/G4 and the iBook.

Exercise 2.2

Find advertisements which illustrate the Apple house style and identify two other organisations that have a house style for their products.

The design department may also be asked to design a completely new product starting only from a design brief produced by the marketing function.

In many industries design can be a very expensive and lengthy process. The design department, therefore, needs to interact extensively with the marketing, production and R&D departments.

Production (service provision)

A **production** function is found in any organisation that directly manufacturers products for its customers, retailers or wholesalers. Within a service organisation, this function may be called **service provision**.

The responsibility of this department is to take raw materials, parts and facilities and use them to create the final product or service to be supplied to customers. The production department, therefore, needs to communicate regularly with *all* other functions.

ICT services

The **ICT services** function within an organisation is concerned with the provision of computer services within that organisation and both internal and external data communications. The hardware facilities provided will vary, and may include stand-alone and networked PCs, microcomputers, minicomputers, mainframe computers, and **LANs** and **WANs**.

This department is also responsible for the support and maintenance of software within an organisation, and hence needs to communicate with all other departments that make use of ICT services.

Activity 2.7

Within your school or college, find out who provides ICT services and what their role is.

Administration

The functions that an **administration** department performs vary considerably, because the term is often used for the department which controls those functions that do not naturally fit into any of the other departments in the organisation.

This department normally has responsibility for the functions that relate to the day-to-day running of an organisation, such as buildings and facilities, general maintenance and cleaning, fleet management, utilities, etc. Often, the HR and ICT services functions are part of the administration function.

Because of the wide-ranging brief such departments operate under, they need to exchange information, in varying amounts, with all other functions in the organisation.

Activity 2.8

Within your school or college, identify the information that is handled by each function or department. Also, produce a list of the appropriate human resources to annotate your structure diagram (see Activity 2.9 on page 72).

The structure of organisations

Most organisations of more than a very few people are, of necessity, hierarchical (see Figure 2.1 on page 62).

Generally, the larger the organisation, the larger and more complex the hierarchy. However, the number of levels that make up that hierarchy will vary.

▼▼▼▼▼▼▼▼▼

Hierarchical organisation
has a number of levels of management, generally organised in some form of tree structure.

▲▲▲▲▲▲▲▲▲▲

The two most extreme levels are a true **hierarchical** structure and a **flat** structure: a true hierarchical structure has many levels of management; a flat structure has only one or two. The more hierarchical a structure is, the more people within it are responsible for managing people or functions. The expression 'too many chiefs and not enough indians' is often used to describe organisations that have a very hierarchical structure. There are many managers, the 'chiefs', and relatively few people doing real day-to-day jobs for the organisation, the 'indians'. The trend in modern-day business, even in very large organisations, is to reduce the number of management levels and move towards a flatter structure.

However, it is important to understand that, as organisations grow and develop, it inevitably becomes necessary to introduce additional levels into the management structure. This may be due simply to the fact that one individual can only effectively manage the activities of a finite number of staff, or that changes in the business require additional skills or a change of responsibilities.

A corner shop is a good example of a flat structure. The Civil Service is still a very good example of a hierarchical structure.

Exercise 2.3

Suggest two other examples of hierarchical organisations and two other examples of flat organisations.

Three organisations, one structured hierarchically and the other two flat are shown in Figures 2.3, 2.4 and 2.5.

To determine how ICT can support the organisation, the responsibilities of the different levels of managers, team leaders, department heads and staff should be evaluated. This is best done by finding out with whom they need to communicate – both upwards and downwards in the organisation – and what information they need to communicate in each direction. The degree of responsibility for decision-making that exists at each management level is also important.

Generally the lower the level in an organisation, the more detailed will be the information required, but in a relatively specific area. At higher levels, information will probably relate to broader areas but be summarised for more senior managers.

A salesperson selling a particular group of a company's products needs access to the prices, availability, specifications and discount structures for all the products that he or she sells. Another salesperson for a different group of products, needs the same detailed information but for different products. The person who manages these two salespeople probably needs to know the prices and discount structures for both groups of products, but may not need to know the detailed specifications or availability of individual products. The sales director for the company does not need any of this detailed information on a regular basis, but does need summaries of total sales by product, product group, sales team and salesperson. This is shown in Figure 2.2.

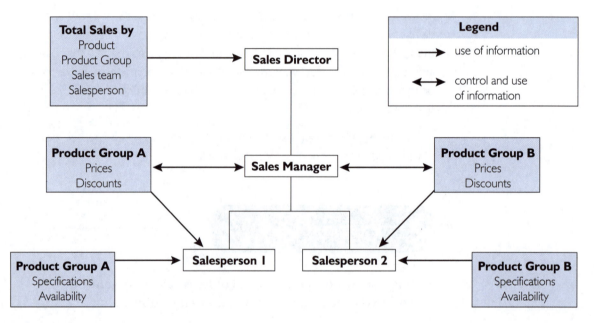

Figure 2.2   *Levels of detail of information*

Exercise 2.4

Suggest another example where the information by different levels of staff is different.

You may want to consider the Head/Principal of your school or college and a member of the teaching staff.

Media Direct

Media Direct is a hierarchical organisation with many levels of management. Because of the size and complexity of the organisation, in which a large number of departments exist to provide different forms of client services, only one part, the account management function, is considered here.

Different levels of responsibility are allocated to each tier of management. The prime responsibilities of the Client Services Director, who reports directly to the Managing Director, are to ensure that the financial business objectives of the group are met, and that the day-to-day management of all of the business activities of the group is carried out. Other key functions include the development and maintenance of long-term plans both for the group and for major clients, and the allocation of staff into teams, each one headed by an Account Director.

Each Account Director is responsible for managing and maximising the business of the clients within his or her team, which may be comprised of any combination of Senior Account Managers, Account Managers and Account Executives. As such, the Account Director manages the project finances for the clients. An Account Director is allowed to make decisions on all but the major issues on charging.

continued

continued

At a lower level, a Senior Account Manager has similar responsibilities but is normally concerned with a specific part of the business of a larger client, or with the whole of the business of a smaller client.

Account Managers are usually responsible for running individual jobs for clients and for managing the costs of these. Again, these relate to a small part of a larger client's business, or to the whole of the business of a smaller client. The Account Manager's direct manager will make all other decisions.

The responsibilities of the Account Executive are generally limited to managing small jobs, and as such have little or no financial input or responsibility.

An outline of the organisation structure of a typical account management group is shown in Figure 2.3.

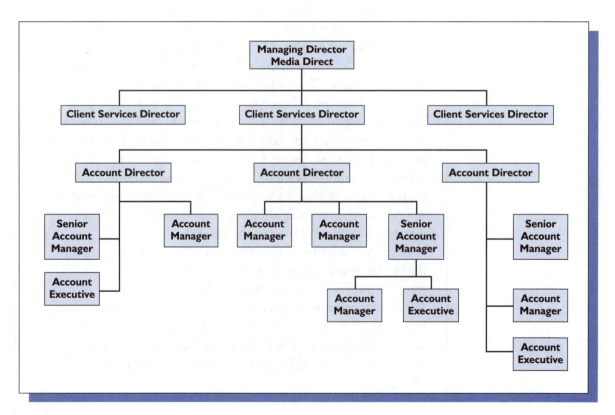

Figure 2.3 *A hierarchical organisational structure – Media Direct account management department*

Browns Transport

Browns Transport is essentially a flat organisation with only three levels involved in day-to-day operations. There are eight key personnel as shown in Figure 2.4.

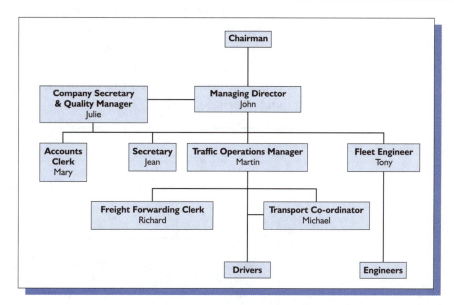

Figure 2.4 *A flat organisational structure – Browns Transport*

I-Spy Security

I-Spy Security is a truly flat organisation with only two levels in its structure (Figure 2.5). Two people manage all aspects of the business; Peter, who is nominally the Managing Director; and Gurmeet, who is the Company Secretary. In practice, they run the business jointly, with decisions being made by whoever is available at the time.

I-Spy employs four engineers: Tim, the Senior Engineer, and Mike, Bill and Deepak. There are also three part-time office staff: Mary, Jane and Helen. Mary and Helen are the wives of Peter and Gurmeet, and are also directors of the

continued

continued

company. Currently, all staff report directly to Peter and Gurmeet.

Peter and Gurmeet also do all of the selling for the company, and they have recognised that the amount of time they spend on this has been reduced as the business has grown, because more and more time has had to be devoted to the management of the engineers. They are therefore considering introducing an extra level into their organisation to oversee the day-to-day management of the engineering function.

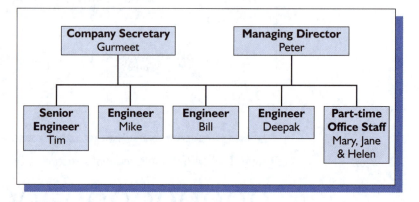

Figure 2.5 *A flat organisational structure – I-Spy Security*

Exercise 2.5

Which organisational structure best describes your school or college?

Activity 2.9

Produce a structure diagram for your school or college.

Decision making

The final factor that has an impact on the flow of information within an organisation is concerned with the level of delegation of responsibility and with management and staff participation in higher level decision-making. Often, the flatter the organisation, the more decision-making and responsibility is delegated to lower levels.

Organisations that make extensive use of team structures often delegate the responsibility for a particular task to a specific team. The way in which this task is achieved (and the responsibility for deciding which individual within the team does what) is then decided by the team members. Such high levels of delegation often have a considerable impact on information flow, as more information must be provided to all members of the team to enable them to make decisions.

Hierarchical organisations generally provide a more restricted subset of information to lower levels of staff, sufficient only for them to function in their day-to-day job. More information tends to flow between different managers at the same level.

Media Direct

The account management groups, while being hierarchical organisations, are also based on teams; each team having control over its own income, costings and billings.

The Account Directors, therefore, have a high level of authority in making decisions regarding the charging of their own clients.

Even at the lower levels of Senior Account Manager and Account Manager, the capability for making decisions normally taken at a higher level may be delegated if an individual shows the appropriate level of responsibility in making such decisions.

I-Spy Security Systems

When Peter and Gurmeet originally set up I-Spy some eight years ago, they did so by taking considerable personal financial risks. Each decision made at that time had to be taken between them after careful consideration. The management style of I-Spy therefore evolved with Peter and Gurmeet being the only members of the organisation who were empowered to take any decisions.

Most of the employees have been with the company since those early years and this has resulted in even the most minor of decisions still being referred back to Peter or Gurmeet. This is part of their problem: having insufficient time to sell and thus expand the business. They recognise that only by adding an additional level of management and giving up some of the decision making, will they be able to develop the company.

Let us return to the example of the sales team on page 68. In this hierarchical structure, decisions on prices and discount structures are taken at the level of sales director. The information is then provided for the sales managers and individual salesmen to apply rigidly.

A different organisation selling similar products may decide to give its sales team the responsibility for achieving a specific level of revenue and profit from a group of products. In this case, the sales team needs access to considerably more information, e.g. the cost of each product. The sales team would decide how many they should aim to sell, at what price and at what discount structure, to achieve the required level of revenue and profit.

Exercise 2.6

Suggest another example where staff are organised in project teams.

Information and its use

Most organisations use ICT systems to control the flow of information either internally or externally, and have a number of different systems to achieve this. This may simply be due to history, a defined development strategy or organisational factors. It is important to understand not only how these systems work, but also how they interact to support the organisation.

Systems that do not interact well may cause inefficiency or even damage to an organisation.

Probably, the worst example of this is when an organisation keeps the same information in different databases, and these are not kept consistent. However, even something as simple as having different versions of the same word processing package can cause considerable problems in the efficient flow of information.

Reasons for the use of ICT systems

Apart from controlling the flow of information, there are many other uses for ICT systems within organisations.

- ✪ The storage and management of information
- ✪ The maintenance of up-to-date information
- ✪ Speedy and accurate processing of multiple repetitive and complex calculations
- ✪ Standardisation of procedures
- ✪ Forecasting and decision-support
- ✪ Communication of information both internally and externally
- ✪ Statutory or legal requirements
- ✪ Direct management
- ✪ Management information and report production

Exercise 2.7

Suggest two other reasons why organisations use ICT systems.

Media Direct

Being an organisation that is highly dependent on information as a key business resource, Media Direct are very heavy users of ICT systems. With the exception of the accounts function, most departments have access to a PC LAN network based on a dedicated server.

Most individuals in the account management department have the use of a PC with access to Microsoft Excel for financial planning of client management; Microsoft Word for proposal and letter writing; and Microsoft Powerpoint for the production of client presentations. A number of laptop PCs with Direction facilities are also available for presentations on client premises.

Browns Transport

Browns make extensive use of computer systems. The main program they use is called System 4. This program has been written specifically for the company (a bespoke program). They also use off-the-shelf accounting and payroll programs and the secretary has access to standard word processing and spreadsheet software.

System 4 provides input screens for logging freight transport jobs. Once input, the system immediately generates the traffic sheets (Figure 2.13 on page 95) and the driver's traffic sheets (Figure 2.14 on page 96).

When each job has been completed, further details such as mileage and expenses are entered and the system then calculates the driver's wages and the costs and earnings for each truck. System 4 also automatically generates and prints an invoice for each customer.

At the end of each month a report is generated which

continued

continued

includes details of all customer invoices. The report is checked and converted to the correct file format for the accounting package by a specially written link program. This is exported into the sales ledger in the accounts package. Purchase invoices are entered manually into the accounts package.

Apart from the Personnel records, the system also stores records on tractors, trailers, product codes, trip pay rates and maintenance stock and labour costs.

Activity 2.10

Identify examples of how ICT is used in your school/college.

Find out what hardware and software is used and why.

Features of information systems

This section looks at typical applications of information systems and their features. It is extremely unlikely that you will find examples of all of these ICT systems being applied to support the organisation that you choose to investigate. However, it is important that you understand the key features of each system and, more importantly, the reasons for their use:

- ✪ Types of data and how it is organised
- ✪ Methods of data collection and data capture
- ✪ Methods of data processing, e.g. batch, on-line, real-time transaction, multi-access
- ✪ Data handling processes, e.g. sorting, merging, amending
- ✪ Types of software, e.g. application packages, bespoke systems.

▼ ▼ ▼ ▼ ▼ ▼ ▼ ▼ ▼ ▼

Relational structure

Data is stored in separate tables that are related to one another.

Serial structure

all data is stored in a single table in the order in which it was input.

Indexed

Each employee's record has a unique index or key. These are stored separately from the data. This allows the records to be sorted more quickly.

▲ ▲ ▲ ▲ ▲ ▲ ▲ ▲ ▲

These features are identified in the descriptions of typical information systems in the sections that follow.

Personnel and training systems

The **personnel record system** within an organisation is almost certainly linked to both the payroll and training record systems should they exist. Typically, it holds details of each employee's name, reference number, address and telephone number, personal details, current position and employment history, education, skills, etc. Most of this information will have been collected initially from the employee's job application form and entered via a keyboard.

Depending on the size of the organisation, the information may be held in either a simple **relational** or **serial** structure, or it may be **indexed**. The processing carried out may include sorting records in order, selecting employee records that match specified criteria or searching for a specific employee record.

All employees in one branch of an organisation have the same contact details. Rather than repeat these for each employee, the branch details are stored in a separate table that is linked to the employees' table.

Some of the information held within the personnel records may also be used as an input to **management information systems (MIS)**. This is particularly true in service organisations that rely heavily on the skills of individual employees.

The information stored is confidential and subject to the Data Protection Act (1998) and, as such, must be protected by appropriate security measures.

Activity 2.11

Collect the non-confidential personnel information for all the members of one department in your school or college.

Respect the confidentiality of information. See page 338 of the Good Working Practice Guide.

Training records are a natural extension of personnel records. Generally, only large organisations that have established staff development policies will maintain training records and training plans for employees. However, smaller companies who wish to achieve certain levels of ISO (International Standards Organisation) accreditation will find it a **statutory requirement** to maintain training records and may feel that it is simpler to do so as an extension of the personnel or employee records systems.

Such records will generally consist of simple tables and include details of training levels reached on particular products or skills.

Activity 2.12

Find out if your school or college keeps staff training records and, if so, what is recorded.

Accounts, finance and payroll systems

All organisations have some form of accounting or financial systems. Such systems require speedy and accurate processing of multiple repetitive calculations in a standardised way but, unlike payrolls, are generally achieved using **online processing**.

Small organisations are most likely to use an **application package** for their accounting and financial systems but larger organisations are most likely to have a **bespoke system** developed specifically for them through the processes of systems analysis and software development.

Activity 2.13

Find out if your school or college uses an applications package or a bespoke system for its financial systems.

Financial and accounting systems are designed to track and process the money that comes into and goes out of an organisation. As such, these systems form the cornerstone of the financial management of the organisation, and provide the basis for any financial planning or budgeting systems.

▼▼▼▼▼▼▼▼▼

Balance sheet

is a statement that shows the commercial position of a company by balancing the company's assets (property, money in the bank, etc.) with the claims on those assets (e.g. money owed).

Income and expenditure statement

summarises the money coming in to the company and the money paid out in a certain period.

▲▲▲▲▲▲▲▲▲

Media Direct

The accounting systems are currently based on an in-house mini system, but purchase orders and invoices are still paper based. This system needs to be replaced in the near future and, with this in mind, Media Direct are currently developing a fully integrated management information system.

Control of the payments coming in to an organisation from its customers is achieved using the sales ledger, and of those going out to its suppliers and other creditors, using the purchase ledger. These are combined, together with other items of expenditure and income such as payroll and bank interest, in the general (or nominal) ledger to summarise the accounts. The general ledger also allows the preparation of **balance sheets** and **income and expenditure statements**.

To be successful, indeed to stay in business, all organisations need to ensure that they are profitable in the long term, and that they control their cash flow in the short term. The information stored for such systems varies from simple relational data to highly complex data structures, depending not only on the size of the organisation, but also on the way in which the organisation's financial accounting procedures are arranged.

Financial and accounting systems are generally linked internally to most other systems within the organisation, particularly with such systems as order processing, stock control and management. In larger organisations, these systems may also have external links to the Bankers Automated Clearing System (BACS), and sometimes direct links with customers and/or suppliers.

Because much of the information contained within financial and accounting systems is not only sensitive within the company, but could also be of value to other organisations, they will often be protected by some form of security.

Most organisations have a computerised **payroll system**, whether this be in-house or run by an external bureau. It is very often also the first system that an organisation computerises. This is because a payroll system needs speedy and accurate processing of multiple repetitive and relatively complex calculations in a standardised way, generally using batch processing.

Tax codes, rates of pay and hours worked are all linked to the employee's reference number. This information can be the subject of regular changes and needs to be kept up to date to ensure the accuracy of the payroll calculations.

The payroll information will usually be held in a simple relational *or* serial format.

Often there are links to communicate information externally to both the Inland Revenue and to BACS (to pay employees' wages directly in to their bank accounts), and to communicate information internally to the organisation's finance systems. The system also produces payslips automatically that may be mailed or given to the employee (Figure 2.6).

All payroll systems contain particularly confidential information to which rigorous security should be applied.

Most payroll systems are based on application packages, but even bespoke systems rely on standard sub-routines for tax and National Insurance calculations.

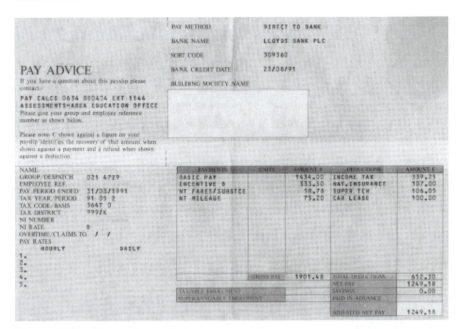

Figure 2.6   *Example payslip*

Browns Transport

As this is a fairly small company, there is no separate personnel department. Personnel records are kept on the computer system including details of holiday days owed and rates of pay. Wages sheets are created for each trip and the total pay due is passed to the accounts office. A payroll program is used to calculate the wages, which are paid directly via BACS into the employee's bank account using an Autopay program.

Research, design and development

Many of the systems used in the **research and development (R&D)** and **design** departments of large organisations will have been developed to meet the specific needs of the organisation's products or services.

However, many such departments also use other software:

- 2-D and 3-D modelling tools
- Graphic design packages
- CAD systems
- Production and project scheduling systems

Sales and purchase order processing

Sales order processing (often called **SOP**, or just **order processing**) is responsible for the management of orders and contracts placed by the customers of an organisation. This is often implemented as a separate computer system, which generates an input link to the sales ledger when the product or service has been delivered and an invoice has been raised.

It is likely that the order processing system has a direct link into the **stock control** and production systems should they exist. Many order processing systems are integrated within an applications package with stock control.

The purchasing department within an organisation is responsible for raising purchase orders for all goods and services from suppliers. As such, it creates the input for the purchase ledger system. These purchase orders are used to check invoices received from suppliers.

Stock control systems

Stock or **inventory control systems** are generally found in organisations that either hold large numbers of items or small numbers of high value items, in store. Each type of item is given a unique code either generated internally by the organisation, or as a code provided by a supplier.

A newsagent chain may allocate their own stock code to items of stationery, but would use the ISBN for books and magazines that they have on sale.

Bar coding is often used as the prime method of data capture for such stock codes. Figure 2.7 shows an example of a bar-coded ISBN.

Figure 2.7   *Bar-coded ISBN*

Exercise 2.8

What do you think ISBN stands for? Suggest two other uses for bar codes.

Other information held in stock control systems includes number in stock, location, re-order levels, cost price, sales price and date received. For high value items, there is usually a requirement to record individual item serial numbers. Depending on the number of different items held in stock, the information is stored in either a relational or an indexed format.

Stock control systems often have internal links to such systems as order processing and production systems. Sometimes they are linked to robotic picking systems within warehouses, but almost always have on-line or paper-based links.

Very often stock re-ordering is an automatic process. Purchase orders are automatically generated to be sent out by the purchasing department. In larger organisations and where delivery timescales are critical, direct external links are made with suppliers.

Exercise 2.9

Suggest organisations that are most likely to have direct links to their suppliers for re-ordering stock.

If you telephone to order items from a mail-order warehouse or catalogue, the person you speak to is almost certainly using some form of computerised SOP system linked to stock control. This enables these organisations to ensure that customer orders are dealt with speedily and accurately.

Some form of security often protects these systems, because the information contained in them is sensitive both internally and externally.

Internal e-mail systems

More and more organisations are using e-mail as the prime method for internal communication with their employees. It is very useful, not only to standardise procedures using selective mailing lists, but also to ensure fast communication of information. However, this is a system that requires careful management to ensure that only the right people receive the right information.

With an increasing number of people working either full-time or part-time from their own home, linking an organisation's internal e-mail system with the Internet allows efficient two-way communication (Figure 2.8).

Most e-mail systems are based on applications packages, often integrated within office systems.

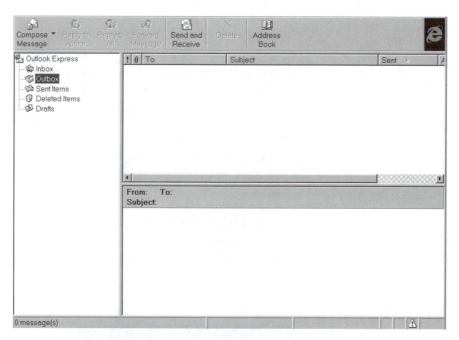

Figure 2.8 *E-mail screen*

Internet and Intranet

The **Internet** and **Intranet**, together with private **LANs** and **WANs** provide enormous opportunities for organisations to achieve speedy and efficient communications both internally and externally.

The Internet has provided organisations with the ability to provide not only access for its employees to external websites and information providers, but also the opportunity to promote its activities relatively easily and cost-effectively to a potentially enormous marketplace (Figure 2.9).

An Intranet provides a further opportunity for organisations to communicate information within an internal closed network to all their employees. Increasingly, larger organisations are making use of Intranet facilities across their own private networks alongside standard ICT systems.

Organisations use many other ICT systems that depend on communications networks.

- ✪ **Video conferencing systems** provide an organisation with the facility for its employees in different locations to not only talk to each other but to see each other as they do so. In such systems, not only voice but video information are transmitted across a private network or the Internet. Such systems are used to reduce travel costs and to arrange meetings at short notice.

- ✪ **EPOS** (electronic point of sale) information is communicated across networks by many retail organisations. This enables such organisations to keep up-to-date information on all stock levels, prices and special discounts, etc. in all their head office and sales outlets.

- ✪ **Fax on demand** provides an organisation with the ability to offer potential customers the facility to telephone one of a number of dedicated telephone numbers, and by leaving their own fax number, receive the information associated with the selected number automatically.

Exercise 2.10

Suggest examples of organisations that make use of communications services such as video conferencing, EPOS and fax on demand.

▼▼▼▼▼▼▼▼▼▼

Dumb terminal
consists of a keyboard and monitor that are connected to the main computer. It has no processing power of its own.

Multi-user
system consists of a central computer with a number of terminals – either dumb or PCs – that allow a number of people to use it at the same time.

▲▲▲▲▲▲▲▲▲▲

Browns Transport

The computer system currently being used is a simple **multi-user** system. Some staff still access this using **dumb terminals**, although many now use a PC (personal computer) to access the system. Some, such as the secretary, have other software such as Windows and word processing software on the hard disk of their PC, but this cannot be accessed from other computers and there is no link with System 4 or the other packages.

continued

continued

There is a modem linking the computer system to the telephone line. This allows access to the computer system in the office in Calais although it is not possible to input data into the French system or to print from it. Most of the communication with the French office is by telephone or fax.

System 4 is being continuously updated by the company's programmer who lives in Devon. He uses the telephone lines and modem to download any upgrades to the software as they are developed.

The company also has its own site on the World Wide Web. See Figure 2.9. This is currently used purely for advertising the company and is essentially an electronic copy of the company's brochure. In future, it may be possible for customers to book freight directly via the website.

The company is currently planning to upgrade to a networked system with links to France through an ISDN line. System 4 will also be updated to run under Windows rather than DOS as at present. This will provide a number of advantages to the company. It will be possible for all staff to have access to all the software available and will enable data to be transferred more easily between the different programs. It will also mean that staff in both offices will have full access to both the English and French systems.

Figure 2.9 *Browns Transport homepage*

Product manufacturing systems

The term **manufacturing systems** is used to describe any of the wide variety of systems that are provided to support organisations that actually make products. Any information system that automates any part of the production cycle is classed as a manufacturing system.

▼▼▼▼▼▼▼▼▼▼

Bill of materials
is a list of the parts needed to manufacture a single product.

▲▲▲▲▲▲▲▲▲▲

Such systems vary from simple systems that carry out **bill of materials** processing to systems that fully automate a complete production line.

Many manufacturing systems are based on packages but, in most cases, they are tailored considerably to meet the needs of a particular organisation.

In many industries, without the aid of these information systems, it would be impossible to manufacture certain products cost effectively.

JIT (just in time) production systems are a very good example of a manufacturing system. They use sophisticated production scheduling techniques to enable an organisation to minimise stock holdings while still meeting customer demand.

Exercise 2.11

Suggest an organisation that might use JIT.

I-Spy Security

Despite being the smallest of the three organisations considered in these case studies, I-Spy make the most use of ICT systems to support the different functions of their business. They are currently in the process of implementing an integrated system based on Microsoft Access database running under a Windows environment on a stand-alone PC. This system is not yet fully operational within I-Spy. This is because of the sheer volume of data that has to be entered in setting up the system, particulary customer, installation and inventory data. However, when

continued

continued

fully live the system will automate most of the business operations.

★ Sales order processing and sales reporting

★ Automatic invoice production

★ Customer records

★ Customer inventory management and reporting

★ In-house stock control

★ Product returns to and from customers and suppliers

★ Product reliability history

★ Supplier and product records

★ Scheduling of engineering work – for installation, planned maintenance and call-outs

★ Simple personnel records

Note that one business function of I-Spy is not to be implemented on this system: purchasing. Due to the close control maintained over costs at any one time, the company uses a number of different suppliers for cameras, VCRs, etc. so it is not practical to automate the purchasing process.

The system is entered via a simple interface allowing the user to select one of seven main options.

1 Table data entry – essentially only used to set up the system

2 Table data update – for maintenance of the database

3 Order entry – for input of new customer orders

4 Monthly reporting – for selection of a series of monthly reports

5 Selective reporting – to request special reports

6 Service calls – for input of call-outs

7 Queries – to access a number of pre-formatted regularly used queries

continued

continued

At each level as the user progresses through any of these options there are a series of selection screens.

To take one example and follow it through, if the user selects order input, they are presented with a further series of five options (Figure 2.10).

1   New customer

2   New installation – the order is for a new branch or location of an existing customer

3   Existing customer – an order for an addition or upgrade to a CCTV system already installed

4   Order confirmation – for the input of additional charges that need to be applied after a system is installed, and for the input of the installation date

5   Main switchboard – this quits order input and returns to the main log on screen

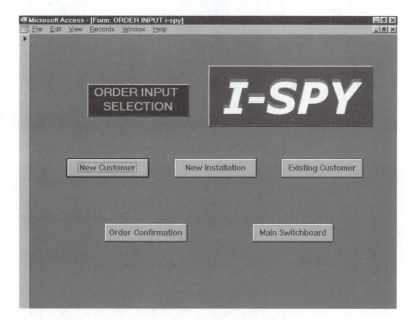

Figure 2.10   *I-Spy order input selection screen*

If the user takes the new customer option they are presented with the main customer details screen to input

continued

continued

company name and address, contact name, telephone number, etc. On completion the system automatically allocates a customer number and a new installation number. The user is then given the option of continuing with order entry or returning back to the main screen. See Figure 2.11. (At all stages in the system, the user has similar options to quit the process and start again.)

Figure 2.11 *I-Spy customer order input screen*

If the user decides to continue with data entry, a screen for the input of the product details is presented. This screen is backed up by a series of look-up tables for product codes and descriptions and product prices. (The system makes extensive use of look-up tables to make the user's job easier.) These look-up tables can be overwritten by the user.

When the input of all the products for a particular order has been completed, the user has the option of continuing to a service order input screen, for customers who have taken up a maintenance contract, or to start entry of a new order.

The service order input screen, again based on look-up

continued

continued

tables, allows the user to input the level and frequency of maintenance services that the customer has chosen. If the user decides to start data entry of a new order, they are returned to the main order entry selection screen.

A similar process is followed for the input of orders for a new installation or for an existing customer.

All of the other functions within the system offer the same facilities to the user in terms of look-up tables and simple selection processes.

Information flow

In addition to being able to describe the reasons for and features of all of the above systems, you should also be able to use **charting techniques** to show the flow of information in these systems. As part of your information flow analysis, you will have found out who needs what information, and you can then draw diagrams to show how they interact.

Obviously, the size and complexity of the organisation, its internal structure, and the number and diversity of its external contacts affect the flow of information. Most importantly, that flow of information must support the business objectives and requirements of the organisation.

It is important to recognise that investigating the flow of information in an organisation starts with determining who needs the information, where and when they need it, and how it should be best presented to them. Information may need to flow simply from one person to one other person within the organisation or from one person to many. The same information may need to be sorted, collated, summarised or restricted in the way it is presented to different people in the organisation.

Information can be passed on verbally, on paper or electronically. When charting the information flow within an organisation, it is essential to differentiate between the different methods of passing these three types of information.

- ✪ Face to face
- ✪ Documents, via internal or external post
- ✪ EDI or e-commerce
- ✪ LAN or Internet e-mail

- Telephone
- Facsimile (fax)
- Centralised database systems

Exercise 2.12

Suggest types of information that could be passed using each of these methods.

Media Direct

When a client requests a new piece of business from Media Direct, the data flow starts with the request from the client which comes in to Media Direct via the account manager responsible for that client. This is referred to as a client brief, and, in this case, we are considering a client brief for a new mailing to 'cold prospects', i.e. potential new customers for that client who will be selected by Media Direct, and sent a mailshot on behalf of the client.

The account manager passes the client brief to the three other main departments that have responsibilities for answering this type of client request: the planning, creative and production departments.

The planning department has the responsibility for deciding which of the many mailing lists available should be used and thus producing information on the quantities to be mailed, the likely response percentage, etc., and the costs. The creative department is responsible for the design and content of the actual mailshot, and the production department for the final construction of the mailing pack and its costs. At this stage, there is considerable information flow between all three departments and the account management department with the quantities, designs and resultant costs being modified to develop and finalise the proposed mailing and to establish the costs to the client.

When this initial stage is finished and a proposal and

continued

continued

quotation has been produced for the client, the Account Manager is responsible for the presentation of this information to the client. If the client agrees this proposal, then Media Direct will set in motion the appropriate actions for the production and distribution of the mailshot.

If however the client does not agree, then effectively the process starts again at the beginning, albeit probably only on the basis of some form of amendment to the original brief. The information flow diagram for a new client brief is shown in Figure 2.12.

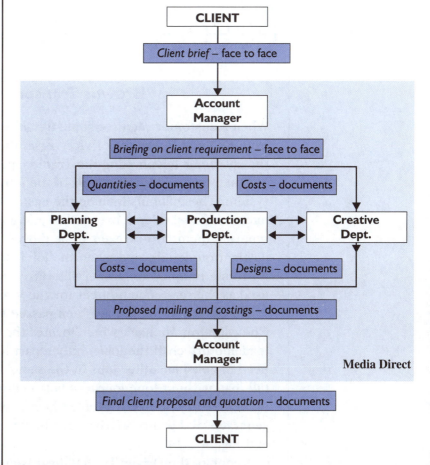

Figure 2.12 *Information flow diagram – Media Direct account management client brief*

continued

continued

Most of the information flows described here are essentially paper based although, since extensive use is made of a local area network of PCs, much of this information is available in a computerised form. In the future, it is likely that much more information will be passed using this PC network when a new MIS is completed.

Browns Transport

When a customer requires some freight to be transported from England to France or vice versa, the job is initiated by the customer telephoning the Traffic Operations Manager, Martin. Martin logs the details of the job onto the computer system. These details include the customer's company name, address, telephone number and contact name, the type and quantity of freight to be moved, the pick-up and destination details, and when the job is to be done. The job is given a unique Freight Service (FS) number, which is used as the reference number for the job.

The details of the job are then passed to the Transport Co-ordinator, Michael, who allocates the job to a particular load and driver. If the job is only a part load, Michael will need to consider other jobs in the same area to make up a full load without long journeys between the different pick-up or delivery points. A Traffic Sheet is produced that generates and prints a Driver Traffic Sheet. See Figure 2.13 and Figure 2.14.

A copy of the Driver Traffic Sheet is given to the driver who fills it in during his journey. On his return, he hands

continued

continued

```
Browns Transport Ltd          Traffic Sheet                    10/01/98
--------------------------------------------------------------------------
Traffic Sheet No.    :   86501                  Reqd. date :   /  /

Driver ID   : KV  Name : VENABLES               Tractor ID : 31 N298 BKL

Trailer no. : BTL 415                           Tacho. no. :

Prod.code: BTO1BTL        Desc. : TANKERS CHARGING TRANSPORT      DPO :

Prod.code   : BTO1BTL         Tip : N  Customer  : BROWNS TANKERS INT. LTD
                                  Reference :

Prod type  : J        Unit :    O      Unit cost :    0.00         Costs

Prod.desc  : TANKERS CHARGING TRANSPORT      Quant.:

Notes      :


Comments   :
                                                   Total cost :

Invoice num :          VAT code : Z                VAT @       :

                                                       Totals  _/mile
Mileage - Start :            kms    Tractor Earnings :
          Finish :           miles  - Tractor costs  :
                                    Gross Margin      :
                                    - Admin/Trail     :
                                    Nett Margin       :

--------------------------------------------------------------------------
Payment to other contractors  :    0.00                    VAT :

Linked sheets for costing     :
```

Figure 2.13 *Traffic sheet*

the sheet to Michael along with any paperwork such as delivery notes. The wages owed are calculated and the sheet is handed to Jean, the Secretary, who logs all the FS numbers and the Traffic Sheet number. This enables the computer system to work out the costs and earnings for each truck.

The delivery notes are passed to Martin, the Traffic Operations Manager, who clips them to a copy of the Traffic Sheet with the invoice value and an invoice is automatically generated and printed. The Traffic Sheet is checked against the invoice. Proof of delivery is attached to the invoice, which is sent to the customer by post. The bottom copy is filed along with a printed copy of the job records.

continued

continued

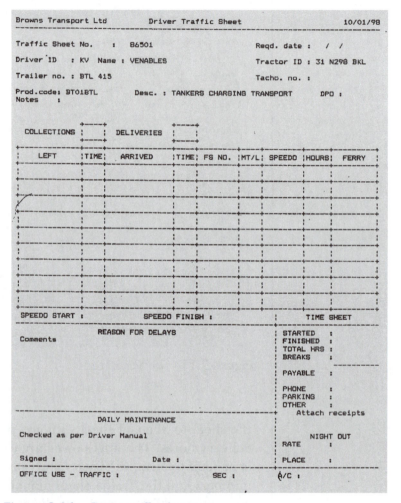

```
Browns Transport Ltd        Driver Traffic Sheet              10/01/98

Traffic Sheet No.   :   86501          Reqd. date :   /  /

Driver ID  : KV  Name : VENABLES       Tractor ID : 31 N298 BKL

Trailer no. : BTL 415                  Tacho. no. :

Prod.code: BT01BTL      Desc. : TANKERS CHARGING TRANSPORT      DPO :
Notes    :

          +---+      +---+
COLLECTIONS :  : DELIVERIES :  :
          +---+      +---+

  LEFT      :TIME: ARRIVED    :TIME: FS NO. :MT/L: SPEEDO :HOURS: FERRY

SPEEDO START :          SPEEDO FINISH :           :      TIME SHEET

              REASON FOR DELAYS                : STARTED  :
Comments                                       : FINISHED :
                                               : TOTAL HRS :
                                               : BREAKS   :
                                               :---------------
                                               : PAYABLE  :
                                               :
                                               : PHONE    :
                                               : PARKING  :
                                               : OTHER    :
                                               :+     Attach receipts
              DAILY MAINTENANCE                :
Checked as per Driver Manual                   :       NIGHT OUT
                                               : RATE    :
Signed :              Date :                    : PLACE   :
OFFICE USE - TRAFFIC :              SEC :        A/C :
```

Figure 2.14 *Driver traffic sheet*

The other main information in Browns relates to the purchase of goods and services:

★ Ferries

★ Sub-contractors

★ Workshop supplies

★ Office supplies

★ Diesel and tolls

continued

continued

Each day the company receives faxes from the ferry companies detailing which vehicle used which ferry crossing. Jean enters this into the job screen. Weekly purchase invoices from the ferry companies are checked against these details by Jean and then passed to Mary, the Accounts Clerk, for payment.

All drivers are issued with company credit cards, which they use to purchase diesel. When the purchase invoices for these card transactions are received, they are checked against the Driver Traffic Sheet before being passed for payment.

Tax and NI payments are sent to the Inland Revenue monthly, and full details of wages paid and tax and NI deducted are sent at the end of the year. Details of value added tax (VAT) paid and charged are sent to Customs and Excise.

Activity 2.14

Draw an information flow diagram for a process within your school or college. For example, consider the process of a prospective student applying for a place at the college or the recruiting of a new member of staff.

> You need to find out what information is passed, from whom, to whom and in what form

Management Information Systems (MIS)

The term MIS is used to cover the very wide variety of ICT facilities that provide support for managers and executives in forecasting, planning, organising, controlling and decision-making within an organisation. As such, these ICT facilities can be provided in a variety of different ways.

At their simplest level MIS may simply be a series of forecasts that have been manually input and collated across a department or team. A spreadsheet forecast which enables a manager to change variables on a 'what if' basis is another simple form of MIS. A report showing year-to-date performance in a particular area is yet another.

Exercise 2.13

Suggest two other examples of management information systems.

Browns Transport

System 4 is able to print out a range of reports, which are used by the Managing Director and Chairman when they need to make management decisions.

Generally, however, MIS bring together information from a variety of sources, both internal and external, sorting, collating, merging and analysing it as necessary to provide only the relevant and necessary information to the manager or executive concerned.

MIS systems are specific to the person or persons that they support so they are usually bespoke systems, but again using standard facilities such as database management, graphics and spreadsheets.

Media Direct

By integrating accounting systems, in addition to the budgetary and planning features of conventional MIS, the new system will provide further facilities.

continued

continued

★ Computerised job and project management

★ On-screen cost control

★ On-screen invoice control and production

★ Time management and time charging facilities

This system is being developed in-house as a bespoke system. This is because of the variety of services that Media Direct provides to its clients, and the consequent complexity of charging for such items as production, design, consultancy and media purchasing.

Two specialist forms of management information systems are important: executive support and decision support systems.

▼▼▼▼▼▼▼▼▼
Strategic planning decisions
are those which relate to the longer-term aspirations of the organisation in important areas.
▲▲▲▲▲▲▲▲▲

Executive support systems are targeted at senior executives who have to make **strategic planning decisions** but who are not expert in the use of ICT and do not make use of spreadsheets or databases. As such, executive support systems provide a simple graphical interface and the facility to change parameters quickly and easily. Typically these systems also include their own database and modelling base and use data from both inside and outside the organisation. This may include specialist information such as economic indicators and share prices.

An example of the sort of decision-making process that such systems are designed to support might be the director of a UK company trying to make a decision as to whether they should start selling their products in Europe.

Exercise 2.14

Suggest two other decision-making processes that an executive support system might be used to support.

Decision support systems are really a form of logistics system for the support of management decision making. These systems are generally relatively complex and will require training to become proficient in their use. Decision support systems only make use of information from within the organisation and this is organised within the system in a structured format. The processing that is carried out on this information uses specialist tools such as traffic flow and statistical analysis. Typically these systems are used in such areas as new product planning or work flow planning.

A very simple example of a decision support system is the system in use in many schools and colleges for the production of timetables.

Exercise 2.15

Suggest two other uses of decision support systems.

Revision questions

1 What are the main differences between the three organisations in the case studies?

2 What is the main function of each organisation?

3 Who are the customers of Browns Transport and who are the suppliers?

4 What information passes between Browns Transport and their customers and suppliers?

5 Give three types of information provider.

6 What is the function of the accounts or finance department in an organisation?

7 Use the example of a sales department to describe the different detail of information needed by different levels of management.

8 What is the function of the human resources department in an organisation?

9 What is another name for the HR department?

10 Describe how decision making differs between Media Direct and I-Spy Security.

11 How can ICT systems sometimes hinder the efficiency of an organisation?

12 What are the key features of a stock control system?

13 What services may be provided by communications networks?

14 Draw an information flow diagram for Browns Transport to show what happens when a customer requires some freight to be transported from England to France, from the customer making the request to them paying the invoice.

15 What extra facilities will Media Direct's new MIS provide?

Spreadsheet Design

3

- Designing spreadsheets to produce required information
- Preparing standard spreadsheets that others can use to produce required information
- Learning and applying good design and test principles

To complete your portfolio for this unit, you need to create a spreadsheet to meet the specified requirements of a user. To do that you need to complete five stages:

1. Understand clearly what it is the user wants.
2. Produce a written document describing what the spreadsheet will do and agree this with the user.
3. Design and create a spreadsheet.
4. Test your spreadsheet to make sure it works correctly and can cope with being used both correctly and incorrectly.
5. Write some documentation for your spreadsheet, both for the user and technical documentation, explaining how your spreadsheet works in case someone other than yourself needs to correct or update the spreadsheet.

Stage 1 is important, unless the spreadsheet you produce does what the user wants all your effort will have been wasted. You also need to remember that your spreadsheet should be designed for a user who is not an IT professional.

This chapter covers five topics:

- ✪ Spreadsheet activities
- ✪ Design and presentation
- ✪ Programming
- ✪ Analysis and specification
- ✪ Testing and documentation

You will meet new technical terms in each of these topics. Some of the words may be familiar but have a specialised meaning in this area of study. You need to know how to use these terms correctly. You should adopt standard ways of working and be aware of security procedures; these are covered in the *Good Working Practice Guide* that starts on page 335.

This unit relies on case study material. The four case studies used here are:

- ✪ Cellphone World
- ✪ Bus passes
- ✪ Costs of car ownership
- ✪ Financial sales

You also need to produce a spreadsheet solution for a specified user.

> *Start looking for a suitable user now!*

Cellphone World

Cellphone World sells mobile phones to the public. There are different makes and models of mobile phones and you can connect these phones to different service providers (e.g. Vodafone, one2one).

Each service provider has different tariffs (a tariff sets out how you will be charged) to suit different mobile phone users.

- ★ One tariff may suit people who make a lot of calls in the evening and not many during the day.

- ★ Another tariff may suit a business user who makes all their calls during the day and hardly any in the evening.

continued

continued

The cost of buying a cellphone can be made up of several different parts too:

★ **The basic phone**

★ **'Hands-free' kit for use in a car**

★ **Initial connection charge to the service**

★ **Various accessories such as spare batteries or a leather case.**

Advising customers which mobile phone, which service and which tariff is best for them is a complex job – but one that is ideal for a spreadsheet.

Spreadsheets are a powerful business tool because they allow people to keep track of financial data. This helps them to predict what might happen in the future. Two main uses of spreadsheets are called **budgeting** and **modelling**.

If in the future you decide you would like to run your own business, you may need to ask your bank manager for a loan. Before s/he would be willing to loan you money to start your business, s/he may ask to see a cash flow forecast (Figure 3.1). This kind of budgeting is ideal for a spreadsheet because not only does it make all the calculations easy but it makes it easy to play the 'what-if?' game. So you can quickly see the answers to questions like 'what if I made twice as many sales in the first 3 months?', or 'what if I only employed one person to help rather than two and halved my wages bill?'.

However, financial applications are not the only use for spreadsheets.

Your local council will have a highways department whose job it is to look after the roads in your area. They might wish to improve a particularly busy stretch of road. Having collected data on traffic flow by doing a survey, they could use a spreadsheet to model what would happen if they modified the road by widening it or changing the timing of traffic lights.

A motor racing team uses electronic sensors to collect data on the performance of their car's engine. This data is fed into a spreadsheet and used to see how the engine's performance would change if alterations were made to the car's electronic engine management system.

People who run their own business, manage budgets within a department of a large company, or tune racing cars, find spreadsheets very useful

Cash flow forecast - Cellphone World				Month:	Jan 1999
	Week 1	Week 2	Week 3	Week 4	Monthly Total
Income					
Sales of phones	£600	£620	£650	£670	£2,540
Other sales	£450	£450	£500	£500	£1,900
Repairs	£200	£200	£220	£220	£840
Total Sales	£1,250	£1,270	£1,370	£1,390	£5,280
Outgoings					
Wages	£300	£300	£320	£320	£1,240
Purchases	£200	£210	£210	£220	£840
Rent	£500	£500	£500	£500	£2,000
Other	£150	£150	£150	£150	£600
Total Outgoings	£1,150	£1,160	£1,180	£1,190	£4,680
Profit/loss	£50	£110	£190	£200	£350

Figure 3.1 *Example cash flow forecast*

tools, but these people are not IT professionals. Their spreadsheets need to be easy to use and the design should discourage them from making mistakes.

Although when producing a complex spreadsheet application, specifying and designing your spreadsheet is always your first step, you need to understand more about how spreadsheets work before looking at the process of design and specification.

Spreadsheet activities

A spreadsheet presents the user with a sheet made up of **rows** and **columns** as shown in Figure 3.2. Columns are named letters of the alphabet and rows are numbered. The box where a row and column meet is called a cell and the **cell reference** or **address** is made up of its column letter and row number.

Exercise 3.1

What happens after 26 columns, when there are no more letters of the alphabet left? What is the maximum number of rows and columns on the spreadsheet you are using?

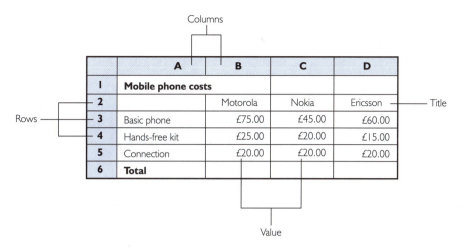

Columns

	A	B	C	D
1	**Mobile phone costs**			
2		Motorola	Nokia	Ericsson
3	Basic phone	£75.00	£45.00	£60.00
4	Hands-free kit	£25.00	£20.00	£15.00
5	Connection	£20.00	£20.00	£20.00
6	**Total**			

Rows

Title

Value

Figure 3.2   *Spreadsheets: basic terms*

Each cell can be empty or can contain one of three things: text, a number or formula.

Sometimes called row or column titles or labels, **text** cells are used to help spreadsheet users to understand what the numeric data in the spreadsheet shows and how to use the spreadsheet. In Figure 3.2, cell A1 contains a main title, cells A3, A4, A5, A6 contain row titles, cells B2, C2 and D2 contain column titles.

Sometimes called values, **numbers** can be formatted in a number of ways e.g. currency or percentage. The value 0.12 formatted as a percentage is displayed as 12%.

Figures 3.1 and 3.2 both show numbers displayed in currency format.

Formulae are the real power of a spreadsheet. They allow calculations not only by a fixed value but by reference to a cell address.

=B2+B3 adds together the values found in cell addresses B2 and B3.

Activity 3.1

Find out what other formats are available for numbers on your spreadsheet.

You will probably find these listed in the help facility.

**Activity
3.2**

Cellphone World have asked you to create a simple
spreadsheet to calculate the total cost of different
types of mobile phone. Enter the data shown in Figure
3.2 using your spreadsheet software.
  To calculate the total cost of a Motorola phone, enter a
formula into cell B6. The formula adds together the
contents of these cells.

For Activity 3.2, you could have taken advantage of another spreadsheet facility
called a **function**. The SUM function adds up all the values between two cells,
so =SUM(B3:B5) has the same effect as =B3+B4+B5. Now you need to
add up the cost of the other phones. Here you come across another
important spreadsheet facility: **copying formulae**. Rather than entering
another formula in C6 and another in D6 you can copy the existing formula.
When you do this the formula changes as you copy it.

The way the cell addresses change when the formula is copied is called
relative referencing (or relative addressing), because the address changes
relative to where it is copied. Note that if you copy a formula down the rows
rather than across the columns then the row number changes.

This relative referencing effect, where the cell addresses change as you copy
the formula is often what you want to happen. However, there are
circumstances when you do *not* want this to happen.

The spreadsheet you have created does not calculate the VAT that needs
to be added to the total cost of the phone. VAT is a fixed rate (currently
17.5%).

The formula to enter in B7 to calculate the VAT is =B6*E3 – total cost for the
Motorola phone multiplied by the VAT rate. However, if you copy that formula
to C6, it changes (due to relative referencing) to =C6*F2. The C6 is fine, that
is the total cost of the Nokia phone, but F2 does not contain the VAT rate,
which is a fixed value and is in cell E3. In this case, you want to turn off the
relative referencing effect on the E3 cell address.

To turn off the relative referencing effect, you use a special symbol (the $ sign)
to use **absolute referencing** instead. So the original formula should be
=B6*E3. This copies to C7 to become =C6*E3 and to D5 to become
=D5*E3. The E3 cell address remains the same because the $ symbols
indicate it is an absolute reference that is not to change when the formula is
copied.

106   CHAPTER 3   SPREADSHEET DESIGN

★   Enter in cell B6 the formula as =SUM(B3:B5).

★ Copy this across cells C6 and D6.

★   Now inspect the formula in C6 and check that it has changed. As you have copied it across a column (from column B to column C), the cell addresses also changes so in C6 the formula now reads =SUM(C3:C5). When the formula is copied into D6 you see the column part of the addresses changes again to =SUM(D3:D6).

> The spreadsheet totals should now look the same as in Figure 3.3.

	A	B	C	D	E
1	**Mobile phone costs**				
2		Motorola	Nokia	Ericsson	VAT rate
3	Basic phone	£75.00	£45.00	£60.00	17.5%
4	Hands-free kit	£25.00	£20.00	£15.00	
5	Connection	£20.00	£20.00	£20.00	
6	**Total**	**£120.00**	**£85.00**	**£95.00**	
7	VAT				
8	**Grand Total**				

Figure 3.3   *Results of Activity 3.3*

Add the text shown in rows 7 and 8 and column E on Figure 3.3 and the formulae for B7. Copy the formula from B7 to C7 and D7. Inspect the values displayed in B7, C7 and D7 to check that the absolute referencing has worked.

In some circumstances, when you copy a formula, you may want the column address to change (relative referencing), but the row address to be fixed (absolute referencing) or vice versa. In these cases you only place the $ sign in front of the part of the address (column letter or row number) you want to fix. This is called **mixed referencing.**

> When the formula =B5+E$8 is copied, relative referencing affects all parts of the formula except the row number 8, which is fixed by the $ preceding it.

With a complex spreadsheet with lots of formulae, it can sometimes be difficult to see how it works. This is particularly the case if you have been asked to correct or modify a spreadsheet someone else has created. In cases like these the **audit** function found on Microsoft Excel is very useful. To see how the formula in a particular cell depends on or affects other cells, all you need to do is place the cursor in that cell then, from the Tools menu, choose the auditing option. A submenu then pops out and you can choose to trace the cell's precedents (arrows appear on the sheet showing which cells provide the data for the formula) or trace its dependants (which cells use the current cell for their data). Knowing which cells depend on a particular cell is important because, if you make a change to that cell, you may unwittingly also affect other cells that depend on it.

More on formulae

So far we have only considered formulae using the + operator for addition, the * for multiplication, and the SUM function. There are four other arithmetic operators:

−	for subtraction	
/	for division	
^	for exponentiation	e.g. $3\char94 2$ is the same as 3*3
%	for per cent	e.g. 10% is the same as 0.1

There are also the relational operators:

>	greater than
<	less than
<>	not equal

The addition of an = sign to the greater or less than signs provides the greater than/less than or equal to operator, e.g. >= means greater than or equal to. For an example, see the IF function on page 110.

There are three logic operators: AND, NOT and OR.

- ✪ **AND returns the value TRUE if** *all* **its arguments are TRUE**
- ✪ **OR returns the value TRUE if** *any* **of its arguments are TRUE**
- ✪ **NOT reverses the logic of its argument**

When a formula has more than one operator, the order in which the operations are done (evaluated) is important.

You might expect the value is 10 (2+3 is 5 multiplied by 2 gives 10), however, it actually displays the value 8. This is because the spreadsheet does not do the sum in left-to-right order but uses the **order of mathematical precedence**.

Therefore, in the formula the 3*2 part is done first (giving 6), then 6 is added to 2, giving 8. If you want to force the evaluation of operators in a different order you can use brackets, since whatever is in the brackets is done first.

Exercise 3.2

How can you get the answer 10 from the example formula in Activity 3.5 by using brackets?

Functions

As well as the SUM function, most spreadsheets have a large number of other functions covering a range of mathematical, statistical, engineering and financial operations. You can find out about what the functions do and how to use them by using the Help facility on your spreadsheet. Some of the more commonly used functions are now explained.

The **AVERAGE function** returns the average (arithmetic mean) of the contents of a range of cells.

In the spreadsheet in Figure 3.4 =AVERAGE(A1:E1) returns the value 3.4 (=(2+2+3+4+6)/5).

	A	B	C	D	E
1	2	2	3	4	6
2					

Figure 3.4 *Example of the AVERAGE function*

The **IF function** allows you to test a **condition** (e.g. is the value in cell A3 greater than 10?) and then carry out one action if the condition is true and another if it is false.

Activity 3.6

The local bus company only issues student bus passes if the student is over 16 but under 21. To show which students in your group can have a bus pass create a spreadsheet like the one shown in Figure 3.5.

	A	B	C
1	**Bus Passes**		
2	**Name**	**Age**	**Bus Pass?**
3	Andrews	17	
4	Clements	15	
5	Davidson	22	
6	Evans	18	
7	Patel	20	
8	Wilson	23	

Figure 3.5 *Bus passes spreadsheet*

A formula is needed in C3 that displays 'Yes' if they are eligible for a bus pass and 'No' if they are not. In 'English', the formula would need to say 'If age > 16 and < 21 then display 'Yes' otherwise display 'No'. In fact, the spreadsheet formula is very similar: =IF(B3>16 AND B3<21, 'Yes', 'No').

Activity 3.7

Enter the formula in cell C3. Then, copy your formula down through cells C4 to C8 and check it displays the correct information in the cells.

Increments: Spreadsheets like Microsoft Excel allow you to fill out lists based on the initial values.

Activity 3.8

★ Enter the number 1 in cell A1 and 3 in B1, then select these two cells.

★ Using the autocopy handle on the current cell pointer (the little black box at the bottom right corner) drag out this selection across C1, D1 and E1.

The series should be continued in these cells for you; see Figure 3.6.

	A	B	C	D	E
1	1	3	5	7	9
2					

Figure 3.6 *Autofilling sequences*

This works not only with numbers but with days of the week and months. So, if you enter Monday in A1, then autocopy that across B1 to E1, it fills in the other days of the week for you.

The **MEDIAN function** returns the median (the number in the middle of a set of numbers). Using the example in Figure 3.6, =MEDIAN(A1:E1) returns the value 5.

The **MIN function** returns the minimum value in a range, while the **MAX function** returns the maximum value in a range.

Consider the spreadsheet in Figure 3.7:
=MIN(A1:E1) returns the value 3, whereas MAX(A1:E1) returns the value 7.

	A	B	C	D	E
1	6	7	3	4	6
2					

Figure 3.7 *Using MIN/MAX functions*

The **MODE function** returns the mode (the most commonly occurring value). Using the example in Figure 3.7, =MODE(A1:E1) returns the value 6.

The **COUNT function** counts the number of values in a range.

In the spreadsheet in Figure 3.8 putting the formula =COUNT(A1:D1) in cell E1 returns the value 3.

	A	B	C	D	E
1	6		3	4	3
2					

Figure 3.8 *Using COUNT*

The **INT function** rounds a number down to the nearest integer (whole number). So =INT(3.8) displays the value 3.

You can display a number as a **percentage** using the percentage format. Most spreadsheets have a button on the formatting toolbar to apply percentage format to the current or selected cells. This format divides the cell value by 100 and adds a % sign.

You can use the **RAND** function to display a **random number**, which is greater than 0 and less than 1.

You can use the exponentiation operator to provide the **square** of a number.

▼ ▼ ▼ ▼ ▼ ▼ ▼ ▼ ▼

PI function
returns the value of π
(3.14159265358979)

▲ ▲ ▲ ▲ ▲ ▲ ▲ ▲ ▲

*To find the area of a circle with a radius of 5 cm, use the formula =**PI**()*(5 ^ 2).*

The **SQRT function** returns the **square root** of a number.

SQRT(16) returns 4.

Activity 3.9

Find out about how these functions work (some you will use later).

IsNumeric
Now()
Today()
Concatenate

A good place to start looking is the Help facility.

You are thinking of buying a car and are concerned about the costs of running it, so you decide to look at the costs of running various different types of car over a year.

Your fixed costs are:

Road tax	£155
MOT	£65
Petrol per litre	85p

Your variable costs depend on the type of car:

Type of car	Insurance (per year)	Litres per kilometre
Economy car	£380	10
Sports car	£550	7.2
4 × 4 (jeep)	£420	8.5

You are not sure how many miles you will do each year but want to see the total annual costs for running each type of car if you did 600, 800 and 1000 kilometres per year.

Produce a spreadsheet model to show the total annual costs.

> Save this spreadsheet – you will need it later.

Formatting

The way data in your spreadsheet is formatted is important. You want the people who are going to use the spreadsheet to be able to understand what they are seeing on the screen and be able to print out the data in a way which is meaningful to them.

Displaying text

It is important that text can be clearly read on a spreadsheet. In particular, you may need to adjust the width of a column so the text is displayed properly. What happens to text if it is too long to fit into its column depends on what is in the cell next to the text. If it is empty, the text just flows into that cell, which may be fine. However, if the cell contains something then the part of the text that does not fit into the previous cell is not displayed. You may need to adjust column widths to avoid this problem.

Activity 3.11

What happens if the data in a cell is too long for the width of the cell? The answer is different depending on whether the data is text or numbers. Experiment with different length text and numbers and different column widths.

Displaying numbers

The way numbers are displayed determines their meaning. You may have noticed that when you type a number into a cell it automatically sits on the right side of the cell (while text sits on the left). This is normally the way you want numbers shown, because the magnitude of a number is shown increasing from the right with all the decimal points aligned.

There are a variety ways of formatting numbers in a spreadsheet:

Decimal number display allows you to control the number of digits displayed after the decimal point.

If accuracy is important you might want to display a number like this: 10.841. However, if you are dealing with numbers where accuracy is less important, you can reduce the number of digits after the decimal point. The spreadsheet then rounds the result, so 10.841 with no fractional part (as an integer) is displayed as 11.

Numbers displayed as **currency** are shown with a currency symbol (£) before the numbers and 2 digits after the decimal point (e.g. £10.84).

Numbers displayed as **percentages** are multiplied by 100 but are then shown with a % sign after them. The value 0.15 formatted as percentage is displayed as 15%.

Scientific format is used for representing very large or small numbers, it is also called exponential format. It shows very large or small numbers in a more compact form.

The Earth is 159,000,000 km from the Sun, which in scientific format is shown as 1.59E+08, which represents 1.59 * 10 ^ 8.

Dates: Spreadsheets usually provide a wide range of date formatting options.

Microsoft Excel automatically recognises dates in most of the common formats (24/11/76, 24/11/1976, 24-Nov-76 etc.) and formats these as dates using one of its default date formats.

Although dates are displayed as dates they are stored (by Microsoft Excel and other spreadsheet software) as numbers. This means you can do arithmetic with dates. So, if you need to know how many days there are between two dates (perhaps in a library you might want to know whether an item is overdue) then you can simply subtract one date from the other.

Custom formats: As well as using the built-in formats for numbers, you can create your own custom formats.

If you want to display mobile phone numbers with a dash between the first 5 numbers and the last 6 (e.g. 07955–544999) then you could create a custom format that would automatically enter the dash for you. (This can be useful to speed up data entry and avoid errors.)

Custom formats use format codes to represent digits and special characters. The format code for the example above is 00000–000000. The format code of 0 displays insignificant zeros. If a number has fewer digits than there are zeros in the format (e.g. if you entered less than 10 digits) the format pads the number out with zeros; if you enter 123, the format displays 0000–000123. There are also other formatting codes:

\#   displays only significant digits; does not display insignificant zeros.

?   adds spaces for insignificant zeros on either side of the decimal point, so that decimal points align. You can also use this symbol for fractions that have varying numbers of digits.

In Figure 3.9, the number 5.3 is shown in A1, B1 and C1 and 5.25 is shown in A2, B2 and C2. The general number format is used in column A, and the fraction format # #/# is used in column B. To align the division symbols, the fraction format # ??/?? is used in column C.

	A	B	C	
1	5.3	5 3/10	5	3/10
2	5.25	5 1/4	5	1/4

Figure 3.9 *Custom formats*

Design and presentation

The presentation of your spreadsheet is important because a well-designed spreadsheet is easier to use:

- ✪ present users with simple but effective ways of inserting data, by providing input boxes and checking the validity of the entry;
- ✪ provide users with helpful prompts;
- ✪ make effective summaries, models, forecasts, tests of hypotheses and simulations;
- ✪ compose two- and three-dimensional charts, graphs and tables.

Sometimes an entry is required. To remind the user what input is needed, a data entry box should be provided (Figure 3.10).

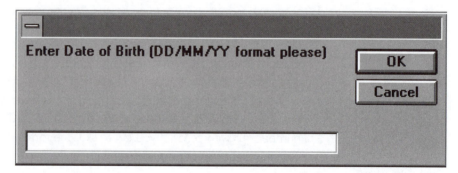

Figure 3.10 *Using data entry boxes*

Display formatting

Spreadsheets have a variety of facilities you can use to improve the way the spreadsheet looks. Don't be tempted to use these facilities just for the sake of it, but rather to make the spreadsheet easier to read by emphasising important titles or values. To apply formatting to a range of cells, you must select the cell(s) first. These are some of the facilities you can use:

▼▼▼▼▼▼▼▼▼

Fonts
have names like
Times New Roman or
Arial and are available
in different sizes
(called point size).

▲▲▲▲▲▲▲▲▲

Fonts

There are a wide range of fonts, or typestyles you can use in a spreadsheet. Some fonts are quite fancy in appearance (called display fonts) and can be used to create a more eye-catching, informal look, while others (like Times New Roman) are more formal looking. You should avoid using too many different fonts in a spreadsheet. More than two different typestyles can make your spreadsheet look complex and messy. Use larger point sizes for titles and headings, and make sure whatever you use is easy to read, because some fancy display fonts are difficult to read at small sizes.

Most fonts can be displayed in **bold** type if you choose. This makes them stand out more. You can use bold as an alternative to a larger size to make headings or other important details, like totals, more eye-catching.

Justification

This refers to the side of the cell that data (text/numbers) sits. You can choose between left, centre and right justification. Choose the justification for a title that matches the values it refers to.

If a column of numbers is aligned to the right of the cell (as numbers usually are), the column title at the top would look wrong if it was left aligned. Right or centre aligned headings fit better with the numbers below them.

Borders or boxes

These can also make your spreadsheet easier to read by splitting up the areas of the spreadsheet (e.g. titles from values) and drawing the user's eyes to important areas (e.g. totals).

Shading and colour

You can use different shading and different colours – for cell backgrounds and contents – to make your spreadsheet easier to read and more attractive. Remember that if the spreadsheet is going to be printed on a black and white printer, you need to check that the colours do not translate into shades of grey that make the spreadsheet difficult to read when it is printed.

There are two general rules for using these features:

✪ **Don't overdo it**. Formatting can make a spreadsheet easier to read. Too much formatting makes the display look complex and can confuse the user.

✪ **Be consistent**. Have some sort of hierarchy of formatting and stick to it. Use one font size for headings, another for column titles and totals, then make sure all the column titles are formatted the same way.

Activity 3.12

The spreadsheet in Figure 3.11 contains no formatting. Copy the spreadsheet, correct the formatting errors it contains and use formatting features such as number formatting, bold and borders to make the spreadsheet look clear and professional.

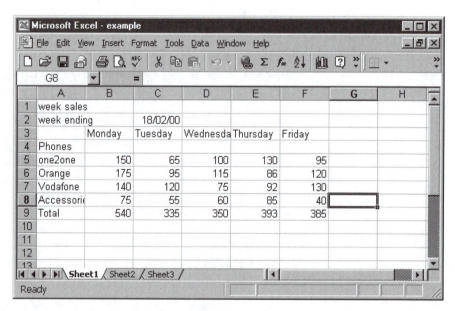

Figure 3.11 *Unformatted spreadsheet*

Print formatting

Most spreadsheets need to be printed at some stage. As well as the formatting you have added to make the spreadsheet easy to read on the screen, you need to consider what formatting you need to add to make it easy to read when it is printed and to give it a professional appearance.

Margins

Reducing the size of the margin allows you to fit more of your spreadsheet on a page, but if the margins are too narrow the page may look very crowded.

Orientation

If your spreadsheet is wider than its height (i.e. more columns than rows) it will fit on fewer pages if it is in landscape format.

Pagination

When a spreadsheet covers more than one page you need to consider the issue of pagination – where one page ends and the next starts. You need to make sure this doesn't split your spreadsheet in an awkward place. You may find that all your spreadsheet fits on one page except one column which prints on one page by itself (called an **orphan**). There are a number of ways you can avoid this. Depending on the shape of your spreadsheet changing the paper orientation may help. Alternatively, reducing the size of the margins may solve the problem. You may also be able to choose page set-up options which allow you to shrink the size of the spreadsheet so it fits onto a certain number of pages.

Headers and footers

Headers are text that prints at the top of every page, while footers print at the bottom. You can, if you wish have text that prints on the left, centre and right within the header and/or footer. Headers and footers are commonly used for information like page numbers, spreadsheet titles, file names or printing dates.

Graphs

A spreadsheet filled with many rows and columns of numbers can be very hard to read and make sense of. A graph is an excellent way of summarising such data so you can make instant comparisons and easily spot trends.

In a cash flow spreadsheet, it may not be immediately obvious how much your costs are rising in comparison to your sales, but a graph would show this information well.

Spreadsheets provide easy to use facilities for graph creation.

Usually, all you need to do is select the row and column titles and the data they relate to, click the graph wizard button, then follow the on-screen instructions. You are asked various questions about the graph, such as what type of graph you want (bar, line, pie, etc.), and you need to select the option you want, then click the Next button to move on to the next set of questions. When you reach the end, click the Finish button and the graph is created for you. A completed example graph, along with the data used to create it, is shown in Figure 3.12.

Did You Know?

Microsoft Excel has a graph 'Wizard'.

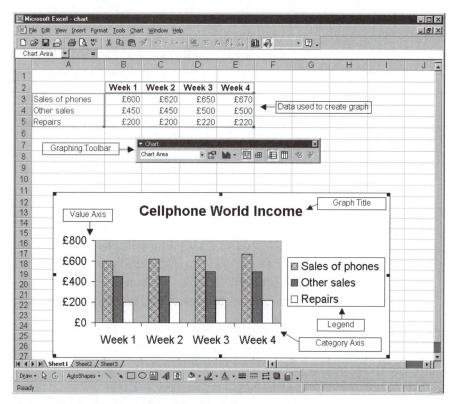

Figure 3.12 *Using a spreadsheet to produce a graph*

Cellphone World want you to create a spreadsheet so that sales assistants can demonstrate to prospective customers how much their monthly cellphone bill might be. This depends on a number of things:

★ Monthly connection charge.

★ Charge per minute for peak rate and cheap rate calls.

★ How many minutes of calls the person may make both at peak times and at cheap rate times.

Items 1 and 2 can be collected from the advertising literature provided by the service providers. Item 3 is entered by the sales assistant based on what the customer tells him/her.

To modify the format of any part of the graph, you can double click on the part you want to change. A dialogue box then appears showing you the formatting options available. When the graph is selected, the graphing toolbar appears and allows you to change the type of graph.

Figure 3.13 shows a 3D pie chart. Pie charts can only show one category (unlike a bar chart which can show several), therefore only Week 1 income data is used to create the graph.

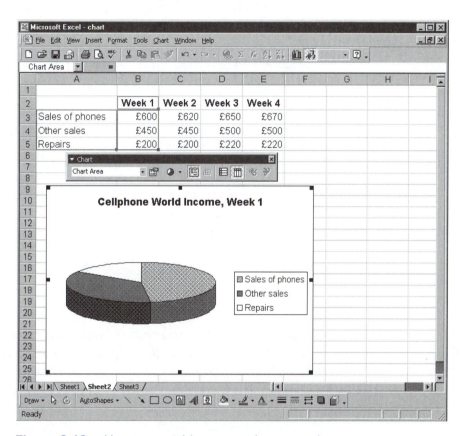

Figure 3.13 *Using a spreadsheet to produce a pie chart*

Activity 3.14

Create a spreadsheet similar to that shown in Figure 3.14:

★ Enter formulae to cells C9, D9 and E9 to calculate the monthly bills correctly.

★ Choose appropriate display formatting to make the spreadsheet clear to read and attractive to look at.

★ Decide on print formatting so the spreadsheet looks good when it is printed.

	A	B	C	D	E
1	**Cellphone Cost Calculator**				
2	Service:		Cellnet	Vodafone	one2one
3	Connection Charge		£35.00	£25.00	£32.00
4	Peak rate charge per min.		£0.20	£0.25	£0.30
5	Cheap rate charge per min.		£0.12	£0.15	£0.10
6	Number of minutes of peak rate calls per month:				
7	Number of minutes of cheap rate calls per month:				
8	Total monthly bill for:		Cellnet	Vodafone	one2one
9					

Figure 3.14 *Cellphone cost calculator*

Activity 3.15

Jim would like to see a graph showing the costs of owning different types of cars. Open up the spreadsheet you created earlier (Activity 3.10) to calculate car ownership costs and create a graph showing the relative costs of running the different cars.

Using help

Spreadsheets have a huge range of features and no one expects you to know about them all. Use the Help facility when you need to use a facility you haven't used before. Help gives descriptions and examples and has a search option to help you find features if you don't know precisely what they are called.

Activity 3.16

Find out how to use these facilities by looking them up using your spreadsheet's Help facility:

★ Probabilities
★ Multiple sheets and creating links between them
★ Sorting lists and tables
★ Correlations
★ Named ranges
★ Protecting cells by locking and hiding
★ Multiple views and windows
★ Histograms
★ Look-up tables

Programming

Spreadsheets need to be used by non-technical people who use the spreadsheet as a tool to help them in their work. Spreadsheets you create for these people need to be easy to use, even though they may be complex in their functions. One way you can simplify complex spreadsheets is by using a **macro**. You can also use macros in word processing and database programs. Macros are a type of program, and have many similarities with programming done in languages like Pascal and Java.

Here are some typical uses of a macro:

- **Controlling what the user can do** – spreadsheets are complex programs so you may want to prevent a user from doing things they are not familiar with.
- **Making sure the user carries out actions in a certain order, e.g. completing data entry before printing the spreadsheet.**
- **Doing complex calculations.**
- **Making sure the user enters valid data, such as a date in a valid format.**
- **Providing the users with buttons to perform certain functions.**

Like programming in other languages, macro programming requires that you design your macro before you write it. You must be clear about what the macro is supposed to do and write a design document describing it before you begin to produce your macro.

Exercise 3.3

Suggest other uses of macros.

Creating macros

Spreadsheet programs normally allow you to record macros, and then refine and add to them by editing them like normal programs. Recording a macro involves switching on a facility called a **macro recorder**. Then you carry out the actions you want to record (e.g. select cells, choose menu options, etc.) and the macro recorder records whatever you do. Once you switch off the macro recorder you can then replay your recorded actions whenever you want. It's rather like recording a short play on a video camera. Just as you would read the script and rehearse before you video record a play, you need to make sure you understand the design of the macro and practise the actions you want to record before you actually record it. If you don't do this, you may well end up recording mistakes in your macro, which may result in your having to record it again or edit out the mistakes.

Having recorded a macro, you can then create a button or a short cut key to make it easy for the spreadsheet user to run the macro.

Let's look at an example. The spreadsheet you created for Cellphone World to estimate monthly bills is fine, but now let's automate some of its functions using macros.

Activity 3.17

The first macro to create clears the spreadsheet of its previous entries. When a customer wants to see an estimate of their monthly bill, the sales assistant wants to be able to click a button to remove the previous customer's entries for the number of minutes they expect to use at peak and cheap rates. This is a simple macro but creating it may help you to understand the basic principle of creating macros.

You need to start off with your spreadsheet looking like Figure 3.15:

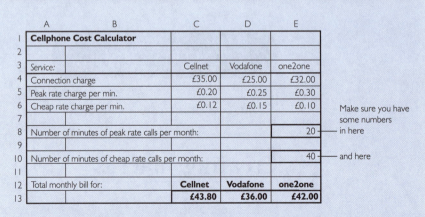

	A	B	C	D	E	
1	Cellphone Cost Calculator					
2						
3	Service:		Cellnet	Vodafone	one2one	
4	Connection charge		£35.00	£25.00	£32.00	
5	Peak rate charge per min.		£0.20	£0.25	£0.30	
6	Cheap rate charge per min.		£0.12	£0.15	£0.10	Make sure you have
7						some numbers
8	Number of minutes of peak rate calls per month:				20	in here
9						
10	Number of minutes of cheap rate calls per month:				40	and here
11						
12	Total monthly bill for:		**Cellnet**	**Vodafone**	**one2one**	
13			**£43.80**	**£36.00**	**£42.00**	

Figure 3.15 *Creating a macro – starting spreadsheet*

To record the macro, follow these steps:

★ Go to the **Tools** menu and select the **Macro** option. A sub-menu should pop out and you need to choose the **Record New Macro** option. You should see a

continued

dialogue box asking you for the name of the new macro. Type the name CLEAR_ENTRIES into the box (see Figure 3.16). From now on, whatever you do is recorded in the macro, so be careful to do only the things you want in it.

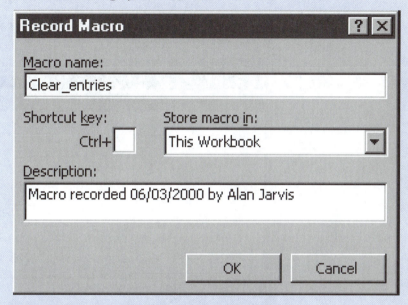

Figure 3.16 *Using the Record New Macro option*

★ Click on Cell E8 (which contains the number of minutes of calls at peak rate) and press the delete key to remove the entry.

★ Then click on cell E10 and press delete again to remove the entry in that cell.

★ Finally, choose the **Tools** menu again, select the **Macro** option and from the sub-menu choose **Stop Recording** (or click the stop recording button in the macro toolbar, which appears when you start recording a macro).

You have now created your first macro. You can test it by using the spreadsheet as if you were a sales assistant at Cellphone World. A customer asks for an estimate of his/her bill, so you enter the number of minutes they think they will use at peak time and the number at cheap rate. Later on, another customer asks for an estimate. To clear the previous entries, use the macro. To run the macro as it is at the moment, you need to go to the Tools menu, select the Macro option then the Macros sub-option, click on the macro name in the box that appears and then click the Run button. The macro should, if you have recorded it properly, remove the previous entries. At the moment, to run the macro takes more keystrokes than deleting the entries yourself, without the macro, would take! To make the macro easy to run, you need to create a button to run the macro or set up a short-cut key.

First, let's have a look at the code created by the macro recorder for our macro. To do this select the Tools menu again, the Macro option and Macros sub-option and you should see the Macros dialogue box (Figure 3.17).

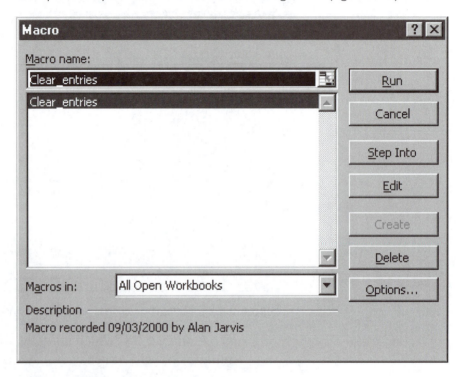

Figure 3.17 *Macro dialogue box*

Click the macro name (Clear_entries), then click the Edit button on the right and the Visual Basic editor program should start in a separate window with the macro code shown on the right (Figure 3.18).

Creating buttons and short-cuts

To add a **button** to run a macro the correct toolbar must be shown on the screen. In Microsoft Excel for Office 2000, this is the Forms toolbar.

Once the correct toolbar is displayed, click on the create button. Then move to the place on the spreadsheet where the button is required and drag out the button. When the button has been created, a dialogue box appears asking which macro the button is to run. Click on the CLEAR_ENTRIES macro, then click OK. Now change the name on the button by clicking inside it and removing the existing name (Button 1) and typing the name 'Clear Entries'. The completed spreadsheet with button is shown in Figure 3.19.

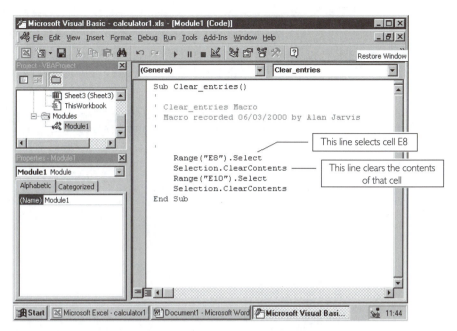

Figure 3.18 *Clear_entries macro*

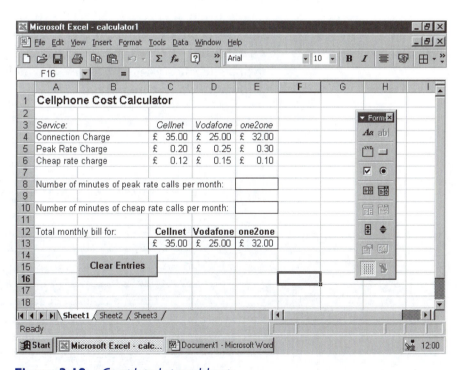

Figure 3.19 *Completed spreadsheet*

Every time you click on this button, it runs the macro.

A **short-cut key** is particularly helpful when the spreadsheet operator may be already using the keyboard when s/he wants to run the macro, as s/he could then run the macro directly from the keyboard rather than having to use the mouse.

To use a short-cut key with the macro, return to the Tools menu, Macro option Macros sub-option, select the CLEAR_ENTRIES macro, and when the dialogue box appears, choose the Options button. In the box marked Short-Cut key, type in the key to be used. It is always used in conjunction with the CTRL key, e.g. if 'Z' is entered as the short-cut key, pressing CTRL+Z runs the macro. Click OK and close the Macro dialogue box. Test the short-cut key by entering some values into the cells the macro clears, then press the short-cut key combination chosen and check to see if the macro works.

Activity 3.18

Cellphone World want a slightly modified version of the original spreadsheet that estimates bills. Rather than showing the different costs of different services all at the same time, they want a spreadsheet that has buttons allowing the sales assistant to select which services are to be shown on the estimated bills.

First modify the original spreadsheet so it looks like Figure 3.20.

	A	B	C	D
1	Cellphone Cost Calculator			
2				
3	Service:			
4	Connection Charge			
5	Peak rate charge			
6	Cheap rate charge			
7				
8	Peak rate calls per month:			
9				
10	Cheap rate calls per month:			
11				
12	Total monthly bill for:			
13				£ -

Figure 3.20 *Spreadsheet for Activity 3.18*

continued

continued

Next, to record a macro called SET_VODAFONE, carry out these actions:

- ★ Print the text 'Vodafone' in D3
- ★ Enter the value 25 in D4
- ★ Enter the value .25 in D5
- ★ Enter the value .15 in D6
- ★ Print the text 'Vodafone' in D12

Once you have created and tested this macro, create two more, one called SET_1TO1 and another called SET_CELLNET. They should set the contents of the cells as shown in Figure 3.21:

Cell	SET_1TO1	SET_CELLNET
D3	one2one	Cellnet
D4	32	35
D5	0.3	0.2
D6	0.1	0.12
D12	one2one	Cellnet

Figure 3.21 *Cells to change for Activity 3.18*

Then, create buttons for each of these macros so that, when the button is clicked, it sets the charges for the particular service.

The completed spreadsheet should look like Figure 3.22.

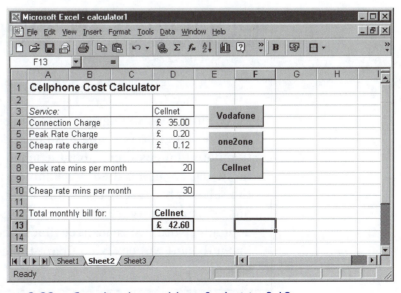

Figure 3.22 *Completed spreadsheet for Activity 3.18*

Analysis and specification

This crucial first stage in creating a complex spreadsheet application involves defining exactly what the user wants. The process now has to be considered in detail. It is often helpful to think of the user's needs in terms of a business problem that you need to solve. If the end result doesn't make some task that the user has to perform easier, quicker or more accurate, then you have not succeeded.

The analysis and specification stage should help you to decide four things.

- ✪ The main information the user wants
- ✪ How the user currently obtains that information
- ✪ How you should present that information
- ✪ Whether you need to report on the likelihood of success

Analysis

Before you can understand a particular business problem, you need to spend some time with the user getting to know their business by asking them questions, watching them work and making notes.

- ✪ How do they currently perform the task you are going to automate with the spreadsheet?
- ✪ What is good about it (so you can preserve these aspects)?
- ✪ What are the problems are with it (so you can improve these)?

As an example, consider this case study.

Peter Piper: Financial Sales

Peter Piper sells savings and pension schemes and has explained that he is losing business because, having talked to a potential customer about a scheme they are interested in, he has to phone them back later with the exact costs of the scheme because it takes him a long time to work them out by hand. However, his competitors use a laptop computer with a spreadsheet that calculates the costs instantly and can easily compare the costs of different schemes.

Peter Piper's problem is that sales are being lost because competitors are able to do the same job more quickly and provide more information (comparisons of different schemes).

You need to find out several things from Peter:

Data input

How does data get into the system, and what format is it in? There is a general principle in computing known as **GIGO**.

If the input data is incorrect, then the output certainly will be. Peter gets the data from his potential customer, such as how old the person is, how much they earn and whether they are married.

Data capture

Data capture is where the data originated from – a form filled in by the customer, or a leaflet of rates. Sometimes data is collected automatically, e.g. using a bar code.

Data processing

You need to know how to process the raw data once it has been input or captured. This may be a case of doing simple arithmetic on the data, or it may be more complex, like calculating averages or percentages.

Data flow

Your spreadsheet may form part of a larger system. Data flow is about where the data from your spreadsheet comes from and where the results go. For example, if the customer accepts the quotation from Peter, the data collected may be sent (perhaps by modem) to head office so that policy documents can be issued and bank debits set up.

Data output

Having processed the data and produced a result, the output may be a printed report or be shown on the screen. You need to agree with Peter what is actually shown and how it is to be presented. You may also want to discuss with him the possibility of presenting the output data in ways that are not possible with the current method he uses, e.g. as a graph.

The specification

The end result of all this discussion and information collection is a document called the **specification**. It describes exactly what the spreadsheet does, and it needs to be **unambiguous** and **non-technical**.

You might say: 'The spreadsheet will show the total cost clearly'. However, what is 'clear' to one person may not be clear to another. It is better to specify: 'The spreadsheet will show the total cost formatted with a leading £ sign and two digits after the decimal place. It will be displayed in a box in bold type'.

You need to avoid using technical computer terms, or provide explanations of their meaning.

You also need to estimate how long it may take you to produce the spreadsheet and how much it will cost. The end-user of the spreadsheet may actually be your customer and will be paying you or your company to do this work. In this situation, once the specification has been agreed, it becomes subject to a legally binding contract. This means that if you don't produce what the specification describes then your customer could sue you or your company. This is one reason why it is very important to get the specification right!

In some circumstances, particularly if what you are being asked to do is rather complex, you may be asked to do a **feasibility study**. This is where you investigate whether it is possible to solve a problem using an IT solution. You look into how long it would take to create a solution and how much it would cost. Sometimes, although an IT solution to a problem is possible, it may be too expensive, or take too long to create to make economic sense.

Cellphone World

Cellphone World now want the spreadsheet that estimates monthly bills to be turned into a customised application that guides the end-user through the process of doing the estimate step by step. The first step is to analyse and specify the problem using **top-down design**. This is a process whereby you define the problem simply, then break it down into a number of smaller sections. Each of these sections is successively split and refined until they are small enough to be programmed.

So the simple definition is:

A system is needed to calculate estimated bills which is to be used with menus and buttons, and prevents the end-user entering invalid data.

This can be broken down into five steps:

- ✪ **Display an opening screen**. Here a worksheet can be used, with a title displayed and a button attached to a macro which takes the user to the next sheet.

- ✪ **Select which service company is to be used**. This is on a separate worksheet and contains buttons to select the service company the user wants to use. These buttons are attached to macros which set the appropriate costs, similar to the macros written before.

- ✪ **Enter the number of minutes at peak and cheap rates**. This step involves displaying an input box where the user enters the number of minutes of use at peak and then at cheap rates. You need to make sure the user enters only a numeric value (i.e. no text).

- ✪ **Display total estimated bill**. This shows the estimated monthly bill as done on previous spreadsheets.

- ✪ **Exit options**. The user needs to be able to choose to redo the calculation, either for a different service, or with different numbers of minutes usage. Or to exit to the opening screen, ready to do a calculation for a different customer.

Programming a complex spreadsheet application

Now the simple design process has been completed, the creation of the spreadsheet and programming the macros can be attempted.

Step 1 – Display an opening screen

Various display formatting facilities can be used to create an opening screen for the system and then record a simple macro to select the next worksheet. Call the macro SWAP_SHEET. As before, you can then create a button on your opening screen which runs the macro. This is shown in Figure 3.23.

Step 2 – Select which service company is to be used

This involves creating a worksheet where the connection, peak rate and cheap rate costs are shown, along with the calculation to work out the estimated bill.

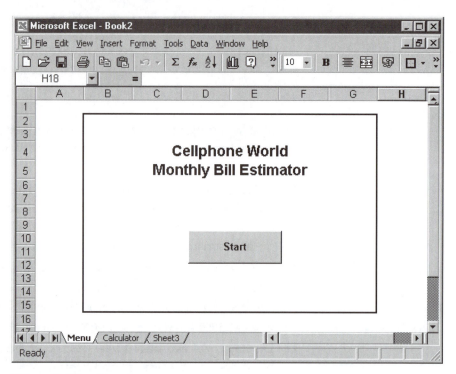

Figure 3.23 *Opening screen*

As done previously, macros need to be recorded to set the prices for the different services and attach them to buttons. You should end up with something similar to Figure 3.24.

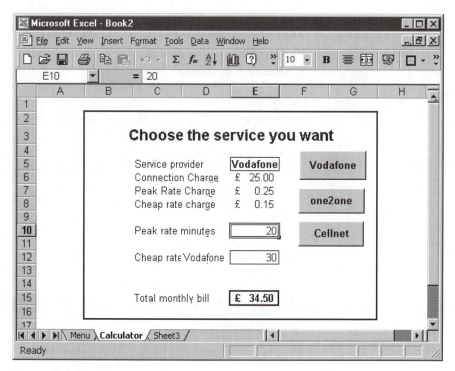

Figure 3.24 *Menu screen*

Step 3 – Enter the number of minutes at peak and cheap rates

Now comes the more complex part. Input from the user needs to be accepted and validated. For example, if the user types 'thirty' instead of '30', the calculation will not work. To create this more complex macro, first record a simple version of it, then edit the Visual BASIC code to refine the macro. The end result of the macro is to insert a number in cell E10, representing the number of peak rate minutes.

Activity 3.19

★　First, make sure the cell pointer is *not* in E10.

★　Then start the macro recorder, calling the macro SET_PEAK.

★　Move to cell E10, type in a value (any value will do, in the example the value of 20 was entered).

★　Stop the recorder.

★　Click the *Edit* button on the Macro dialogue box to start the Visual Basic editor to inspect your macro.

It should look like Figure 3.25.

```
Book2 - Module1 (Code)

(General)                              set_peak

Sub set_peak()
'
' set_peak Macro
' Macro recorded 06/03/2000 by Alan Jarvis
'


    Range("E10").Select
    ActiveCell.FormulaR1C1 = "20"
    Range("E11").Select
End Sub
```

Figure 3.25 *Macro SET_PEAK*

At the moment, this macro places a fixed value (in this case 20) in E10. The user needs to be able to specify this amount, and because this varies, depending on the customer, a **variable** is used to store the value.

The value stored in the variable is not known until the macro is run, but the box (or variable) is given a name so it can be referred to in the macro. In this case, the variable is called PEAK_MINS. An input box is also needed to collect the real value from the user. Finally, the contents of the variable need to be placed in cell E10. The modified macro should look like Figure 3.26.

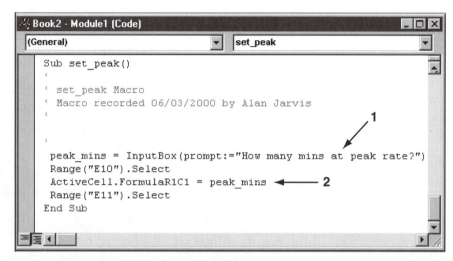

Figure 3.26 *Modified macro SET_PEAK*

1 This new line of code uses a variable called PEAK_MINS. The contents of this variable are collected from an input box that appears on the screen with the message (prompt) 'How many minutes at peak rate?'

2 In this modified line, rather than having the 'Active Cell' (E10 here) set to 20, which was the value that was typed in when the macro was recorded, it is set to whatever is contained in the variable PEAK_MINS.

If you run this macro, you should see that it displays the input box and places whatever value you type into the box in cell E10. However, it does *not* validate the entry, so if you leave the input box empty or type in text, it still accepts this and is happy to put text in E10, although this prevents the formula that calculates the total bill from working correctly and displays an error. Any entries that are non-numeric therefore need to be rejected.

To do this, you not only need to check if the entry made is numeric, you also need to send the macro around in a **loop**.

In this case, the loop displays the input box and checks the entry to see if it is numeric. If the entry is not numeric, the loop continues. The only way out of the loop is if a numeric entry is made. For this, you use a type of Visual Basic loop called a Do-Until loop – it does the loop until a numeric entry is made. The macro code needs to be modified (Figure 3.27).

1   This new line uses a new variable, NUM_CHECK, which holds the result of testing PEAK_MINS to see if it is numeric. This is done by a function called IsNumeric. If PEAK_MINS is numeric it returns the value True, if it isn't, it returns the value False.

2   This is the Do-Until loop. Everything between the Do-Until statement and the Loop statement is repeated until NUM_CHECK is true.

3   This statement displays a message box on the screen, showing the message in quotes. The 0 at the end indicates that the message box contains an OK button to remove it from the screen.

When you run this version of the macro, you should find that it only accepts a numeric value. Any other entry (including making no entry at all) results in the appearance of the message box demanding 'Numbers only please'.

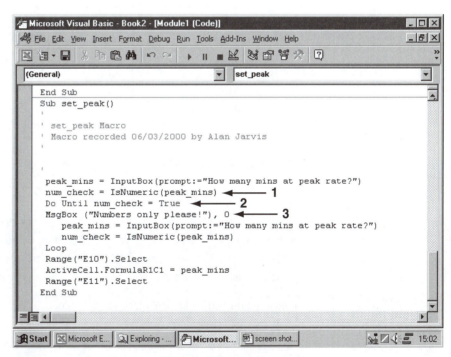

Figure 3.27   *Modified macro SET_PEAK*

Activity 3.20

Test your macro properly by drawing up a test plan. List possible entries a user might make in the input box.

Remember that users may make entries that are obviously wrong or unsuitable (either by mistake or deliberately) and your macro must cope with them sensibly.

Your test data must include values that are normal (i.e. within the range of normal values, though you may need to think about what the range of normal values is), extreme (i.e. way outside the normal range of values) and abnormal (e.g. a text entry where numbers are expected). An example is shown in Figure 3.28.

Possible entries for minutes at peak rate		
Type	**Range**	**Value**
Normal	Upper	200
	Lower	0
Extreme	Upper	9999999
	Lower	−100
Abnormal		Space, text

Figure 3.28 *Test data*

Then list how you think the macro should deal with each entry: basically it should either accept the entry or reject it. Now try out each entry and see if your macro responds the way you predicted. If it doesn't you should consider modifying the macro so it responds correctly. Your test plan should look something like Figure 3.29.

There is one remaining problem with the macro. It has to be run from the Tools menu. The macro needs to run automatically once the service provider has been chosen. To do this, one line of code is needed at the end of both the SET_CELLFONE and SET_VODANET macros to call the SET_PEAK macro:

```
Application.Run macro:="set_peak"
```

Be sure to add this as the last statement before the End sub.

A very similar macro is also needed to collect the number of minutes at cheap rate that the customer expects to use. Rather than going through the same process used to create the SET_PEAK macro, you can simply copy and paste

Test plan			
Entry	**Expected result**	**Actual result**	**Modifications needed?**
200	Accepted	Accepted	No
0	Accepted	Accepted	No
9999999	Rejected	Accepted, but caused answer too large to be displayed	Yes
−100	Rejected	Accepted But caused macro to halt	Yes
Space	Rejected	Rejected	No
ZZ	Rejected	Rejected	No

Figure 3.29   *Test plan*

it, then change every reference to 'peak' to 'cheap', and move the cell references two rows down. Your new macro should look like Figure 3.30.

As with the SET_PEAK macro this one needs to run automatically. So add the line:

Application.Run macro:="set_cheap"

to the end of the SET_PEAK macro so they run one after the other.

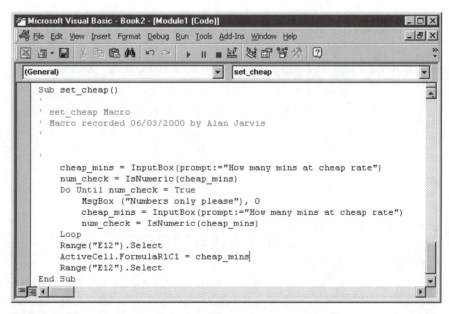

Figure 3.30   *Macro for SET_CHEAP*

Step 4 – Exit options

If the spreadsheet user wants to try a different service provider or change the number of minutes at either rate all they need to do is click the appropriate service provider button to change the costs and re-enter the number of minutes. A macro is, however, needed to clean up the worksheet (delete the previously entered number of peak and cheap rate minutes) and return the user to the menu on the first worksheet. This is a simple macro that can be recorded and attached to a new button. It doesn't need any further refinement.

How could this spreadsheet application be improved? For example, a common scenario might be that a customer, having seen what his/her estimated bill is for one service provider, wants to see what it would be for another. The current application allows this but requires you to enter the number of minutes at peak and cheap rates again.

Exercise 3.4

★ **How could you avoid this unnecessary data re-entry?**
★ **Is the spreadsheet 'foolproof'?**
★ **What else might you have to do before you could give this spreadsheet to someone who had never used a spreadsheet before?**

Testing and documentation

Once you have created your macro it must be thoroughly tested to make sure it works properly in all circumstances, including when used incorrectly. You also need to check that the formulae produce the correct results. Most importantly, you need to check that your spreadsheet does what the original specification describes.

▼▼▼▼▼▼▼▼▼▼

User documentation should help people to use your spreadsheet.

▲▲▲▲▲▲▲▲▲▲

Documentation

You need to produce documentation for your spreadsheet. Two types of documentation are needed: **user documentation** and **technical documentation**.

You need to make sure that the user documentation can be easily understood by non-technical users and that it relates closely to the way they are likely to use the system. Technical documentation describes in detail how the spreadsheet works.

You also need to consider *how* your documentation is provided. Traditionally, documentation has been printed but, more recently, **online documentation** has become popular. There are a number of advantages to online documentation. It is easier and cheaper to produce and update. However, you need to choose a delivery mechanism. Providing a word processed file is the simplest but not really the best method. Users could accidentally (or deliberately) modify or even delete the file and it does not provide very good search facilities. Other options include Windows Help files, Internet Web HTML pages or Adobe Acrobat files. Whichever method you choose, you need to make sure your users can find how to use the chosen method.

So, here is what the technical documentation for the spreadsheet application described in our case study should include:

✪ The original specification
✪ The hardware and software the system requires (Windows 98, Microsoft Excel 2000, etc.)
✪ Listings (prints) of the macros, with descriptions of their purpose
✪ Prints of the worksheets, both with and without formulae displayed
✪ Details of the testing carried out

This is what the user documentation for this case study application should include:

✪ Details of how to load the spreadsheet file
✪ Detailed explanation of how to use the application, including examples. Screen shots from the spreadsheet may reassure the user and make explanations easier
✪ Descriptions of error messages and what to do if they appear

Activity 3.21

Create user documentation and technical documentation for your spreadsheet.

★ User instructions should be detailed and clear, and you should avoid the use of technical language.

★ You might want to consider providing a tutorial which takes the user through several worked examples of how to use the system. You need to make sure the tutorial provides a realistic example of how the system might be used in reality.

★ You should also provide an index for your documentation so that a user with a specific problem can find the place where it is described in the documentation quickly.

Revision questions

1 Explain the terms relative referencing, absolute referencing and mixed referencing.

2 List four different uses of a spreadsheet macro.

3 Give an example of how the function COUNT can be used.

4 List three different ways a user can cause a macro to run.

5 Explain what relational operators are.

6 Describe what this formula does:
=IF(B8>20,"Overdue","On time")

7 Explain the scientific number format.

8 Explain the order of mathematical precedence.

9 What is test data?

10 What does the mathematical operator ^ do?

11 Describe what this formula does:
=SUM(B4:B12).

12 Why is it important to check the widths of the columns on a spreadsheet?

13 List three things you should identify when analysing a user's requirement for a spreadsheet.

14 Explain the term 'data capture'.

15 What does a cash flow forecast show and what is it used for?

System Installation and Configuration

4

- Acquire an understanding of ICT system components and their purpose
- Specify the components of an ICT system to meet user needs
- Install and configure ICT systems
- Install, configure and test new hardware
- Install, configure and test new software
- Configure systems to meet user needs
- Understand and implement safety and security procedures

Introduction

This chapter looks in detail at three topics:

- Hardware components of given computer systems
- Software components of given computer systems
- Safety and security of computer systems

During the course of your work for this unit, you will produce a working computer system to meet a given specification, and modify the hardware and software of existing systems.

As part of the evidence requirements for this unit, you need to produce a record of your work. This record includes the following items.

- ✪ Date of undertaking work
- ✪ A description of work done
- ✪ Specifications and guidance used
- ✪ Components installed
- ✪ Configuration tasks undertaken
- ✪ Faults and problems experienced
- ✪ Solutions applied
- ✪ Support services accessed
- ✪ Diagnostic software used
- ✪ Testing procedures carried out

Activity 4.1

Design a form for recording a log of tasks done and problems encountered. It should allow you to record the information listed above. Compare your design with those of others in your group. Discuss and make improvements to the design. Complete the log as you work through this unit.

Keep this form for inclusion in your portfolio.

Activity 4.2

Schedule a time for weekly meetings of a group to share solutions to common problems. Appoint someone as a secretary – set up a reference manual for your group that contains written copies of the problems and solutions.

Throughout the chapter the emphasis is on the specification of stand-alone systems. The text and exercises are designed to help you to understand a wide range of hardware and software. The activities require you to put this understanding into practice.

It is important to specify a system that will precisely meet a user's needs. It is true to say that computer and related technologies are converging. That is to say that nearly all computers and peripherals can be connected to share data. However, while this means that almost any specification will enable a user to do the job, each item in the system has a very wide range of possible specifications. This range must be carefully examined to ensure that several objectives are met:

- ✪ The system meets the users' needs.
- ✪ Unnecessary expense is not incurred.
- ✪ The system is designed to last for as long as possible before becoming obsolete.

In specifying systems in this unit, you will need to choose suitable solutions in both hardware and software. You will also need to take safety and security into consideration. Throughout the unit, you must have the needs of the user at the forefront of your decisions. You will also be required to keep a log of your work and record problems encountered.

In this chapter, three case studies are used.

Swanage Folk Festival

A folk festival is held in Swanage every September. It is organised by a committee of around ten people. The festival lasts for three days and has around 100 acts performing and 5000 visitors. The committee uses ICT for internal communications and to produce publicity material.

Hyperion-Media

Hyperion-Media publish advertising and marketing material for other companies. Hyperion-Media have offices in the south of England with computers and associated peripherals for data capture, manipulation and production of material. They work with companies of all sizes, from small businesses to large multinationals.

They have contracts for electronic magazines on the Internet, company Intranets and CD-ROM-based promotional material. They also run an Internet café.

ICT system components – hardware

This part of the chapter looks at hardware components that can be specified for a given system.

- ✪ Main processing unit
- ✪ Memory
- ✪ Peripheral devices

   Storage

   Input

   Output

   Printers

- ✪ Connectors
- ✪ Consumables

A system may have communications devices that connect it to other systems.

Main processing unit

The main processing unit is the 'box' that contains the essential electronics that give a computer the ability to receive data from input devices, process that data, and send it to storage and/or output devices. Two common formats for the main processing unit are the **tower** unit and the **desktop** unit (see Figure 4.1). The choice between the two will depend on the space available to the user.

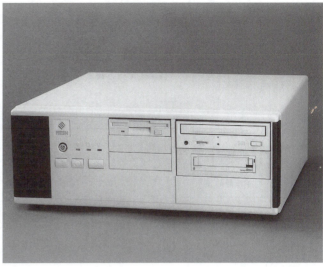

Figure 4.1 *Tower and desktop units*

Motherboard

This is the main circuit board for the computer. Integrated circuits (ICs), or chips, are plugged into the motherboard; other boards can be plugged into or connected to it. The choice of motherboard is determined by the choice of manufacturer and the processor type. Often, spaces are left on the

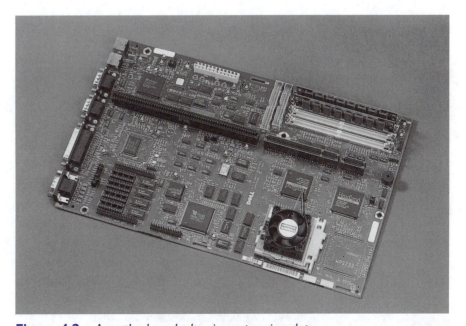

Figure 4.2 *A motherboard, showing expansion slots*

motherboard for additional ICs. Similarly, sockets are provided to insert other circuit boards. These spaces are called **expansion slots** (Figure 4.2).

Processor

The processor is the main IC, or chip, that carries out the processing of data. It contains circuitry for arithmetic and logical operations, and some memory, known as **registers**. The registers are used for a variety of purposes:

✪ To temporarily store data during processing
✪ To store instructions during the execution of a program
✪ To store the status of the computer system
✪ To register the occurrence of events in the system

The choice of processor is usually a balance between cost and speed. The more money available, the faster the processor a user can buy. Personal computers are often described by their processor type and speed, e.g. Pentium III, 500 Mhz.

Co-processor

A co-processor is an IC that provides extra capability to the main processor. Typically, this may allow it to perform mathematical calculations more quickly or to a higher degree of accuracy. Modern processors have co-processors as part of their circuitry. If the user requires extra processing power, it may be better to choose a higher specification main processor rather than an additional co-processor.

Controller

This circuitry controls the other hardware components, the running of programs and the flow of data around the computer. The main processor will come with a particular controller, and it is not usually possible to specify the controller separately.

Cards

Circuit boards that are connected to the motherboard are called cards. These are used for controlling specific peripheral connections, communicating with networks or performing other specialist tasks (e.g. sound). The number and variety of cards needed depends on the user's needs, but will be limited by the number of slots available. When adding a new card to a system, care must be taken to avoid conflicts with any existing cards. Modern operating systems usually deal with this problem automatically.

Conflicts are caused by cards requiring the same resources or being assigned the same interrupt request (IRQ). Find out what resources and interrupts are used by cards in your computer system.

Bus

A bus is a set of connections that carry electronic signals. An **internal bus** runs within a single component, e.g. the **central processing unit (CPU)**. **External buses** carry signals between components and run across a circuit board or between circuit boards. There are three types of external bus (Figure 4.3).

Did You Know?

Bus comes from the Latin word omnibus which means 'carries all'.

- ✪ The **data bus** carries data between the CPU and memory and peripheral controller cards.

- ✪ The **address bus** carries the address to which data is to be sent, or from which it is to be fetched.

- ✪ The **control bus** carries signals between the CPU and the other

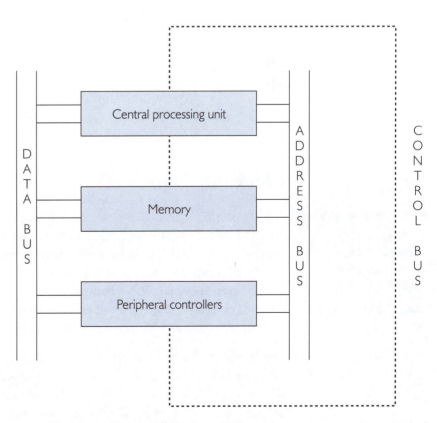

Figure 4.3 *Schematic diagram of conventional bus architecture*

system components. Signals are sent along the control bus to enable and disable devices, and synchronise transmission of data.

The design of the buses is known as the **computer architecture**. A particular architecture may be chosen because of advantages it brings in speed of data transfer or amount of memory that may be directly connected. Various architecture standards have been developed.

ISA (industry-standard architecture) is a 16-bit bus standard for IBM-compatibles. It allows only the first 16 MB of main memory to be direct accessed and was originally referred to as AT bus architecture.

PCI (peripheral component interconnect) is a 33 MHz standard for connecting peripherals to most makes of PC. It can be used in systems based on Pentium, Pentium Pro, AMD 5x86, AMD K5 and AMD K6 processors, and in some DEC Alpha and PowerPC systems. However, it is processor independent and so can work with other processor architectures as well.

▼▼▼▼▼▼▼▼▼

Asynchronously
not in time with the
CPU's internal clock

▲▲▲▲▲▲▲▲▲

Technically, PCI uses a separate bus linked to the standard bus systems through a bridge circuit and controller. It includes buffers to decouple the CPU from relatively slow peripherals and to allow them to operate **asynchronously**.

Other standards include **EISA (extended industry-standard architecture)** and **MCA (microchannel architecture)**.

Activity
4.4

Find out about, and describe, the EISA and MCA architectures.

Clock

▼▼▼▼▼▼▼▼▼

**1 Mhz
(megahertz)**
1 million pulses per
second.

▲▲▲▲▲▲▲▲▲

A quartz crystal that oscillates at a known, fixed rate is used as a clock within the CPU. All processor operations are carried out in time with the beats from the clock. Clock rates are measured in **megahertz (MHz)**. However, having a 200 MHz clock does not mean that the computer can carry out 200 million instructions per second. This is because each instruction takes several clock pulses to complete. The system's performance will also be reduced by bottlenecks as several tasks compete for the same resources.

The number of instructions carried out per second is a better indication of the true speed of a processor. It will depend on the clock speed, the architecture and the instruction set of the processor. A processor quoted as 20 Mips can carry out a maximum of 20 million instructions per second. RISC (reduced instruction set computer) CPUs tend to have simpler instructions than CISC (complex instruction set computer) CPUs but higher clock rates. Processors have been designed that use **pipelining** to execute more than one instruction per cycle. **Parallel processors** use multiple arithmetic-logic units (ALU) to process several instructions simultaneously. The **ALU** is the part of the CPU that carries out calculations and logical operations.

The motherboard is connected to the electrical supply via a **power supply unit (PSU)**. This acts as a transformer to convert the mains signal into low-voltage DC supplier for the power rails on the board. Typically, a circuit board requires voltages of ± 5 or 12 volts.

Alternative battery power sources may be used, for instance on portable computers. Batteries are generally of one or two types: lithium (Li) or longer lasting nickel-metal hydride. To protect a computer system from the effects of power cuts, an **uninterruptible power supply (UPS)** should be fitted.

Activity 4.5

What are the specifications of the computers that you use?

Which feature has the most effect on these computers' performance?

Exercise 4.1

You are asked for your advice on the best specification for a computer that is to be used by a family. What would you advise?

Memory

The amount of memory in a computer system determines the level of complexity of task that the system can handle. A single unit of memory is called a **bit**. A bit can store a single 0 or 1. Eight bits together are called a **byte**. Memory, and data storage, capacity is usually measured in larger units.

Each location in memory is given a numeric **address**. A single address stores a fixed amount of data. For instance, a computer with 32-bit wide memory locations can store 32 bits in each location.

The greater the capacity of each address, the more powerful the computer. This is because more data may be transferred in a single operation (Figure 4.4).

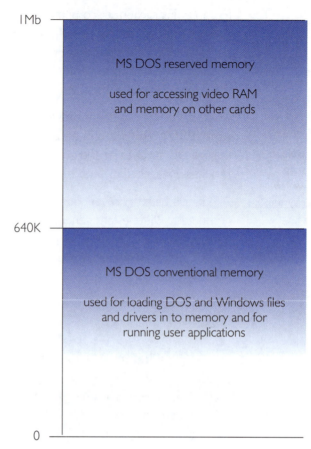

Figure 4.4 *Memory locations and contents*

There are two classes of memory in a computer system.

- ✪ RAM (random access memory)
- ✪ ROM (read only memory)

RAM is memory that can be both read from and written to. It is used for storing data and programs while the computer is being used. This includes most of the operating system, user programs and data, and the contents of buffers.

Most RAM is **volatile**, i.e. it can only hold data while power is supplied. Once power is removed the contents of RAM are lost. System settings such as date and time are stored in CMOS (complementary metal oxide semiconductor) RAM. **CMOS RAM** has a battery to maintain the data contained in it. The settings are therefore not lost when the main power is switched off.

The main part of RAM may be either static or dynamic.

- ✪ **Static RAM** is more expensive but allows for faster transfer of data.
- ✪ In **dynamic RAM**, the contents will decay even with power

supplied and so it needs to be continually refreshed, which slows the system down.

Developments in technology are allowing smaller and faster RAM circuits to be developed. An example of this is EDO (extended data out) RAM that provides for very fast data transfer. **EDO RAM** is often used for transfer of data to and from visual display. This maximises the rate of update of graphical display.

For transfer of data to and from peripherals, some very fast RAM is often provided. This is known as **cache RAM**. In a computer system with a large cache, data transfer times from peripherals are very short. A large quantity of cache RAM is desirable, but adds to the overall cost of the computer system.

ROM (read only memory) contains the start-up sequence for a computer system. This will also include the **BIOS** (basic/input output system). Once the computer is switched on, the BIOS will load up the rest of the operating system to allow the user to use the system.

In some hand-held computers, the whole of the operating system is stored on ROM so as to remove the need to load anything from disk or cartridge. These computers may simply be switched on and used immediately.

The data in ROM cannot be altered or deleted, unless it is erasable and reprogrammable (**EPROM**). To rewrite the data, a special machine is needed. EPROMs are sometimes used to store system settings rather than CMOS RAM. The disadvantage is that the EPROM can only be reprogrammed a fixed number of times before it 'wears out'.

Did You Know?

System settings are known as **BIOS** settings – **B**asic **I**nput **O**utput **S**ystem.

Exercise 4.2

Why is the operating system on a palmtop computer stored in ROM?

Swanage Folk Festival

The festival uses a desktop publishing (DTP) package to produce its publicity. Posters are designed incorporating scanned images of artists performing at the festival. The files are sent to a printing company to produce the posters. The images need to be of the highest quality possible. Currently the committee use a PC with 64 MB of RAM. To obtain the highest quality the images are rescanned by the printing company using a machine with 128 MB of memory.

Exercise 4.3

How much RAM would you recommend as the minimum for a home user of computers?

Computers are available with 64 MB of RAM. Would you recommend this specification to any particular user? What type of applications would run satisfactorily with this amount of memory?

Activity 4.6

Find out the memory specifications of games consoles.

Exercise 4.4

The data in memory is transferred to and from the CPU using the address bus and the data bus. A computer is described as having 'a 32-bit address bus and a 16-bit data bus'.

★ How many memory locations may be directly addressed?
★ How much data (in bytes) can be transferred in one operation?
★ How much memory (in kilobytes) may be connected to the CPU in this computer?

Find out what BIOS settings are stored on the computer that you are familiar with. Which ones, if any, can be modified without knowing a password? Which ones, if any, can be modified only if a system password is known?

Using the log sheet designed in Activity 4.1, keep a record of what you have done with solutions to any problems encountered. This can be included in your portfolio.

Did You Know?

Peripheral means 'on the outside'. The ring road around Paris is called the 'Boulevard Peripherique'.

Peripherals

A **peripheral** is any device connected to the motherboard but separate from it. Usually it is taken to mean anything outside of the box that houses the CPU but, with the design of computers changing, some peripherals may have the CPU built in. For example, the iMac computer has its CPU in the monitor housing. The monitor is still a peripheral device to the CPU.

Storage devices

▼ ▼ ▼ ▼ ▼ ▼ ▼ ▼ ▼

Secondary storage
Storage provided by peripheral devices other than memory.

Primary storage
is the storage provided by memory in a computer system.

▲ ▲ ▲ ▲ ▲ ▲ ▲ ▲ ▲

Secondary storage is required in a computer system for three reasons.

✪ The content of memory is usually **volatile**, which means that if power is disconnected the data is lost.

✪ The capacity (in megabytes) of memory is limited due to the size of address and data buses.

✪ Memory is more expensive than secondary storage.

Several types of **disks** may be used for secondary storage.

✪ Floppy disks

✪ Hard disks

✪ Optical disks (including CD-ROM, writeable CD, DVD)

A **floppy disk** is a low capacity disk which may be removed from the computer. There are two types of floppy disks – those holding a small amount of data (under 3 megabytes) and 'super-floppies' that can hold hundreds of megabytes (sometimes called **ZIP disks)**. Data may be both written to and read from the floppy disk although they usually have a small notch which can be used to make the disk read-only (or **write-protected**). They are small, lightweight and easily transported. This makes them ideal for backups of small amounts of data or for transfer of data from one machine to another. On the other hand, they may be easily misplaced, damaged or stolen!

A **hard disk** is a higher capacity medium, with up to hundreds of gigabytes. They are usually non-removable, but removable hard disks are becoming more common. They can be both read from and written to, and are the standard medium for storing data on computer systems today. The capacity of a hard disk may be increased by using **data compression** techniques which allow large data files to occupy less space. The specification of a hard disk depends not only on its capacity but also the **access time** to data. This is affected by the **rotation speed** of the disk drive. The access time is also affected by the way in which the disk is connected to the motherboard – standards being **SCSI** and **IDE**.

Activity 4.8

Find out the relative advantages and costs of SCSI and IDE hard disks.

Most modern PCs are fitted with a **CD-ROM drive** which allows data to be read from a CD-ROM. CD-ROMs use optical technology to read the data from the surface of the disk. CD-ROM disks are portable and have a large capacity, typically 600 Mb. They are used for software supply and reference material such as encyclopaedias. A read-only medium, hence the name, they are being complemented by **writeable CDs**. These allow for a large amount of data to be written to a CD as well as read from it. They are sometimes known as **CD-RW**. For these, a CD drive is needed which includes write heads as well as read heads.

A **DVD (digital versatile disk)** is a higher capacity version of a CD and DVD drives have a higher transfer rate. DVD disks provide high quality playback of films and audio and they are increasingly found as standard on home computer systems. DVDs may be read only or read/write. They are sometimes known as **DVD-ROM** and **DVD-RAM** respectively.

Backups must be taken of all data on a hard disk. There are several ways of doing this.

- ✪ Mirror disks
- ✪ Zip drive
- ✪ Tape cartridge
- ✪ Writeable CD

Activity 4.9

Investigate some ways of backing up on a hard disk, and any others you can find out about. Make a presentation of your findings – this could be a report or a talk.

Activity 4.10

Find out the specification of the hard disk on two different computers that you use. Explain how the specification affects the performance of the disks.

Input devices

Computer systems will be supplied with a **keyboard** but users may prefer to have a different one installed. For example, keyboards are available with a curved layout for the keys to reduce the risk of **repetitive strain injury (RSI)** (Figure 4.5). There are standard layouts for different character sets (e.g. French, Japanese) and for particular operating systems.

A **concept keyboard** is a flat surface divided into a number of touch sensitive areas (Figure 4.6). Each area may be defined to be a particular key, word or

Figure 4.5   *Different types of keyboard*

Figure 4.6 *Concept keyboard*

action. They are often used with young children or those who find a traditional keyboard layout difficult. They are also used where a wipe-clean surface is required such as in a bar or fast-food outlet. In this context, the operator merely has to press the key corresponding to the item sold. The computer system uses a database to look up the price of the item. It also records the number of items sold to assist stock control.

The **mouse** is a device for tracking a pointer across a screen. The tracking is done by a ball rolling under the mouse. Rollers translate this movement into digital pulses that can then be interpreted as changes in co-ordinates. This allows the user to point at **icons** on the screen before clicking on them to make choices from menus or to launch programs.

File maintenance such as moving or copying a file may be done by dragging and dropping the file's icons. A mouse may have one, two or three buttons that perform different functions when clicked. A double click, two rapid clicks in succession, on a mouse button may also carry out a different function. The mouse's operation is often configurable with users being able to control such things as sensitivity, pointer size, etc.

Mice are available in a variety of shapes for **ergonomic** considerations. They may also have extra features such as a wheel or an extra button. Wireless mice are also available.

▼▼▼▼▼▼▼▼▼

Icon
A small graphic image representing an application or action

▲▲▲▲▲▲▲▲▲

▼▼▼▼▼▼▼▼▼

Ergonomic
characteristics make an object easy and efficient to use

▲▲▲▲▲▲▲▲▲

Exercise 4.5

What are the advantages of having a wireless mouse?
Apple computer systems have one button only on the mouse, PCs traditionally have two and some systems have three. What are the relative advantages of each design?

Activity 4.11

Find out which settings can be configured for the mice on the computer systems you use.

> Using the log sheet designed in Activity 4.1, keep a record of what you have done with solutions to any problems encountered. This can be included in your portfolio.

A **trackerball** is a more expensive alternative to a mouse. The ball is mounted on the topside of the trackerball. Buttons are provided in the same way as a mouse. This provides great security, as the trackerball is less likely to be damaged. It may also be easier to use if fine hand control is difficult for the user.

Activity 4.12

Find some other examples of the use of touch screens, concept keyboards and trackerballs. For each, explain why the particular input device is used.

John Cooper: Financial Adviser

John's laptop computer can be used with a mouse. It also has an input device for pointing and selecting that is built into the casing. When he is in someone's home, John can literally use the laptop on his lap without needing to have somewhere to roll his mouse.

Activity 4.13

What input devices are used instead of a mouse on a laptop computer? Ask users of laptop computers what they like and dislike about these input devices.

Touch screen. In some systems, it is desirable for users to interact directly with the screen. An example of this is in a tourist office where the screen may be placed in the wall of the office so that it is accessible 24 hours a day. The user simply presses the appropriate part of the screen. Doing away with the need for a mouse or other pointing device means that there are no trailing cables or separate components. This makes the touch screen very secure in such an open environment. Touch screens may also be used in 'dirty' environments as they are not as susceptible to dust as a mouse due to their lack of moving parts. They are used in bars and restaurants for similar tasks as concept keyboards.

Scanners are used for the input of images. A light is passed over the image and charge-coupled devices measure the intensity of the reflected light. There are several types of scanner.

- ✪ **Flat-bed scanners** The image to be scanned is placed face down and the light passes underneath it in the same way as a photocopier. These are commonly available in A4 or A3 size. Some models have a scanning area slightly larger than A4 or A3 allowing the whole of the image to be scanned without loss at the edges.

- ✪ **Hand-held scanners** The scanner is moved over the image. For most purposes these do not provide sufficient quality. Although a hand-held scanner may be very cheap, the small extra cost of a flat-bed scanner makes it a better proposition. Hand-held scanners sometimes have motorised paper feeders which gives a better image.

▼▼▼▼▼▼▼▼▼▼

Wand
A hand-held barcode reader

Digitising
Converting data into binary form so that it can be processed by a computer

▲▲▲▲▲▲▲▲▲▲

- ✪ **Specialist scanners** use the same concept of measuring the intensity of reflected light or infrared. They are used in **barcode readers** – either hand-held (**wand**) or mounted in a **electronic point of sale (EPOS)** terminal – and find a high tech use in retina scanning for security purposes. **Three dimensional scanners** have also been produced to capture an image of a solid object. Light is projected onto the object and measured by sensors around the object. Very large images may be captured on a **drum scanner** or by photographing sections of the image and **digitising** them.

Hyperion-Media

Hyperion-Media use a variety of multimedia effects in their website and CD-ROM publications. Images are captured from digital camera and existing CD-ROMs and DVDs. Animations are created using image manipulation software.

Multimedia input. Sound may be input to the computer system from a standard **microphone** or from an audio source such as a CD. Sound may also be taken from the audio-out socket of a video camera or player. With a microphone, the quality of the sound depends critically on the quality of the microphone, the distance from the sound source and the background noise.

Graphic images may be input to a computer system from any of these:

- ✪ Digital camera (still video)
- ✪ Moving video camera
- ✪ Videotape or disk (e.g. DVD)
- ✪ CD-ROM

Exercise 4.6

What are the problems associated with capturing sound through a microphone? How might these be overcome?

Activity 4.14

Create a set of web pages to advertise an event in school, college or your local community. Include sound and graphical images captured from a variety of sources.

Using the log sheet designed in Activity 4.1, keep a record of what you have done with solutions to any problems encountered. This can be included in your portfolio.

Output devices

The **visual display unit (VDU)** or screen is an essential part of all computer systems. Desktop computers use a VDU with a cathode ray tube in which images are displayed by streams of electrons hitting a phosphorescent surface. The position of the streams are controlled by the VDU controller and allow for individual dots (**pixels**) to be displayed independently of each other. Each pixel may be displayed in a range of colours dependent on the **colour mode** set up within the computer. An image may be created in one colour mode (e.g. 256-colours) and then modified to another (e.g. greyscale). The quality of colour is specified by the number of bits used to hold the colour information for a single pixel. 256 colours require 8-bits. Higher quality colour, with a finer range of colours, is obtained by using 16-bit or 32-bit colour. This is sometimes referred to as 'true colour'.

Activity 4.15

Find out how many different colours can be represented by 16-bits and by 32-bits.

The number of pixels on the screen is determined by its **resolution**, the higher the resolution the sharper the image. This is often quoted as a dot pitch size. Standards for resolution and maximum number of colours have been set for VDUs. These standards include VGA, SVGA, etc. and users will need to select an appropriate standard to meet the needs of their work. The standard sets the maximum number of pixels that can be displayed on the VDU. The actual resolution may be modified to values up to this maximum.

The image on a VDU is not static. As a consequence, the user will see a slight flickering of the image. Several aspects of the VDU's specification affect the amount of flickering.

✪ The **scan frequency** is the number of lines of pixels a VDU can display in one second, expressed in kHz (generally between 20 and 100 kHz). The higher the frequency, the less flickering a user will see.

✪ The **refresh rate** is the maximum number of frames that can be displayed on a monitor in a second. The higher the rate, the less flickering a user will see.

✪ **Interlace** mode blends the changes between the repeated displays of images. This makes the display easier to look at by apparently reducing the amount of flickering.

Sound output. Sound may be played through internal or external **speakers** on a computer system. Internal speakers, often housed in the monitor casing or processor box, do not provide very high quality. External speakers or headphones may be connected to an audio-out socket.

Activity 4.16

Investigate the specifications of monitors that you use. Which are easiest to look at for long periods? Why is this?

Find out how to reconfigure the monitors that you use. What settings are you able to change? What values of those settings make the screen easiest to look at?

Exercise 4.7

The laptop VDU technology is also used on some standard desktop computer systems – for example, at a cashier's desk in a bank. Why is this?

Activity 4.17

Find out how sound can be played through a computer system that you use. Can you connect external speakers?

Using the log sheet designed in Activity 4.1, keep a record of what you have done with solutions to any problems encountered. This can be included in your portfolio.

Printers

Printers are available in a wide range of specifications and types. The two most common types are **inkjet** and **laser** printers. An **inkjet printer** works by spraying inks (either black or coloured) onto the paper in a series of tiny dots. The **resolution** of the printer and the accuracy of the image determine its price. A typical maximum resolution is 720 **dpi** although technological developments are producing finer detail through overlaying and interlacing techniques. The quality of output from an inkjet printer is heavily dependent on the quality of the paper being used, as cheap paper will cause the ink to run or bleed.

A laser printer works by spraying an electric charge onto the paper. This charge is in the image of the text or graphics to be printed. Powdered ink, or toner, is then attracted to the paper and bonded by heat (Figure 4.7).

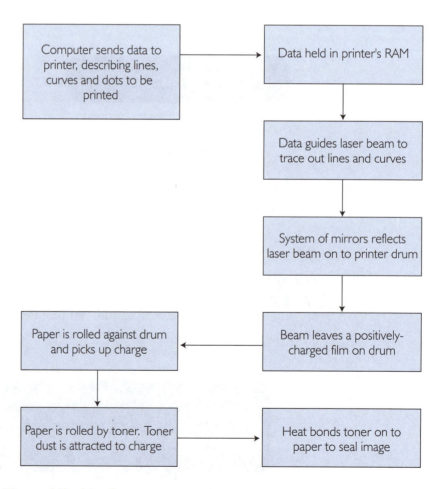

Figure 4.7 *How laser printing works*

The accuracy and resolution produced by a laser printer is usually more consistent than an inkjet printer and less dependent on the quality of paper. They can print more pages per minute than an inkjet printer of comparable price. Laser printers are most often used when high speed, high quality black on white printout is required. The maximum resolution is usually 600 dpi and colour output is around ten times as expensive as the equivalent quality inkjet.

Swanage Folk Festival

The organisers of the festival accept advertisements on paper. Some advertisers use a computer system to produce adverts and then give the organisers a paper copy. These are reproduced in the festival programme and are often quite small. The organisers prefer the advertisements that are submitted this way to be printed on a laser printer, rather than an inkjet. This is because the text and images are sharper and can be more easily read.

Activity 4.18

Use a desktop publishing program to produce an advertisement for an event that you know about.
Print the advertisement on both a laser and an inkjet printer.
Reduce the size of the advertisement. What is the smallest size that is easily read when printed out on each type of printer?

Using the log sheet designed in Activity 4.1, keep a record of what you have done with solutions to any problems encountered. This can be included in your portfolio.

An earlier type of printer is the **dot-matrix printer**. This works by hammering pins against a **ribbon** to produce a pattern of dots to make up a character or graphic. In comparison to inkjets or lasers, dot matrix printers are cheaper but slower. The use of a ribbon as opposed to ink or toner cartridges is also cheaper. The hammering of the ribbon onto the paper is noisy and this is a serious disadvantage in an office. The main advantage of dot-matrix printers is their ability to print onto multi-part stationery. The printer prints the top copy and the action of the pins ensures that the other copies are legible.

A **plotter** produces output by pens drawing directly onto the paper. Up to A3 size, it is usual to use **flatbed plotters**. For larger size plans, **drum plotters** may be used. This is particularly useful in applications such as architectural design.

Exercise 4.8

What is the difference between flatbed and drum plotters? Consider the way in which the paper is held in the plotter and the way in which the image is created.

The CPU can output data to the printer or plotter much faster than it can be dealt with, so a **buffer** is used. This is random access memory (RAM) that is dedicated to storing the data being output. The buffer may be in the input/output circuitry of the CPU or in the printer or both. The processor is free to process other tasks once it has sent the data into the buffer. The printer or plotter can take data from the buffer at its own speed. The larger the buffer, the more efficient the output process. In a similar way, data to be printed may be temporarily stored in a **spool file** on disk, or tape, awaiting output. This technique also frees up the CPU for other tasks.

To speed up the data transfer still further, **double buffering** may be used. In this technique, two buffers are used. While one buffer is being filled, the other is being emptied (Figure 4.8).

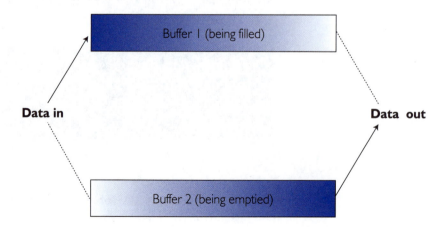

Figure 4.8   *Double buffering*

What type of printer would you recommend for each of these applications? Why?

★ Home use – mainly word processing, some use for designing greetings cards

★ A church that prints 200 copies of a plain-text newsletter each week

★ A business that sends out colour catalogues each month to 1000 customers

Activity 4.19

What is the advertised print rate for the printers that you use (in pages per minute)? What is the actual rate for text? For pictures? Can you increase this rate by reconfiguring the printer? If so, how?

John Cooper: Financial Adviser

John Cooper uses a portable computer and printer to provide his customers with quotes for financial products. He enters details of their current income and expenditure and type of insurance, assurance or investment required. The software then calculates a series of quotes. The portable printer prints these out in draft form. A higher quality printout is produced when John returns to the office. This high quality copy is then posted to his clients.

The computer system is contained in a standard size briefcase so that it can be easily carried into people's homes.

**Activity
4.20**

Investigate the type of monitors that are used on laptop computers. How do the various types differ in the quality of image and the method creating the display? Which type would you recommend for John Cooper?

What type of printer would you recommend for the portable computer? Which type would you recommend for the office? Explain your reasons.

Connecting devices

Ports

These are connections between circuit boards in the main processing unit and peripherals. Data is transmitted through a **serial port** one bit at a time. Data is transmitted through a **parallel port** several bits at a time (Figure 4.9).

The choice of number and type of ports will depend on the user's needs and the peripherals attached to the system. The serial port is used for connecting devices such as modems and for network connections. Computer systems increasingly have a standard serial connection – the **universal serial port**. This allows over a hundred devices to be connected together in one 'daisy-chain' without loss of performance (Figure 4.10).

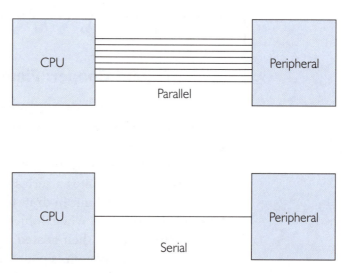

Figure 4.9   *Serial and parallel ports*

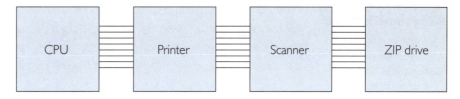

Figure 4.10 *'Daisy chain' of devices*

Connectors

There are various standards for connecting devices together. When connecting using a parallel connector the **Centronics** standard is to use a 36-pin D-shaped plug and socket. This is a common standard for connecting printers to computers. Where **coaxial** cables are used, **BNC connectors** allow for devices to be connected together. A BNC connector is secured by twisting and locking, similar to a light bulb fitting.

To connect devices to telephone lines or networks, the standard connector is the **RJ (registered jack) connector**. The eight-wire RJ-45 is most common for connecting to networks (especially Ethernet local area network (LAN) connections).

Any connector between serial and parallel cables and a data bus can be referred to as a **DB connector**. A 25-pin parallel printer connector can be called a DB-25 using this convention.

Devices sometimes need to be configured for the correct **settings**, e.g. the data transfer characteristics on a printer. This is often done with small two-position switches on the circuit board known as **dual in-line (DIL) switches.** The switches are usually mounted together to form a **dual in-line package (DIP) switch** (Figure 4.11).

Figure 4.11 *DIP switches*

When connecting using a serial port the RS232, and later RS423 and RS432, standards are used. These define the purpose of each of the pins in the plug and socket. These connection standards require 9 pins, but 25-pin connectors are sometimes used with most pins not being connected.

Keyboards, mice and other devices are often connected using round connecting plugs. These are called **DIN plugs**.

Other settings may be set on a circuit board by the use of **jumpers**. These allow connections to be made between two pins on the board. By moving the jumper from one pair to another, a system setting is altered (Figure 4.12).

Figure 4.12 *Jumpers*

Activity 4.21

Find some examples of jumpers and DIP switches on the system that you use. What settings can be altered using them?

Using the log sheet designed in Activity 4.1, keep a record of what you have done with solutions to any problems encountered This can be included in your portfolio.

Expansion cards

To improve the performance of a computer system, it is usually possible to connect additional circuit boards, or **cards**, to the motherboard (see pages 147–8). For example, **video cards** allow the output of data to VDUs. The video card installed in the system, and the specification of the VDU attached, determines the quality of the display (see page 148).

Similarly, **sound cards** allow the output of stereo, multi-channel audio output. The sound card fitted determines the quality of this output. One measure is the number of bits per channel. The higher the number of bits, the 'richer' the sound.

Sound may be input to the computer using a standard **microphone** connected to an input port on a sound card. Output is from the sound card to a **speaker**.

If the computer is to be connected to a local area network (LAN) then a **network card** will need to be fitted. For connection to a wide area network (WAN), it will be necessary to connect the processor to a **modem** or **ISDN router** which will itself require a **serial communications card**.

There are several standards for connecting devices to the motherboard.

- ✪ An **IDE interface** is used for connecting hard disk drives to the motherboard. The interface is an integral part of the disk drive itself, thus reducing the cost of adding the drive to the computer.
- ✪ Hard disks can also be connected using a **SCSI (small computer standard interface)** which offers higher performance. SCSIs can be used both for disk drives and other peripherals such as scanners. They offer high performance as they permit high transfer rates. Many, typically up to seven, devices may use one SCSI.
- ✪ When connecting peripherals, a cheaper solution than SCSI is to connect the external ports of a computer. A scanner, for example, may be connected via a bi-directional parallel port such as the printer port.

Exercise 4.10

What are the advantages of using an IDE interface? What are the advantages of using a SCSI?

Exercise 4.11

What are the problems that you might encounter if a scanner is connected via a bi-directional parallel port?

Activity 4.22

Find out what expansion cards, if any, are fitted to the computers that you use. Practise fitting a card.

Using the log sheet designed in Activity 4.1, keep a record of what you have done with solutions to any problems encountered. This can be included in your portfolio.

Activity 4.23

What settings can you configure on a sound card? How do you do it on the system that you use?

Using the log sheet designed in Activity 4.1, keep a record of what you have done with solutions to any problems encountered. This can be included in your portfolio.

Consumables

In any computer system, there are a number of items that are used up and replacements are purchased. These include paper, ink (toner or cartridges) and ribbons. The cost of these consumables must be taken into account when specifying a system. Items such as floppy disks and backup tape cartridges must also be budgeted for.

Activity 4.24

Find out how much paper and ink are used by the computers in your school, college or at home. How much does this all cost? Compare your answers to other computer users' systems. Which is the cheapest type of printer to run?

Activity 4.25

Take the components of a dismantled IT system and reassemble them to form a working system.

Using the log sheet designed in Activity 4.1, keep a record of what you have done with solutions to any problems encountered. This can be included in your portfolio.

Pay particular attention to issues of health and safety.

Hyperion-Media

When a company starts a contract with Hyperion-Media it needs to provide some artwork and images that can be incorporated into the promotional material or website. To this is added sounds, music and video. Hyperion-Media specialise in the creation of animated effects as part of their published material.

What hardware would you recommend for a company like Hyperion-Media? You should produce a full specification of computers and all associated peripherals and provide an estimated cost.

You will need to research the current availability and prices of hardware in trade magazines and online sources.

ICT system components – software

This part of the chapter looks at the software that may be specified for a given system.

- ✪ Minimum system software and system settings
- ✪ Operating systems
- ✪ User interfaces
- ✪ Utilities
- ✪ Applications
- ✪ Computer programming languages

System software and settings

When a new system is specified, the user will need to have a basic minimum set of software so that communication with the computer is possible. This minimum system software is provided with the processor and forms part of its specification. It includes the operating system provided with the system.

As soon as the computer is switched on, the **BIOS** and **start-up** software will be loaded and run. This software, stored in ROM, will load up the rest of the **operating system** including the **user interface** that will allow the user to use the computer. During this start-up process, it is possible for the user to modify system settings. At the very simplest level, this will allow the user to set the **system time** and **date**. Some of the other settings are described here.

The user will be able to the **set the start-up (boot) disk drive** so that the location of the operating system may be specified. Under normal operation, the start-up disk drive will be set to the internal hard disk but it may be necessary to allow the user to start up the computer from a floppy disk. This is only usually needed if the hard disk, or its interface card, develops a fault or if the operating system on the hard disk becomes corrupted. If a computer is connected to a network, the operating system and user interface will usually be loaded from the network file server. This is usually achieved in one of two ways.

1   A network boot ROM on the network card in the machine effectively sets the boot drive to be the file server.

2   The machine boots from the internal hard drive and then loads network boot software.

If a new or additional disk drive has been fitted then the user must be able to **define a new disk drive**. This would happen if the specification required extra disk capacity to be fitted, or if a new CD-ROM disk drive was to be installed for example. Similarly, any extra peripherals will need to be set up and the processor settings will allow the user to **set up and configure** an expansion card (video, sound, etc.).

It may be necessary for the user to protect a station by requiring a **system password** to be entered before the station can be used. This password is stored in the system settings and often has to be entered before any changes to the settings themselves can be made. A password may also be used to prevent users from accessing a floppy disk drive. This is particularly important if the user is concerned about software being copied from the hard disk, or if the copying of software from floppy disk is to be prevented.

The user will also be able to set up the **memory management** requirements of this system. This provides the opportunity to vary the size of cache and buffers being used, and to allocate various parts of memory to certain tasks. In doing so, the speed of operation can be optimised. For example, a user processing a large volume of graphical images will need to set aside considerable portions of memory for this purpose. It is often possible to load memory management drivers which optimise the use of the memory in the system.

Activity 4.27

Investigate some memory management software by looking through computing magazines or by reading manuals for any such software that you have access to. What are the advertised features of the software?

Activity 4.28

Find out how to modify the BIOS settings on the computer system that you are familiar with. Before you make any changes, it is sensible to write down the current values of all of the settings! This will allow you to reset them if you configure the computer so that it becomes unusable.

You should be able to change the date and time, set up passwords and modify the configuration of peripheral controllers and of memory.

Using the log sheet designed in Activity 4.1, keep a record of what you have done with solutions to any problems encountered. This can be included in your portfolio.

Operating systems

The **operating system** (OS) is the suite of programs that allows the user to communicate with the computer system, and the hardware and software to work together. Different operating systems will provide different facilities for the user, and will be able to control different hardware and software. Usually, the choice of operating system for any given hardware is limited.

Once the operating system has been selected, it must be **installed** on the computer system. On most computers, the operating system is not pre-loaded. It is stored on the computer's disk drive and must be loaded into RAM each time the system is booted.

As with all software, the operating system for a desktop computer may be supplied on floppy disks, on CD-ROMs or downloaded from an online system such as the Internet. The operating system will consist of many files and will set up a **directory structure** for these files (Figures 4.13). It is important that a user's system has a sensible directory structure so that programs and data may be located easily. Each file has a filename which contains the path through the directory structure to reach that file from the root. The full path is not always displayed as it may appear daunting for inexperienced users.

It is often possible, especially on network systems, to set a **virtual drive** or directory. This can be useful, for instance, if each user of the system is to have a separate root directory. Such a directory will appear as the root to a user but will really be a sub-directory on the physical drive. Each user can then see only part of the whole structure (Figure 4.13).

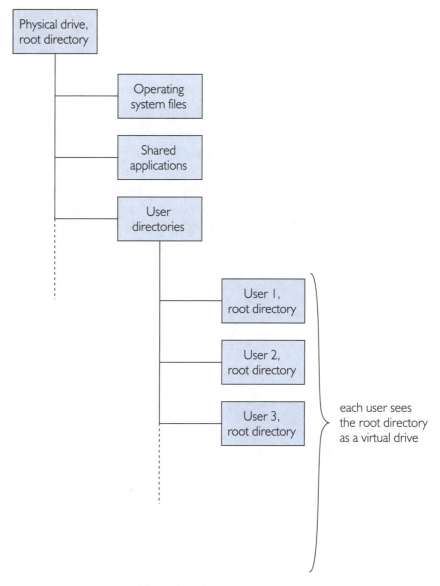

Figure 4.13 *Directory structure, virtual drives and OS files*

If you have access to two operating systems, what are their relative advantages? Are there any features, missing from both, that you would consider desirable?

Once installed, the operating system must be **configured** to provide the facilities that the user requires. The configuration may be stored in CMOS RAM and in files on disk. This will involve selecting appropriate **device drivers** and setting up the **user interface**. A device driver is a program that allows the computer system and the device to communicate with each other. It provides the commands to control the device and configuration options. A common example is a mouse driver, which allows a mouse to be used on the system (Figure 4.14). There may also be a need to **configure peripherals** by, for example, setting DIP switches (see page 169) or, more usually, by configuring the device's driver software.

It is also necessary to set up any **initialisation** or **batch files** (see Activity 4.30). These are programs that allow the drivers to be loaded and to run **menu programs**. They can also be used to set up pathways to **directories** so that software can be located by the system. Any **network connection configurations** will also need to be set up so that a station may communicate with the network operating system. This could include setting station identity, printer connections and queue names, and mail address (Figure 4.15).

```
REM [Header]
DOS=HIGH, UMB
DEVICE=C:\WINDOWS\HIMEM.SYS

REM DEVICE=C:\WINDOWS\EM386.EXE AUTO NOEMS

FILES=100

REM [SCSI Controller]
REM [CD-ROM Drive]
DEVICEHIGH=C:\DRIVERS\CDROM\HIT-IDE.SYS /D:MSCD000
REM [Display]
REM [Sound, MIDI, or Video Capture Card]
REM [Mouse]
REM [Miscellaneous]

[Common]
DEVICEHIGH=C:\WINDOWS\COMMAND\ANSI.SYS
```

```
[MOUSE]
MouseType=PS2
PhysicalButtons=2
HorizontalSensitvity=50
VerticalSensitvity=50
ActiveAccelerationProfile=2
RotationAngle=0
PrimaryButton=1
SecondaryButton=3
ClickLock=OFF
```

Figure 4.14   *Printout of a CONFIG.SYS file and mouse driver file*

Activity 4.30

For one operating system, investigate how it is configured through system and batch files. Experiment with modifying these files. Is there a setting that you consider should be permanently changed? If so, why?

Use your log sheet to record what you have done.

```
@C:\PROGRA~1\NAVDX.EXE /Startup
REM C:\NECSSFW\IRT.EXE
REM SET MSINPUT=C:\MSINPUT
@ECHO OFF
C:\WINDOWS\BOOT>C:\WINDOWS\BOOTLOG.LOG
REM [Header]
REM [System Start]
REM [CD-ROM Drive]
REM [Display]

REM [Soun, MIDI, or Video Capture Card]
SET BLASTER=A220 15 D1 T4
SET SOUND16=C:\OPTISND
SET MIDI=SYNTH:2 MAP:E

REM [Mouse]
REM [System End]
REM [Miscellaneous]
```

Figure 4.15   *Example of AUTOEXEC.BAT file*

User interfaces

User interfaces fall into two broad categories (Figure 4.16).

○ Command interfaces

○ Graphical user interfaces (GUI)

A **command interface** requires the user to type commands rather than using a mouse pointer. In this case, it is possible to alter the font, screen colours and the appearance of the screen prompt. The command is translated, and then executed, by a **command line interpreter (CLI)**.

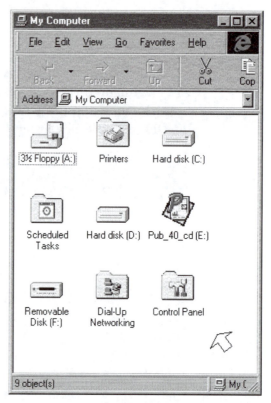

Figure 4.16 *Graphical user interface*

A **graphical user interface (GUI)** allows users to select options by use of a pointing device such as a mouse (Figure 4.16). It makes use of menus and icons so that the selection is user-friendly. Users can modify the **desktop appearance** by choosing icon size, window colours, fonts, etc. Users can usually have their own images as the background for the desktop, associate appropriate sounds to particular operations and select screen savers. All of these changes are made through a **control panel** utility that will also offer more advanced changes to be made to the operating system, such as adding and removing hardware and device drivers.

Users will be able to modify the appearance of **toolbars**, **menu layouts**, **borders**, **rulers** and **scroll bars**. All of these settings will have defaults that are set up when the system is first installed. **Defaults** are the initial value of settings. For example a desktop may be dark blue when a computer system is first set up – this is the default colour.

Exercise 4.12

Give TWO advantages and THREE disadvantages of a GUI compared to a command-driven interface.

Activity 4.31

Survey a group of people that use your computer systems. Find out which settings they prefer for toolbars, menu layouts, borders, rulers and scroll bars. Set up desktops for these users incorporating their preferences. Evaluate their choices.

> Using the log sheet designed in Activity 4.1, keep a record of what you have done with solutions to any problems encountered. This can be included in your portfolio.

Utilities

Utility programs are supplied with the operating system to perform system and file maintenance tasks. For example, the control panel utility described in the previous section provides programs to search for files, an on-screen clock, volume control, etc.

A user can install utilities onto a new system in addition to those provided with the operating system:

- ✪ **Anti-virus software**, which detects and removes known viruses from the system, may be configured to automatically start up and monitor all files and disks used on the system. The anti-virus software may also have the facility to **schedule** events, e.g. to scan all files on the hard disk every week at a set time.

- ✪ **Diagnostic software** allows system faults to be located and system performance to be **monitored**. For example, it will give a reading to show how much RAM is being used by each task.

- ✪ **Disk diagnostics** may be examined if a problem is suspected with a disk drive. The disk may need **defragmenting** to collect together all of the files and the free space on the disk. This usually results in faster file access.

- ✪ **Device drivers** are needed for setting up and installing peripheral devices.

- ✪ **Power management software**, supplied with laptop computers to conserve the battery life. This allows the user to specify the time interval between the last action and the computer going into sleep mode. The user may choose to have the computer save its memory content to disk on entering sleep mode, so as to preserve the data being worked on.

- ✪ **Directory management** software allows users to see the underlying directory structure, create new directories and find files within the structure.

Activity 4.32

Find out how to run diagnostic software on the computer system that you use. Make a note of the readings it gives.

Make changes to the system. For example, reconfigure the BIOS or run a multi-tasking application such as background printing from a word processor.

Re-run the diagnostics software and note the differences in the readings it gives. Does the diagnostics software help you to decide which is the optimum configuration for your system?

Using the log sheet designed in Activity 4.1, keep a record of what you have done with solutions to any problems encountered. This can be included in your portfolio.

Exercise 4.13

What effects of viruses on computer systems have you heard of?

How did the 'Millennium Bug Problem' differ from a virus?

Activity 4.33

Find out how to configure anti-virus software. Make a list of the settings that can be enabled or disabled.

Using the log sheet designed in Activity 4.1, keep a record of what you have done with solutions to any problems encountered. This can be included in your portfolio.

Activity 4.34

Find out what utility software is available on your system. Select three or four, and describe what each does.

Using the log sheet designed in Activity 4.1, keep a record of what you have done with solutions to any problems encountered. This can be included in your portfolio.

Applications

The most important software for the user, and that which varies most from context to context, is the **applications software.** A user may require access to **specialist software** (such as payroll, accounts, bookings) dependent on the business or organisational needs. It is very likely, however, that there will be a need to specify and set up **generic applications software.**

- ✪ Document (word) processing
- ✪ Desktop publishing (DTP)
- ✪ Multimedia reference
- ✪ Multimedia production (authoring)
- ✪ Database
- ✪ Spreadsheet
- ✪ Vector-based graphic images (e.g. geometric objects)
- ✪ Bitmap graphic images (e.g. photo images)
- ✪ Presentation graphics (e.g. slideshows)

You need to know which type of software suits a particular activity, and this is described in some detail in Chapter 2. Refer also to the index for relevant page numbers.

If a **graphical user interface (GUI)** is being used, it is usual to install the applications software. Once this is done, the application can be run from the desktop by clicking on an **icon** or selecting from a **menu**. Alternatively, and in non-GUI systems, it will be necessary to include paths to the applications in the menu structures by amending paths or to provide users with the commands to run the software. When installing applications, care should be taken with the use of directories (folders). It is sensible, for example, to store each application in its own separate directory. This becomes particularly important if the user ever decides to 'uninstall' software. Some software will come with an uninstall routine but this is not always so.

Once the applications have been installed, the user may have particular requirements for its customisation. These can be set up in a **preferences** (or **options**) **file** for the application.

- ✪ The ***start-up appearance*** *(colours, window size, borders, rulers and scrollbars, etc.)*

- ✪ *The path of **default directories** to be used for loading and saving files and for loading clip art, templates and other resources*

- ✪ *A facility to automatically **save** work, the time interval between saves and whether a **backup** copy is to be kept automatically*

- ✪ ***Menus** that can be configured to exclude rarely used options or to include user-defined **macros***

Exercise 4.14

Identify other options for customising applications software and why they are provided.

Within an application, it is often possible to create **macros**. These allow frequently used tasks to be automated so that users have only to press a particular key sequence or select a single item from a menu to perform the task. Some typical uses for macros are given here.

- ✪ *Sorting data into alphabetical order, if this option does not exist*

- ✪ *Querying a database*

- ✪ *Graphing data on a spreadsheet*

- ✪ *Performing a mail-merge*

A macro is created by following this sequence of steps:

1   Selecting MACRO RECORD from a menu or toolbar

2   Naming the macro

3   Assigning the key press that will execute the macro, if required

4   Assigning the macro name to a menu, if required

5   Manually performing the operation that is to be automated

6   Selecting STOP MACRO RECORDING from a menu or toolbar

Once the macro is created, it is executed by selecting its name from the menu that it was assigned to, making the appropriate key press or selecting it by name from the list of macros. A macro is actually a short piece of program code. The application package will usually provide a facility to view and edit this code. Similarly, macros may be created by typing the code in from scratch rather than by using the 'macro record' feature. This is especially useful if the macro is to contain operations that cannot be carried out precisely manually (for example, the operation 'Move to the cell above' is often recorded as 'Move to cell B4').

The user may be helped further by the creation of **templates**. These allow the creation of documents that conform to standard layouts and styles. If the templates match existing paper-based documents, users can often use them more readily. The use of templates is discussed further in Chapter 1.

Activity 4.35

Find out how to install an application on the computer system that you are familiar with. Install a piece of application software and ensure that its set-up meets the needs of prospective users. Save the users' preferences in a configuration file (this is often located under an Options menu).

Using the log sheet designed in Activity 4.1, keep a record of what you have done with solutions to any problems encountered. This can be included in your portfolio.

Activity 4.36

Create a macro to work with the application you have installed. This could be a macro (or batch file) to launch the application, or a macro to automate some frequently used task within the application. Document your macro by explaining what it does and how you created it.

Test your designs by asking someone else to work with your macro and to evaluate its effectiveness. Document your design and the evaluation.

> Using the log sheet designed in Activity 4.1, keep a record of what you have done with solutions to any problems encountered. This can be included in your portfolio.

Activity 4.37

Create a template within the application. This should be designed with a user's specific needs in mind.

Test your design by asking someone else to work with your template and to evaluate its effectiveness. Document your design and the evaluation.

> Using the log sheet designed in Activity 4.1, keep a record of what you have done with solutions to any problems encountered. This can be included in your portfolio.

Write some guidance to the user explaining how to use the system.

★ How to use the templates and macros that you have created.

★ How to modify the preferences.

★ How to keep files secure through backups and, if available, document protection.

Using the log sheet designed in Activity 4.1, keep a record of what you have done with solutions to any problems encountered. This can be included in your portfolio.

Computer programming languages

If the system is to be used for programming then it will be necessary to specify and install language environments. These will include translation and execution tools. These are covered in the optional units of this qualification.

Safety and security

Throughout your work in Vocational A-level ICT you need to consider safety and security. These are covered here and in the *Good Working Practice Guide* , starting on page 335.

Safety

When specifying and setting up a computer system, it is important to consider certain health and safety issues. All **cables** must be placed so as not to cause obstruction. This may be done by use of trunking and conduits to take the cables safely from one part of the installation to another. This applies not just to electrical cables but to those data cables between devices. In addition, all **electrical cables** must be wired to conform to electrical wiring legislation (currently BS7671:1998 in the United Kingdom). There are many provisions in these regulations.

- ✪ Users must be protected against electric shock, e.g. by having no bare wires
- ✪ Cabling must be protected against extremes of heat and cold
- ✪ The circuits must be protected against current overload by adequate fuses and circuit-breakers
- ✪ Suitable switches and circuit isolators must be provided
- ✪ Regular safety tests must be carried out on the equipment

When the computer system is being used, it is important that certain simple guidelines are followed.

- ✪ Clear the space around peripherals and CPU to allow easy access and ventilation
- ✪ Keep area free from drinks
- ✪ Dust down cases and wipe screens regularly
- ✪ Do not open cases without disconnecting power
- ✪ Do not reposition devices without first disconnecting power

When setting out the furniture, **ergonomic** considerations should be taken into account. This applies to the positioning of equipment, its relative height, angle, etc. This will minimise **physical stress.** Users should be aware of the need to take appropriate breaks and to recognise the symptoms of **repetitive strain** so as to take remedial action. Monitors should comply with all current legislation and a label affixed to them to indicate this compliance. UK requirements are contained in the Health and Safety (Display Equipment) Regulations 1992. This includes compliance with maximum radiation levels.

Activity 4.39

Research and collect material on the ergonomic and safe positioning and use of computer equipment.

This may be obtained from the Health and Safety Executive or from your school or college. Many institutions also publish their health and safety policies on the world wide web.

Activity 4.40

Carry out a health and safety audit on the computer installation with which you are familiar. Make copies of, and complete, the forms provided.

> Using the log sheet designed in Activity 4.1, keep a record of what you have done with solutions to any problems encountered. This can be included in your portfolio.

Security

Users of all computer systems can be encouraged to take simple steps to increase the security of the hardware and software. The security of data is probably of more significance to an organisation than that of hardware. This is because hardware can simply be replaced by purchasing new but data would need to be re-entered from source documents if they existed! Data held on a computer system is often private or commercially sensitive. Organisations will need to ensure that it is kept secure to prevent unauthorised access or use.

- ✪ Data and software should be backed up regularly
- ✪ Backup tapes or disks should be kept in a secure location away from the main system
- ✪ Confidential information must be protected by following the provisions of the Data Protection Acts (1984 and 1998)
- ✪ Passwords should be applied to user access to terminals, documents or menus
- ✪ Physical damage should be avoided (fire, water, dust, etc.)
- ✪ Virus checking should be systematically undertaken and anti-virus software regularly updated
- ✪ Copyright of data and software must be maintained
- ✪ Theft of equipment, data and software should be avoided by providing appropriate locks, cameras, passcards, etc.

All of the above points should be made explicit to the user in the specification of a system. They should also be made relevant to the user's particular context.

Exercise 4.15

It is necessary to have good housekeeping routines to ensure that users can locate data files at a later date. Explain how such routines can be set up on the computer system that you are familiar with. Write a statement of good working practice to encourage users to carry out these routines.

John Cooper: Financial Adviser

The financial advice software stores clients' personal details as part of the process for producing customised quotes.

Exercise 4.16

★ How do the provisions of the Data Protection Act (1998) affect the use of a computer system by John Cooper?
★ What advice would you give to a dentist on the procedures carried out to ensure the security of data?

Revision questions

1 What are the functions of the main processing unit in a computer?

2 What is a motherboard?

3 What are the functions of registers in a computer system?

4 Name three types of bus in a computer system and explain their purpose.

5 Why does the clock speed of a computer alone determine the speed of processing?

6 Describe different types of RAM.

7 What is a concept keyboard and what type of applications might use them?

8 What are the key features of (a) scanners and (b) monitors that should be considered when specifying a new system?

9 Compare the relative benefits of laser printers and inkjet printers.

10 What are DB and RJ connectors, DIP switches and jumpers, and what are they used for?

11 What are the differences between IDE and SCSI connections?

12 What are the main functions of an operating system?

13 Name and describe three common utilities found on a computer system.

14 How can a user configure (a) system settings and (b) applications software?

15 What are macros and templates, and why are they used?

Systems Analysis

5

- Understanding the principles of systems analysis
- Investigating problems for clients
- Applying the principles of systems analysis to propose solutions
- Using structured analysis methods to define data and its processing
- Creating feasibility study reports and system specifications

Introduction

What is systems analysis?

Organisations such as banks, hospitals and supermarkets, use computer systems as tools to help them to carry out their business. Their computer systems have to be developed, not by the users of the system, but by IT professionals. The computer system must meet the needs of the users, so the IT professionals have to understand those needs in detail. There are two main difficulties systems analysis must overcome:

▮ The users of the system and the developers of the system are experts in two different areas. For example, in a bank the users are experts in banking and finance, and the system developers are experts in IT. However, the users need to be able to

▼ ▼ ▼ ▼ ▼ ▼ ▼ ▼ ▼ ▼

Systems analysis
The process of analysing and understanding user needs is called **systems analysis**.

▲ ▲ ▲ ▲ ▲ ▲ ▲ ▲ ▲ ▲

communicate in detail what the system needs to do, so the system developers need to become experts in the area of banking that the system will address.

2   Computer systems need to model real-world situations, such as withdrawing some money from a bank or buying some goods at the supermarket. These real-world situations are highly complex with many interrelationships with other systems. Ways are needed not only to understand this complexity, but also to describe (model) it in some formal way (such as a diagram).

Systems analysis is of critical importance in the development of a complex computerised system. Errors at this stage may result in a system which, no matter how good the programming or the user interface is, fails to meet the primary goal of any computer system, i.e. to meet the needs of the user.

The software development life cycle

Systems analysis is part of the system development life cycle (Figure 5.1). As the name cycle suggests, it has no clear start or finish but it is useful to think of the start of the cycle as being the point where dissatisfaction with the existing system (either computerised or manual) reaches such a level that a new system is considered. It may be that the existing system is unable to cope efficiently with an increasing volume of work, or it may be that other companies in the same business have introduced systems which give them a competitive advantage (e.g. an Internet shopping service) so a similar (or better) system is needed to regain the competitive edge. This is the point where systems analysis begins: the existing system and its limitations are analysed, the needs of the users are identified and the way forward is investigated.

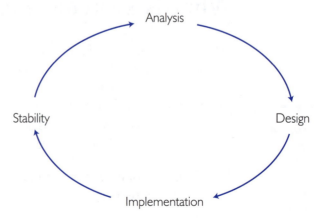

Figure 5.1   *The software development life cycle*

Once the analysis stage is completed, then it is time to start on the detailed design of the required system, followed by the development of the programs, testing and implementation. This chapter concentrates only on the analysis stage, but other units cover the other stages. After the system has been implemented and initial teething problems have been ironed out, the system should enter a period of stability. There will come a time, however, when (due to further increases in work load, new developments or changes in the market) the system will no longer fully meet the needs of its users and the need to develop a new or modified system will arise. So, the whole process begins again. Hence, the use of the term **cycle**.

Case studies

To help you to understand the processes involved in systems analysis, this chapter includes three case studies:

- ✪ the Shoot-Em-Up Games Ltd royalty payment system
- ✪ a serials management system
- ✪ Sunnyside Health Centre

Shoot-Em-Up Games

Shoot-Em-Up (SEU) Games Ltd is a small company that markets computer games for PCs and games machines (e.g. Sony Playstation). SEU doesn't employ its own programmers. Instead, the games are written by freelance (self-employed) programmers who are paid a royalty (a percentage of the sale price) for each copy of the game sold. Currently, the accounts department uses a simple spreadsheet to work out how much royalty money to pay each programmer, but, as the number of games the company sells has increased, this system is time-consuming to use.

Serials Management System

Libraries (not just college libraries) subscribe to a wide range of serials, ranging from daily newspapers, like *The Times* and *The Guardian*, to specialist weekly publications (e.g. *Times Educational Supplement* and *Computing*) and monthly magazines (e.g. *Which*). The subscription to these serials all need to be paid (usually once a year) and the library staff need to check that all copies arrive each day, week and month. They also need to keep back numbers (old copies) for a certain period of time.

Activity

5.1

Go to your local library (school, college or public library will do) and find out what serials they take (daily, weekly and monthly).

★   Do they keep back copies? If so, for how long?

★   Do they have any kind of index to help people find particular copies or articles?

★   Do they have any kind of computer indexing system? Does it include serials or just books?

Once you have collected this information write it up in a report.

Sunnyside Health Centre

This health centre has three GPs (general practitioners), a practice nurse and a receptionist. Patients who want to see a GP or the nurse must make an appointment via the receptionist.

Activity 5.2

Work in groups to find answers to these questions:

★ Whatever system the receptionist uses to book the appointments, what do you think the goals of the system should be?

★ What advantages might a computerised appointments system have over a manual one?

★ What disadvantages might a computerised system have?

The stages of systems analysis

The process of systems analysis can be broken down into four stages:

1 The **feasibility study** is an initial look at an existing system to see how it can be improved. The end result of this stage is a **feasibility report**.

2 **Investigation**: this is a fact-finding stage which involves defining the scope of the system, its boundaries and the user's requirements.

3 Use of **structured analysis tools**: this stage involves using a number of techniques (often utilising diagrams) to model the flow of information and the interrelationships in the system.

4 Finally, the systems analyst needs to draw together the information that has been gathered and analysed in the two previous stages into a document called the **system specification**.

Feasibility study

A feasibility study answers a very important question: can the need for a new system be justified? In other words: is it technically feasible and economically desirable? The feasibility study begins with a preliminary investigation which involves obtaining some general information:

✪ The system currently being used, its benefits and limitations

✪ The additional requirements of the new system

Then, from the information gathered during this preliminary investigation, a report is produced:

- ✪ A statement of the purpose of the system
- ✪ A definition of system scope
- ✪ A list of current deficiencies
- ✪ A statement of user requirements
- ✪ Cost-benefits or limitations of development
- ✪ Conclusions and recommendations

Each of these items is described in more detail below. The primary source of information for the feasibility study is the users of the current system, but an equally important source is the sponsors of the new system, i.e. the management or directors of the organisation who will pay for its development. While both groups will need to be satisfied with the eventual outcome (i.e. the new system), their requirements may be quite different.

A statement of the purpose of the system

This includes a brief description of what the current system does, and an indication of any new developments that are required in the new system.

A definition of system scope

This section establishes the boundaries of the systems analysis process and includes any constraints such as cost of development. It includes all areas of the system that should be developed and identifies any other systems that might be affected by this development or that provide information for this system.

It is important to remember that when a new system is being developed, it is almost certain to be affected by, and have an effect on, other systems that are used within an organisation. Often, when researching one system, faults can be identified with other systems. It is important to establish in this section exactly the limits or 'scope' of this task.

A list of current deficiencies

This section includes all the problems of the current system. However, it is also important to make a note of those parts of a system that are identified as working well, so they can be preserved in the new system.

A statement of user requirements

Clearly, this section needs to be developed in close consultation with the users and there are various ways their requirements can be defined. One way is to ask users to write down or list what they require from the new system. Another is for the systems analyst to interview users to identify what they think needs to be achieved by the new system.

It is important for the users to prioritise the list of requirements, as not all may be achievable due to constraints on time or money.

Using the information provided by the users, the systems analyst then identifies the outputs that are required from the system. That enables him/her to decide on the appropriate data inputs and data capture methods. Finally, once the inputs and outputs are identified, the general processing steps required are outlined.

Cost-benefits or limitations of development

Every software development project has a limit on the funds available to complete the project, and this budget is normally set by the sponsors of the project. During the feasibility stage, the systems analyst may or may not know what this financial limitation is. The feasibility study will need to estimate the cost of completing the project, including things like cost of hardware and software, manpower costs for developing new software, and training costs. The new development will probably also have cost-benefits. These might be tangible cost-benefits such as reduced costs of processing or manpower, increased sales, etc., or they may be intangible benefits like improved customer service. The systems analyst may have to identify what cost-benefits the project sponsors are expecting and to consider these carefully to see if they are achievable.

Conclusions and recommendations

This section of the report clearly lays out the best way forward for developing a new system. By comparing cost-benefits and limitations, the systems analyst makes recommendations that are achievable within an agreed time plan and budget. If the analyst believes a sensible solution *cannot* be achieved, then the reasons why are identified here.

Based on the conclusions and recommendations, the managers decide whether to go ahead with a fuller analysis. If the analyst has recommended that there may not be a workable solution, they need to decide whether:

- ✪ **to remove any constraints that may be causing the analyst to give this recommendation;**
- ✪ **to seek other alternative solutions; or**
- ✪ **to stay with the current system.**

Shoot-Em-Up Games

SEU Games have asked Wendy Jones, a systems analyst, to produce a feasibility report for the development of their royalty payment system. Wendy has spoken to the Managing Director of the company, and some of the staff in the accounts department who use the current royalty system. Using the information she obtained along with her experience of analysing and developing similar systems Wendy has produced her report. The summary of her report is shown in Figure 5.2.

Sunnyside Health Centre

The three GPs at Sunnyside Health Centre have a receptionist who makes patient appointments for them. The patients ring up when they need to see a GP and the receptionist uses a big diary book to find a suitable slot when the GP is free. A page from the book is shown in Figure 5.3.

Twice a day (morning and afternoon surgery) the receptionist needs to copy the list of each patient due from the book onto an individual list for each GP. The receptionist gives the list, along with the patients' notes to the GP at the beginning of the surgery. A copy of the attendance list is shown in Figure 5.4.

This manual system is time-consuming and inflexible, so the Sunnyside Health Centre would like to replace it with a computerised system.

Feasibility Study - Shoot-Em-Up Games Ltd.

System: Royalty payment system

Analyst: Wendy Jones

Date: 24/11/1999

Summary

Purpose of the system
- To record details of programmers to whom royalties are due
- To record, for each game, who royalties are due to and what percentage
- To calculate royalties due
- To produce royalty payment reports
- To produce management reports

System scope
- Needs to run on existing PC in accounts department
- Approximate budget of £4000 for purchase of software and development costs
- Data for the system provided by sales recording system
- System to provide data to the accounting system

Current deficiencies
- Current system requires manual input of data and the process of producing the royalty payments takes too long.
- Mistakes are not easily identified.
- Royalty payments reports sent to programmers do not provide sufficient detail.
- Details of payments made have to be manually entered in to the accounting system.

User requirements
- Faster processing
- Improved accuracy
- Improved detail on reports
- Automatic collection of sales data and output of accounting data

Cost-benefits/limitations
- The new system will reduce the need for overtime payments in the accounts department.

Conclusions and recommendations

A new payment system can be developed using the existing PC in the accounts department with the addition of a database package, which will allow the development of a customised application to meet the user's requirements. The development of the system should take approximately six weeks and be achieved within the budget.

Figure 5.2 *Shoot-Em-Up Games feasibility study*

Sunnyside Health Centre - Appointments Diary

Date: _____

Morning Surgery	Dr Williams	Dr Patel	Dr Jackson
9.00			
9.10			
9.20			
9.30			
9.40			
9.50			
10.00			
10.10			
10.20			
10.30			
10.40			
10.50			
11.00			
11.10			
11.20			
11.30			
11.40			
11.50			
12.00			

Afternoon	Dr Williams	Dr Patel	Dr Jackson
4.00			
4.10			
4.20			
4.30			
4.40			
4.50			
5.00			
5.10			
5.20			
5.30			
5.40			
5.50			
6.00			

Figure 5.3   *Sunnyside Health Centre appointments book*

Sunnyside Health Centre - Attendance list

Date: _____   Doctor: _____

Morning Surgery	Patient	Seen?
9.00		
9.10		
9.20		
9.30		
9.40		
9.50		
10.00		
10.10		
10.20		
10.30		
10.40		
10.50		
11.00		
11.10		
11.20		
11.30		
11.40		
11.50		
12.00		
Afternoon		
4.00		
4.10		
4.20		
4.30		
4.40		
4.50		
5.00		
5.10		
5.20		
5.30		
5.40		
5.50		
6.00		

Figure 5.4 *Sunnyside Health Centre patient attendance list*

You need to produce a feasibility study for the Sunnyside Health Centre system. You will need to do some research into how health centre appointment systems work. You can use your own experience of booking an appointment with the GP. You could also take a trip to your local health centre or GP and see what system they use. You should remember that people who work in health centres are busy people but you may find a receptionist who is willing to spend a couple of minutes with you explaining how the systems (manual or computerised) works. Alternatively, if you have a friend or a relative who works in a health centre they may be able to provide you with some information. You should work in groups to collect this information.

> Remember your feasibility study must cover:
>
> ★ A statement of the purpose of the system
> ★ A definition of system scope
> ★ A list of current deficiencies
> ★ A statement of user requirements
> ★ Cost-benefits or limitations of development
> ★ Conclusions and recommendations

Investigation

If the feasibility study is accepted, then more detailed research is carried out. The systems analyst investigates in detail how the current systems works, including how data is put into the system (input), how it flows around the system and is processed and what types of output are produced. The systems analyst also needs to identify the system boundaries and what its interfaces are with other systems.

The information to be gathered?

This case study shows the information required from SEU, under eight headings that can be applied to any investigation.

Shoot-Em-Up Games

Wendy Jones, the systems analyst, will carry out the investigation. She will need to collect the following information:

1. ***The people involved*** This includes the Managing Director (MD) of SEU, who will be paying for the system development (the sponsor of the system); Steve, who works in accounts and currently does all the royalty calculations on a spreadsheet (the user of the system); all the programmers who receive their royalty cheques (the customers).

2. ***Data capture methods*** How does data get into the system? Does Steve type it into his spreadsheet himself or does the spreadsheet download it from some other database?

3. ***Data types, sources and flows*** For example, where does the information about how many copies of each game is sold come from? How does Steve know what percentage to pay each programmer? Does all the data come from the same place or does it come from different sources?

4. ***Decisions taken and types of processing*** How does Steve's spreadsheet calculate how much to pay each programmer? How often are the payments made?

5. ***Storage methods*** How does Steve store the data he uses? Is it all kept on the spreadsheet? Does he keep historic data? Does he keep paper copies?

6. ***Documents used*** Does Steve use any input documents (e.g. lists of games sold)? What output documents does his spreadsheet produce? Does he produce management reports for the MD to look at?

continued

continued

7 *Types of output* What are the outputs of the system? How is the money paid to the programmers (e.g. by cheque or automatic payment via BACS)?

8 *Manual and automatic operations* What parts of the system are carried out manually? What parts are automatically carried out by Steve's spreadsheet?

Wendy, the analyst, needs to find answers to all these questions, and uses a number of different methods to gather this information.

Techniques for gathering information

A number of techniques can be used to gather the required information:

- Interview
- Questionnaire
- Observation
- Document analysis

One or more of these methods may be appropriate, and different methods are more suitable in different circumstances.

Table 5.1 summarises the advantages and disadvantages of the four main investigation methods.

Activity 5.4

★ Arrange an interview with your librarian (or ask if they can come and talk to your class – your teacher should be able to help you arrange this) to talk about how they manage the serials in your library.

★ Work out a series of questions to ask the librarian to collect the sort of information you would need to analyse a computerised serials management system.

★ Take notes at the interview and, if there are things you don't understand, ask further questions to clarify what is meant.

Method	What you need to decide	Advantages	Disadvantages
Interview	★ Who to interview ★ Where and when to conduct the interview ★ What questions to ask ★ How to record the answers	★ A rapport can be developed with the people who use the system. ★ You can adjust questions as the interview proceeds. ★ You can add additional questions to find more information.	★ Can be time-consuming and therefore costly. ★ Poor interviewing can lead to misleading or insufficient information. ★ In a large organisation, you cannot meet all the people involved in using the system.
Questionnaire	★ Who to ask to complete it ★ What questions to ask ★ How to collate and record the responses	★ Large number of people can be asked the same questions. Therefore comparisons are easy (e.g. 58% of respondents said they were dissatisfied with the current system). ★ Cheaper than interviews for large numbers of people. ★ Anonymity may provide more honest answers.	★ Must be designed carefully. Questions need to be simple and easy to answer, e.g. using tick boxes. ★ Questions cannot be ambiguous and require interpretation. ★ Cannot guarantee 100% return rate; may be much lower with some groups.
Observation	★ What and who you are going to observe ★ Where and when you are going to do the observation ★ How you are going to record the observation	★ The effect of office layout and conditions on the system can be assessed. ★ Work loads, methods of working, delays and bottlenecks can be identified.	★ Can be time-consuming and therefore costly. ★ Problems may not occur during the observation period. ★ Users may put on a performance when being observed.
Documentation analysis	★ Which documents to analyse ★ How to record your analysis	★ Good for obtaining factual information e.g. volume of sales, input and outputs of the system.	★ Cannot be used where input, output and information flow is not document based.

Table 5.1 *Investigation methods*

An analyst has to work closely with the users of the existing system and needs to consider, certainly with the first three techniques, from whom to collect the information. In some circumstances, users may not be keen to see the system change and they may even be hostile to the idea, perhaps due to fears about job losses. In these situations an analyst has to use tact and diplomacy to be able to collect the information successfully.

For each technique, it is important to identify exactly what information is required. Questionnaires and recording documents can then be designed to control the amount and the quality of information gathered.

Shoot-Em-Up Games

Wendy uses all four techniques to gather the required information for the SEU royalty system.

▶ INTERVIEW WITH THE MD

Wendy has a short interview with the MD to clarify what he hopes to achieve by developing this new system. He explains that calculating royalty is not Steve's only job. However it is taking so much of his time, he is complaining that another person should be taken on in the accounts department to do this job. The MD wants to avoid this extra cost by developing a new system. The MD also explains that he wants to improve the service he provides to the programmers. Good games programmers are very hard to find, so he needs to keep them happy by providing regular, up-to-date payments, and by providing more information about how the royalties are calculated (e.g. which games the programmer has written are selling best, and which platforms are most popular for a particular game – Playstation or Dreamcast for example).

▶ OBSERVATION

Steve is a busy man so Wendy decides that, rather than trying to collect all the information she needs from Steve by interview, she should watch Steve doing the royalty calculations using his spreadsheet. She takes notes and asks him some questions as he completes the job.

continued

continued

▶ DOCUMENT ANALYSIS

Following the observation of Steve doing the calculations, Wendy collects examples of all the documents Steve produces, individual royalty payment reports, management reports, etc. and a complete print out of the spreadsheet he uses, including a copy showing the formulae used.

▶ INTERVIEW WITH STEVE

Having reviewed her notes from the observation and analysed the documents Steve provided, Wendy has an interview with Steve to clarify a few outstanding points.

▶ QUESTIONNAIRE

Taking the point the MD made about keeping the programmers happy, Wendy designs a short questionnaire asking the programmers what information they would like to have on their royalty payment reports. She e-mails this to them but receives very few replies. Perhaps the programmers are too busy writing (or playing!) games?

Activity 5.5

★ Design a questionnaire that you think an analyst could use to establish what use is made of the serials in the library by students in your school or college library.

★ You need to try to find out what, if any, use they currently make of the serials. If they don't use them, why not?

★ You should also try to find out what improvement they think could be made to the way serials are provided (for example would they find a searchable computerised index helpful?).

Structured analysis tools

Once all the information described in the investigation phase has been collected the next step is to analyse it. The aim here is to take the unstructured information that has been collected and use a variety of tools to describe or model the system in a structured way:

- ✪ High–level data flow diagrams (DFDs)
- ✪ Process specifications
- ✪ Entity–relationship diagrams (ERDs)
- ✪ Low–level (detailed) data flow diagrams
- ✪ Entity–attribute definitions
- ✪ Data dictionary

Data flow diagrams (DFDs)

DFDs
are a diagrammatical way of representing the flow of information in a system.

It is normal to create a series of **DFDs** starting with the highest level, which gives a general overview of the information flow, and then progress to more detailed and complex diagrams (low-level DFDs).

To draw DFDs correctly you must follow certain rules about how the boxes, circles and arrows that make up the DFD are drawn.

High-level DFDs

Context diagram
A high-level DFD (sometimes called a **context diagram**) shows how the system interacts with the outside world.

To construct a high-level DFD first identify all the sources and recipients (input and outputs) of data that are *external* to the system. These are called the **external entities**. These external entities may be people or they may be other systems.

Having identified the external entities, you then list the data that flows to and/or from these external entities.

Shoot-Em-Up Games

For SEU Games, there are four external entities:

1   The sales system
2   The programmers
3   The accounting system
4   The managing director

The next step is to take a piece of A4 paper and draw each of the external entity names in an ellipse around the outside of the paper. In the centre of the page, a single process box is drawn, with the name of the system in it. The beginning of a high-level DFD for SEU Games is shown in Figure 5.5.

Notice the number 1 in the process box is its identifier. All process boxes are numbered so you can easily refer to them. Now arrows are added to indicate the data flows that have been identified. With input data flows, the arrow must point into the process box; output ones point to the external entity. Each arrow must be labelled with the data flow name.

The complete high-level DFD for SEU Games is shown in Figure 5.6.

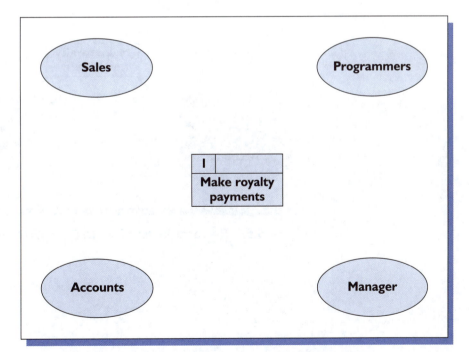

Figure 5.5   *The beginning of a high-level DFD for SEU Games*

Shoot-Em-Up Games

For SEU Games there are six data flows:

1   Sales – number of games sold (input)
2   Sales – details of new games (input)
3   Programmers – royalty payments (output)
4   Programmers – details (input)
5   Accounting – payment details (output)
6   Managing director – summary report (output)

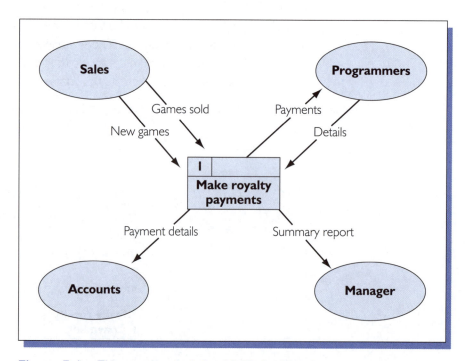

Figure 5.6 *The complete high-level DFD for SEU Games*

Activity 5.6

Create a high-level DFD for the Serials Management System. Use the following external entities:

★ Librarians

★ Library users

★ Serials suppliers (the companies that supply the newspapers and magazines)

And these dataflows:

To/from the librarians

★ Register new serial (i.e. the library wants to start taking a new serial) – input

★ Cancel serial – input

★ Register new issue (i.e. the librarian wants to register the arrival of a new issue of a serial) – input

★ Notify missing serial (i.e. the system notifies the librarian that a serial issue that should have arrived has not been registered) – output

To/from student

★ Input search list (i.e. the student inputs criteria for a search for serials with a particular article) – input

★ Receive search list (i.e. the system supplies a list of serials which match the student's search criteria) – output

To/from serials suppliers

★ Request subscription – input

★ Subscription payment – output

Activity 5.7

Working in groups, attempt to identify the external entities and dataflows for the Sunnyside Health Centre appointments system. Then draw the high-level DFD for the system.

Low-level DFDs

The high-level DFD then needs to be broken down (decomposed). To do this, a single process (e.g. make royalty payments) is divided into several, more detailed processes. The analyst refers to the information obtained in the investigation stage about the decisions made and processing carried out which should allow him/her to break down the single process into several steps.

As a rule of thumb, there should be a single process dealing with each data flow attached to an external entity.

Shoot-Em-Up Games

The single process of making royalty payments in the high-level DFD of SEU Games can be broken into six processes in the low-level DFD:

1   Calculate payments (take the data about the games sold and calculate how much to pay each programmer).

2   Make payments (take payments details and print cheques for each programmer).

3   Update accounts (take payments details data and transfer that information to the accounting system).

4   Create reports (take payments details and print a management summary report).

5   Record new game (take details of a new game from the sales system and record them).

6   Record programmer details (take programmer details and record them).

This is shown in Figure 5.7.

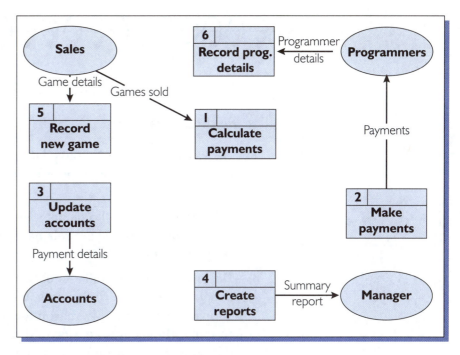

Figure 5.7 *The first step in creating a low-level DFD*

A new component is also introduced in the DFD along with the external entities, processes and data flows we have already used: the **data store**. It is important to remember when drawing DFDs that only a process can write or read data to or from a data store, and that each data store must be written to and read from at least once. A data store is drawn as an open-ended box, see Figure 5.8.

Like process boxes, data stores are numbered for identification purposes. The one shown in Figure 5.8 is number D1.

D1	**Customer details**

Figure 5.8 *A data store*

Shoot-Em-Up Games

There are three data stores:

1   D1 Payment details – holds data about how much to pay a particular programmer for the sales of a particular game.

2   D2 Game Details – holds data about all the games the company sells (e.g. their name and which programmer wrote them).

3   D3 Programmer Details – holds data about the programmers (e.g. their name and address). D3 is shown twice. The only reason for this duplication is to make the diagram easier to draw. Without it a data flow arrow would have to cut across several other data flows, making the diagram messy and difficult to follow. Duplicate data stores are shown by an additional bar inside the box containing the identifier.

The completed DFD is shown in Figure 5.9.

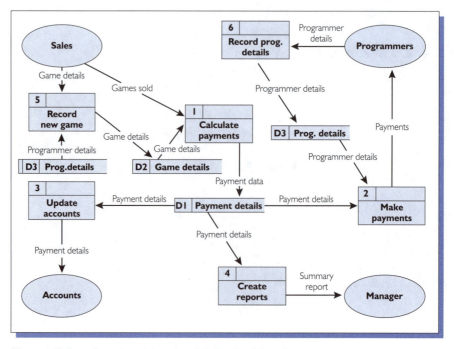

Figure 5.9 *Completed low-level DFD for SEU Games*

It is important to remember that, when creating a low-level DFD, the same external entities and data flows in and out of the external entities appear as in the high-level DFD. If you realise you have missed out an external entity and/or data flow you must go back and redraw your high-level DFD.

Activity 5.8

Working in groups, produce a low-level DFD for the serials management system.

> Don't be tempted to divide the process into too many processes or the diagram will become too complicated. Your low-level DFD needs to easily fit onto a single sheet of A4 paper.

Activity 5.9

Working on your own, attempt to draw a low-level DFD for the Sunnyside Health Centre appointments system. Then compare your attempt with other students and discuss the differences in an attempt to produce an agreed diagram.

> You may find it helpful to practice drawing DFDs in small groups so you can discuss different ways of drawing the diagrams.

Creating DFDs can be quite difficult and requires practice. It may take several attempts to get the DFD right and although there are rules about how to draw the DFD diagrams, there is not necessarily one right diagram for a particular system.

Although this course only looks at two levels of DFDs, an analyst may go on decomposing the processes in the DFD to show even more detail.

Entities, attributes and ERDs

When an analyst has used the DFDs to identify the processes and data stores in the system, the entity-relationship diagram (ERD) can be produced. These diagrams are used to model the relationships that exist between different entities in the system. A brief description of this technique is given here; more detail can be found in Chapter 6: *Database Design*.

Entities are usually real-world things (customers, products, computer games) that need to be represented in the system. Entities have **attributes** – elements that define a particular entity. Table 5.2 shows some simple examples.

Table 5.2 *Entities and possible attributes*

Entity	Possible attributes
Customer	Name
	Address
	Credit limit
Product	Description
	Type
	Price
Computer game	Name
	Platform (e.g. PC, Playstation, Dreamcast)
	Price

An **occurrence** (sometimes called a **record**) of the entity customer might be:

Name:	John Smith Office Supplies
Address:	10 Main Street, Watford
Credit Limit	£1500

▼▼▼▼▼▼▼▼▼▼

Primary key
is used to uniquely identify a particular occurrence of an entity.

▲▲▲▲▲▲▲▲▲▲

One (or more) of the attributes of a particular entity is normally defined as the **primary key** attribute. To guarantee uniqueness numbers are normally used for primary key attributes. So, for example, on a database recording details of the entity student, the attribute student number would be the primary key. The system would need to ensure that each student received a unique number.

Exercise 5.1

Why is the student surname *not* used as a primary key?

Most systems have a number of entities within them. Entities often have relationships between them. For example, the entity Customers and the entity Orders are related, because every order a company receives comes from a customer. The relationship between two entities can normally be described by a verb. In this example, the verb is *place*, because customers *place* orders (see Figure 5.10).

Note that in an ERD, the entity name is in capitals and contained in a round cornered box.

Figure 5.10   *The relationship 'Customers place order'*

How do we know which orders were placed by a particular customer? One of the attributes of the entity customer is the customer number. This unique number identifies each customer and so is the primary key of that entity. When that customer places an order, an occurrence of the orders entity is created. So that it is possible to tell which customer placed the order, the customer number is inserted into that occurrence of the orders entity. This is called a **foreign key** (because the key value belongs to another entity) – see Figure 5.11.

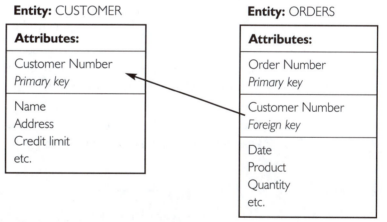

Figure 5.11   *Primary and foreign keys*

Each customer would have a least one and probably many more orders that they placed. So, for one customer, there would be many occurrences of the orders entity. This type of relationship is therefore called a **one-to-many relationship**. In an entity-relationship diagram, this is shown by a forked end to the line at the 'many' end that joins the two entities, as shown in Figure 5.12.

Figure 5.12   *A one-to-many relationship*

Activity 5.10

Two of the entities needed in the Serials Management System are Magazines and Issues. The Magazine entity stores information about each magazine, its name, its price etc. Issues stores information about individual copies of a magazine, its date, articles contained in it, etc.

How are these two entities related? Draw an ERD for them.

One-to-many relationships are the most common type of relationship between entities, but it is not the only type.

Imagine a company that has a system to store data about its employees. The entity employee would have attributes such as name, address, salary and the primary key would probably be employee number. The sales people who work for the company are provided with a company car. That gives us another entity, company car, which has attributes such as registration number, make, model, etc. There is a relationship between these two entities, which can be described by the verb, *uses*, a salesperson *uses* a company car. However, each salesperson is assigned only one company car at a time, so this isn't a one-to-many relationship, this is a **one-to-one** relationship. The ERD diagram for this type of relationship is shown in Figure 5.13.

Figure 5.13   *A one-to-one relationship*

This example also introduces another concept. A newly employed salesperson may not receive his/her company car until he/she has finished training, so the relationship between the two entities is **optional**, in other words, a salesperson does not have to have a related record in the company car entity. Likewise, when a salesperson leaves the company his/her car will remain unassigned to a salesperson until it is either sold or assigned to a new salesperson. Therefore the relationship is optional at both ends. However, with the previous example of customers and orders, an order must be related to a customer (otherwise who could have placed the order?). This relationship is **mandatory** at the 'many' end. Since a new customer could register their details with the company without placing an order, a customer does not have to have a related occurrence on the orders table (although most will) so it is optional at the 'one' end.

There is a third type of relationship between entities. This is called a **many-to-many** relationship.

Sunnyside Health Centre

In the Sunnyside Health Centre, as well as looking into an appointments system, they are also investigating a system to keep track of which drugs have been prescribed to patients. Two of the entities that would be defined are Patients and Drugs. For each patient, at various times, the GP may prescribe different drugs.

This appears to be a one-to-many relationship as one patient can take (or be prescribed) many drugs. However, if we look at it from the point of view of the drug entity, then one drug can also be prescribed to many different patients. It is therefore a many-to-many relationship. These sorts of relationships would cause a problem in the system. Remember that, with a one-to-many relationship, the way we identify which particular occurrence the 'many' side is linked to is by inserting the foreign key from the 'one' side of the relationship. However, if the entity could be linked to many different occurrences, which foreign key would we insert?

The problem with many-to-many relationships is that for a given occurrence in one entity it is not possible to tell to which occurrence in the related table it is related. For this reason, many-to-many relationships have to be re-thought to identify a link entity which contains the foreign keys from both the two original entities. Thus the two original entities both have one-to-many relationships with the link entity. In this example, we might call the link entity Prescription. This is shown in Figure 5.14.

In an ERD, this would be shown as in Figure 5.15.

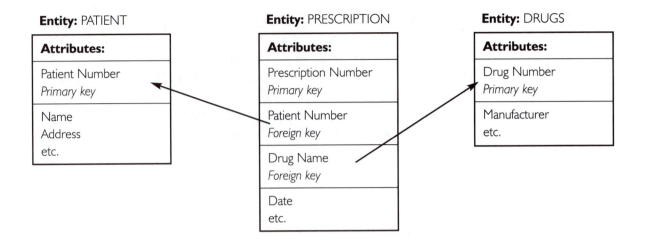

Figure 5.14 *Coping with a many-to-many relationship*

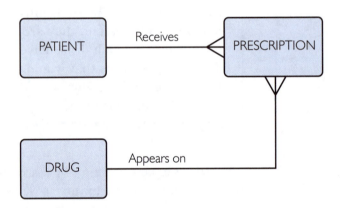

Figure 5.15 *Replacing a many-to-many relationship*

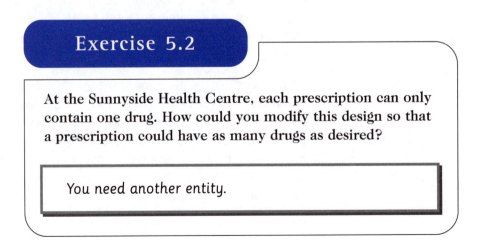

Exercise 5.2

At the Sunnyside Health Centre, each prescription can only contain one drug. How could you modify this design so that a prescription could have as many drugs as desired?

You need another entity.

Shoot-Em-Up Games

For SEU Games three entities can be defined:

- ★ Games
- ★ Programmers
- ★ Payments

A simple ERD with the relationship between these entities is shown in Figure 5.16.

Figure 5.16   *ERD for SEU Games*

The diagram shows two relationships:

1   A one-to-many relationship between Games and Programmers, i.e. each game is written by one programmer, but programmers can write many games.

2   A one-to-many relationship between Programmers and Payments, i.e. each programmer can receive many payments (over time) but each payment is made to one programmer only.

SEU Games has three entities: games, programmers and payments.

★ What attributes might these entities have?

★ What could be the primary key for these entities?

★ What foreign keys would you need to include in the entities?

Suppose some games were written by more than one programmer.

★ What kind of relationship would that create between games and programmers?

★ Can you work out what you need to do and redraw the ERD?

> You might find it helpful to complete this exercise in small groups.

Activity 5.11

Decide what entities there should be in the Sunnyside Health Centre.
Work out how they are related, and draw an ERD.

Data dictionary

▼▼▼▼▼▼▼▼▼▼

Data dictionary lists the entities in a system, the name and description of each attribute and the relationships between entities.

▲▲▲▲▲▲▲▲▲▲

Once DFDs and ERDs have been created, this information about the data in the system can be summarised using a data dictionary. Many **CASE** (**Computer Aided Software Engineering**) tools create data dictionaries for the analyst or programmer automatically. However, you can create simple data dictionaries yourself.

Shoot-Em-Up Games

Figure 5.17 shows the data dictionary for the payment details file of SEU Games.

Entity Name: Payment Details			
Relationships:			
Related to:	**Type**	**Which end?**	
Programmers	I to many	many	
Attributes:			
Name	**Key Type:**	**Format**	**Length**
Payment number	Primary	Numeric	6
Date	-	Date	
Programmer number	Foreign	Numeric	6
Total amount	-	Currency	5
Payment flag	-	Bolean	

Figure 5.17 *Data dictionary for SEU Games*

Exercise 5.4

Complete the data dictionary entries for all the entities of SEU Games.

Activity 5.12

Create a data dictionary for all the entities you identified for the Sunnyside Health Centre.

Process specifications

Having identified the processes needed within the system using the DFDs, it is time to create a process specification for each process. A variety of different methods can be used to create process specifications:

- Structured English
- Decision tables
- Flow charts

Typically, you would choose one of these techniques to describe a particular process, rather than using all three.

- **Flow charts** are good for providing a general outline of the processing involved, but often don't relate all that well to the actual code that is eventually written.

- **Structured English** on the other hand is much more detailed (sometimes too detailed for this stage) and is closely related to actual programming code.

- **Decision tables** are useful where there are a lot of different options to choose and you want to identify what happens in each circumstance.

Structured English

Structured English is a 'half way house' between actual program code and normal spoken English. It is used to describe the steps in a process without having to worry about the exact programming syntax. It is sometimes referred to as **pseudo-code**.

Start-Em-Up Games

Figure 5.18 shows the Make payments process for SEU Games. To help you understand this structured English example you should look at SEU Games' low-level DFD (Figure 5.9) and the data dictionary (Figure 5.17). The names in capitals come from these items.

Table 5.3 explains the steps in the example.

Figure 5.18 shows use of the construct REPEAT UNTIL …LOOP to cause the process to loop through each programmer on the Programmer Details file until the end of the file is reached (the construct DO WHILE provides an alternative but similar method e.g. Do While not end PROGRAMMER DETAILS).

Two other Structured English constructs are often used to control loops:

```
1    Open PAYMENT DETAILS file
2    Open PROGRAMMER DETAILS file
3    Repeat until end of PROGRAMMER DETAILS file
4            Read next PROGRAMMER DETAILS
5            Select PAYMENT-DETAILS where PROGRAMMER-NUMBER = PROGRAMMER
             DETAILS.PROGRAMMER-NUMBER and PAYMENT-FLAG = unpaid
6            Repeat until end of selected PAYMENT-DETAILS
7                    Cheque-total = Cheque-total + PAYMENT-AMOUNT
8                    Set PAYMENT-FLAG to paid
9                    Rewrite PAYMENT-DETAILS record
10           Loop
11           Print using cheque format PROGRAMMER-NAME, PAYMENT-TOTAL, DATE
12   Loop
13   Close PROGRAMMER DETAILS file
14   Close PAYMENT file
15   End
```

Figure 5.18   *Structured English example*

Table 5.3   *Explanation of pseudo-code in Figure 5.18*

Lines	Purpose
1,2	The two files (data stores) containing the payment details and the programmer details are opened.
3,4	Each programmer record needs to be read in turn, so the section between lines 3 and 12 is repeated until the end of the programmer file is reached.
5	For each programmer, the payments recorded on the payments file for that particular programmer (PROGRAMMER-NUMBER = PROGRAMMER DETAILS.PROGRAMMER-NUMBER) need to be selected. In addition, only those payments that have not already been made (PAYMENT-FLAG= unpaid) are to be selected.
6–10	This loops through each of the selected payments and totals up the payment amount, sets the payment flag to paid, and writes the details back to the payment-details data store.
11	This line prints out the cheque using a pre-defined cheque template.
13–14	Close the two files.

1   IF ... THEN ... ELSE is used where a choice needs to be made based on some condition. This construct takes the form:

   If (condition) Then (action)
   Else (alternative action)

2   SELECT CASE...END SELECT – used instead of multiple IF statements where there are many different choices to be made. See the example (see Figure 5.20 on page 230).

These looping constructs are used in conjunction with:

The relational operators		and	the logical operators
equals	=		AND
Less than	<		OR
Greater than	>		NOT
Less than or equal to	<=		
Greater than or equal to	>=		
Not equal to	<>		

You should have met these operators already in Chapter 3: *Spreadsheet Design*.

Exercise 5.5

Describe what the following Structured English does:

```
Enter monthly_sales
If monthly_sales > 200 then discount = 10%
If monthly_sales > 800 then discount = 25%
Else discount = 0
Endif
```

The **AND operator** is used in line 5 of the Figure 5.18 on page 227:

5   *Select PAYMENT-DETAILS where PROGRAMMER-NUMBER =
      PROGRAMMER DETAILS.PROGRAMMER-NUMBER and PAYMENT-
      FLAG = unpaid*

Here it is used to make sure that only those occurrences are selected from the payment details file which have the same programmer number as the current occurrence of the programmer file AND their payment flag was set to unpaid, i.e. *both* conditions have to be true. Using OR instead would have meant that occurrences were selected when *either* conditions were true.

Some examples of the use of the relational operators (=, > and <) are given in the SELECT CASE example in Figure 5.20 on page 230.

There are no exact rules on how to use Structured English, but you need to use your experience of real programming languages and keep in mind that the result should avoid any ambiguity. As with the other techniques in this section, you need practice to become proficient.

Activity 5.13

Choose one of the other processes defined in the DFD for SEU Games (Figure 5.9 on page 216) and create a process specification for it using Structured English.

> Vague statements like '**Process PAYMENTS DETAILS file**' should be avoided; instead, you should try to identify exactly what processing is required.

Decision tables

Decision tables are useful where the processing step includes a range of true or false conditions. Depending on the combination of conditions, different actions need to be taken.

A decision table is made up of two parts:

- ✪ The **conditions** are listed at the top of the table (you must list all possible combinations).
- ✪ The **actions** (i.e. what to do in each condition) are listed in the lower part of the table.

Shoot-Em-Up Games

At SEU Games, rules as to how the royalties are calculated are based on the number of sales (sales above 1000 per month earn a higher percentage royalty) and whether there is both a Playstation and Dreamcast version of the game (games that are available for both machines also earn a higher percentage royalty). Figure 5.19 shows the decision table for all possible combinations.

Some applications can be developed directly from decision tables using a program generator that allows entry of information in the form of decision tables.

Conditions				
Both Playstation and Dreamcast versions are available	**Y**	**Y**	**N**	**N**
Sales over 1,000 per month	**Y**	**N**	**Y**	**N**
Action				
5% Royalty				✓
7% Royalty			✓	
9% Royalty		✓		
10% Royalty	✓			

Figure 5.19 *Decision table*

Another option for analysing this kind of processing is using Structured English as previously described. The Structured English for describing the same royalty calculation is shown in Figure 5.20.

```
Select Case Royalty-calculation
        Case (both-versions = no) and (sales-total < 1000)
            Payment-total = sales-total * 5%
        Case (both-versions = no) and (sales-total < 1000)
            Payment-total = sales-total * 7%
        Case (both-versions = yes) and (sales-total < 1000)
            Payment-total = sales-total * 9%
        Case (both-versions = yes) and (sales-total > 1000)
            Payment-total = sales-total * 10%
End-select
```

Figure 5.20 *An example of the CASE statement*

You can probably see that decision tables facilitate the identification of actions to take in all the different combinations of conditions. It is certainly easier to write the Structured English once you have the decision table to guide you, and you are less likely to omit possible combinations.

Sunnyside Health Centre

The health centre has decided to set up a number of specialist clinics for particular groups of patients:

★ Well Woman's Clinic – for women aged between 19 and 100

★ Over-60s Clinic – men and women over 60

★ Men's Health Clinic – for men aged between 19 and 100

 Activity 5.14

Draw up a decision table which will show whether a particular patient is eligible for each clinic.

Flow chart

Flow charts are another method of representing the processes of a system in a pictorial form using different shaped boxes to represent different types of actions (Figure 5.21).

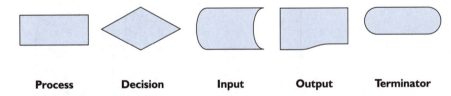

| Process | Decision | Input | Output | Terminator |

Figure 5.21   *Basic flow chart symbols*

Flow charts can be used to model all kind of systems, not just computer systems. They model human thought processes quite well and can help you to break down a process into smaller steps. They are also relatively easily understood by people who are not programmers or IT professionals. However, flow charts don't translate well into program code and can became so complex they are hard to follow. For these reasons, flow charts are best used to give a generalised overview of the functions of a process, with decision tables or structured English used to describe the detail.

Shoot-Em-Up Games

A flow chart for the Calculate Payments process is shown in Figure 5.22.

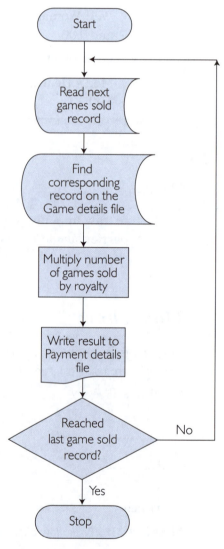

Figure 5.22 *Flow chart for SEU games*

Note that this simplified version of the flow chart omits the detail about how different royalty percentages are used to calculate the payment (as described in the section on decision tables). If that detail were included, additional decision boxes would be required and the diagram would become much larger and more complex.

Activity 5.15

A pharmacist prepares drugs from a GP's prescription. The rules on whether or not the patient has to pay for the prescription are as follows:

★ People under the age of 17 and over the age of 60 do not have to pay.
★ Women who are pregnant do not pay.
★ Everyone else must pay.

Draw a flow chart describing the processing required to decide if the patient has to pay.

System specification

The final step of the analysis phase is for the analyst to produce a system specification. This document draws together the information and analysis done and adds details about the inputs and outputs of the system:

✪ A high-level data flow diagram
✪ A low-level data flow diagram
✪ Entity-relationship diagrams
✪ Data dictionary
✪ Process specifications
✪ Input specifications
✪ Output specifications
✪ Details of resource implications

The diagrams, data dictionary and process specifications are described in earlier sections of this chapter. Here, the specifications are considered.

Input specification

An input specification includes descriptions of the following:

✪ Data sources
✪ Methods of data capture

- Data input forms and/or screen layouts
- Verification methods applied during input
- Validation methods applied after the data is entered

The data sources will identify where each piece of information is coming from.

Shoot-Em-Up Games

The information about how many games have been sold comes from another computer system within the organisation – the sales system.

Serials Management System

The source of data about which newspapers have arrived each day comes from the librarians themselves who make a manual check.

The method of data capture describes how the data enters the system. Clearly, understanding where it comes from is important in deciding how it can be captured.

Shoot-Em-Up Games

The sales data in this system will need to be captured by a network link and will require some programming effort on both the sales system, to provide and transfer the file, and the royalties system to accept and, if necessary, convert it.

Serials Management System

The likely data capture method here would be manual data entry by the librarian, in which case a suitable data entry screen will have to be developed for the system.

There are many data capture methods (see page 57 in Chapter 4), such as bar-codes, magnetic strips, etc. It is important that the best method is chosen to suit the system requirements so take these factors into account:

- ✪ Accuracy of input
- ✪ Reliability
- ✪ Cost
- ✪ Ease of use

The specification of input forms and screen layouts only requires written information about what detail should be included in such documents or screens. The actual drawing of these forms or screens will be carried out during the design stage of the system development. However, the analyst may provide some guidance on how such forms and screens may look by including one or two examples:

- ✪ **The title of each screen to be used for entering data into the system**
- ✪ **A brief description of purpose**
- ✪ **A list of data items that will be collected using the screen or form**
- ✪ **Any data items that are printed/displayed on the screen/report before or during use with details of where these data items are obtained from**
- ✪ **Instructions to help the user**
- ✪ **Error messages**

Ensuring the accuracy of data entered is very important. The analyst must include in the specification methods of checking that data has been entered correctly and that the data is reasonable. It is easy for an operator to misread information from a source document or to mis-key the data, and steps must be taken to avoid these errors entering the system.

Verification is the method of checking that the data entered on to the system is the same as that on the original source. Methods used to check this include requesting the operator to enter important data twice and then checking to see if both entries are the same. This method is usually needed for high volumes of numeric data that are very difficult to 'read'. Another method is to re-display entered information and ask the operator to check it and confirm that it is correct.

Validation is the process of checking that data entered into a system is reasonable and in the correct form. A common example is dates, a date such as 34/4/2001 is clearly incorrect and a system should always check that dates are reasonable.

Data items like account numbers or employee numbers are not so obvious when incorrect, although it may be possible to check them against a database of valid numbers. In these cases, there are a number of other types of validation checks that can be made:

A **check digit** is a digit at the end of the number which is calculated from the other digits in the number. When the complete number is entered into the system, the check digit is calculated again and compared with the check digit that was entered. If they are the same, the number is probably valid, if not, the number has been entered incorrectly.

All books come with an identification code known as the International Standard Book Number (ISBN). This number consists of a 10 digit code, i.e. 0340394536. The final digit (6) is the check digit.

To calculate the check digit, multiply each digit by its position number counting downwards (start at 10 × 0 and finish with 2 × 3) and then add these numbers together and divide by 11. This sample calculation uses the ISBN number 0340394536 (6 is the check digit).

0	3	4	0	3	9	4	5	3	**Total**
0 × 10	3 × 9	4 × 8	0 × 7	3 × 6	9 × 5	4 × 4	5 × 3	3 × 2	
0	27	32	0	18	45	16	15	6	= **159**

159 divided by 11 gives 14 remainder 5, then subtracting this remainder from 11 gives the check digit of 6.

Check digits are powerful validation tools because they can detect common errors in entering numbers (such as transposition) as well as pressing incorrect keys.

Suppose an operator entered the same ISBN into a system but transposed the first two digits so it was entered as 3040394536. The system would calculate the check digit as 3, which is different from the check digit entered (6), so an error would be identified.

A **type check** checks that only acceptable characters are used for an attribute.

A National Insurance number comes in the form WA742099A and the system needs to check for two alpha characters followed by six numerical digits followed by a single alpha character.

In some database applications, an **input mask** can be set to allow only acceptable patterns of digits and numbers to be entered.

A **length check** is used to check that the correct number of characters are entered. A **range check** is used when an attribute has boundary limits set.

A college course only accepts people who are over 17 and under 21 on 1 September 2000, so each student's date of birth must be after 2/9/1979 and before 1/9/1983.

> ## Activity 5.16
>
> Using your low-level DFD (see Activity 5.9 on page 217), take all the inputs to the Sunnyside Health Centre system and create an input specification.
>
> ★ Where will the data come from?
> ★ How will it enter the system?
> ★ What input screens may be needed?
>
> > You could use the form creation facilities in a program such as Microsoft Access to create an example input screen.
>
> ★ What attributes may need verification or validation?
>
> > Use the data dictionary you created to identify the attributes that will be input.

Output specification

An output specification is a description of all the information that is produced by the system:

- ✪ The data required for output
- ✪ Screen display layouts
- ✪ Printed report layouts

For each screen or printed report, it is necessary to provide the following information:

- ✪ **Type** – screen display, printing or screen display with an option to print displayed data
- ✪ **Purpose** – who is it for? What is it to be used for?
- ✪ **Data required** – the attributes to be shown, any calculated data items to be displayed. Are processes such as sorting or grouping of data needed? If so, which attributes should be used for these processes?

Shoot-Em-Up Games

An example output specification for a management report in the SEU Games royalty system is shown in Figure 5.23.

Reaching conclusions

This section is produced by the analyst to help a manager or company director to decide whether to proceed with producing the system. The analyst will provide information regarding hardware, software and personnel. For each of these, the analyst needs to consider the following factors:

- ✪ Alternative solutions available
- ✪ Any constraints affecting choices available
- ✪ Any risks in carrying out the changes to the existing system
- ✪ Benefits of developing a new system

Using these factors, the analyst will produce a **cost–benefit analysis** which shows the pros and cons of each alternative solution. Cost–benefit analysis is not just looking at the financial aspects of developing the new system; it is also a question of balancing gains and losses of each alternative solution against the present system.

SEU Games - Output Specification		
Report R-1		
Name:	Monthly payment summary report	
Type:	Printed report	
Purpose:	Management report which lists each month's royalty payment and shows totals	
Data required:	**Source**	**Sort/Group**
Platform (eg Playstation, Dreamcast etc.)	Games detail file	The report is grouped by platform
Game name	Games detail file	Sorted alphabetically
Monthly sales	Payments file	
Programmer	Games detail file	
Royalty amount	Payments file	
Total sales	Calculated field showing total sales per platform	
Total payments	Calculated field showing total royalty payments per platform	

Figure 5.23   *Example output specification for a management report*

The cost–benefit analysis could include information that looks at the cost of each alternative compared with the gains made in the speed of processing, capacity for expansion of the amount of information handled, etc.

Once the cost–benefit analysis is completed, the analyst makes recommendations based on all the information, even if the recommendation is not to proceed further, or to proceed only if a constraint such as cost can be renegotiated.

Revision questions

1. Explain why the software development cycle is called a cycle.

2. List the topics that should be covered in a feasibility study.

3. Why is it important to define the scope of the system in the feasibility study?

4. List four techniques that a systems analyst can use to investigate a system.

5. For two of the techniques listed above, explain the advantages and disadvantages.

6. List four structured analysis tools.

7. Name the three components of a high-level DFD.

8. In a supermarket stock control system, what might the external entities be?

9. In a low-level DFD, data stores can only be read from and written to by what?

10. In a hospital database system, each ward has several beds. What kind of relationship would exist between the entities WARDS and BEDS? Draw the ERD describing the relationship.

11. Explain the meaning of the term foreign key.

12. Explain what many-to-many relationships are and why they have to be removed.

13. What information is contained in a data dictionary?

14. What is a decision table and what is it used for?

15. Describe the purpose of an input specification.

Database Design

6

- Explore the use of record-structured databases used in organisations
- Explore how information is structured for database storage and processing
- Understand and use logical data modelling
- Learn and apply the principles of relational database design
- Design, implement and test a relational database to meet a given specification
- Produce user documentation

The assessment of this unit will be by means of an assignment, which will require you to produce a relational database application including design notes, technical documentation and user instructions.

This chapter looks in detail at seven topics:

- ✪ Database concepts
- ✪ Logical data modelling
- ✪ Normalisation
- ✪ Relational database structures
- ✪ Relational database construction
- ✪ Testing
- ✪ Documentation

These topics are explained through a series of case studies of database systems used in these organisations:

- ✪ A hospital trust
- ✪ A leisure centre
- ✪ A library
- ✪ A college
- ✪ A video store
- ✪ A driving school

Database concepts

Data and information

Data consists of the numbers and other symbols that are used to record and communicate **information.** If data is to provide useful information it must be structured and organised, and computers are ideal tools to help to do this.

A single hard disk on a PC can now hold several **gigabytes** of data. Modern processors enable vast quantities of data to be processed at enormous speed.

Computer systems have traditionally organised data into **records** that give structure to the data, and **files** that are related sets of records. This is very similar to manual systems for storing paper records in file folders in filing cabinets.

Examples of information requirements can be seen in the case studies used in this chapter.

- ✪ The hospital trust administrator needs to be aware of patient numbers and availability of beds.
- ✪ The leisure centre manager needs to know how well the facilities are being used.
- ✪ The librarian needs to know when books are overdue.
- ✪ The college staff need to keep track of students' progress on Vocational A-Level programmes.
- ✪ The video store owner needs to know which videos are the most popular.
- ✪ The driving school manager needs to know how much to pay the instructors.

Choose one of the above case studies, or another of your own, and make a list of the information needs of the organisation.

In addition to understanding how well their organisation is performing, managers need operational information for setting performance targets, decision making, modelling and forecasting. This information is generated from **transactions** that are the normal, daily events of an organisation.

Transactions

A transaction is generally an event in which some goods are sold or a service is provided, usually in exchange, directly or indirectly, for some form of payment.

In the private sector, goods and services are usually sold directly to customers for money. In the case of public sector organisations, such as hospital trusts, the police and local authorities, the provision of a service is paid for from public funds.

In all cases, the managers of these organisations need to be aware of the frequency and nature of these daily transactions so that, over a period of time, they are able to judge whether their organisation is operating efficiently, either providing the best service, or for private companies, operating profitably.

Table 6.1 lists examples of transactions in the case studies.

Table 6.1 *Transaction examples*

Case study	Transaction example
Hospital trust	Registration and discharge of patients
Leisure centre	Booking of facilities
Library	Issue and return of books
College	Recording of students' completion of Vocational A-level units
Video store	Customers' payments
Driving school	Recording of instructors' working hours

For each of the six case studies, give three further examples of transactions that might be required.

Competition and the requirement for greater public accountability has created a need for organisations to be able to process vast amounts of transaction data precisely, reliably, and at very high speed. A well-structured computer system is able to do just that. It can log transactions, perform calculations and automate the process of producing analytical reports quickly and reliably.

Hospital Trust System

In a hospital trust, data is held and maintained by different departments as shown in Figure 6.1.

★ The Medical Records department maintains the information on patients.

★ The Personnel department maintains staff records.

★ The Finance department handles salaries and wages.

★ Each ward organises the monthly staffing schedules.

The files held in each of these areas contain the data shown in Table 6.2 (page 246).

In maintaining staff records, the Personnel department creates a new file entry for each new member of staff, and needs to keep the details of existing staff up to date, e.g. noting a change of address or a change of grade. Personnel and Finance hold their own staff files independently of each other, so there is a risk that the data in the two files may not be consistent. If the data becomes inconsistent, then the efficiency of the overall system is affected, which results in an inaccurate and unreliable operation.

Administrative staff frequently need to check and double check any reports produced, and decisions made by senior management may be made on the basis of information that

continued

continued

is inaccurate or out of date, and may be seen eventually by some managers as too unreliable to use.

Even if the data is consistent, there is a great deal of unnecessary, or redundant, data being stored, resulting in excessive use of disk space and unnecessary processing.

Sharing of data between departments is difficult because each department uses specially written programs to access its own data.

The hospital trust wants to develop new applications but finds that any change to the current data files, such as adding a new field or changing the length of an existing field requires modification to existing programs which use the data.

To overcome such difficulties, the hospital trust has decided to implement a database.

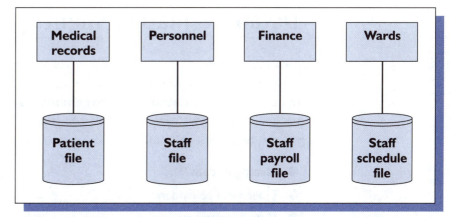

Figure 6.1   *Hospital trust administration system*

Exercise 6.2

The personnel department of the hospital trust is informed that a nurse has been promoted to a higher grade, but the finance department receives the change of grade note too late for the next pay run. What is the result for

★ the nurse?
★ the finance clerks?
★ the finance director?

Table 6.2 *Hospital trust files*

Medical records	Personnel	Finance	Wards
Patients:	*Staff:*	*Staff payroll:*	*Staff schedule:*
Admission number	Employee number	Employee number	Employee number
Surname	Surname	Surname	Surname
First name	First name	First name	First name
Address	Address	NI number	Date
Date of birth	Date of birth	Tax code	Start time
GP	Grade	Salary per annum	End time
Next of kin	Date commenced	Contracted out?	
Admission date	Department	Gross pay year to date	
Ward	Weekly overtime hours	NI deducted year to date	
		Tax deducted year to date	
Consultant number		Address	
		Bank details	

Database management systems

A database comprises the entire collection of data that is required by all departments of an organisation. Selective access to the database is controlled by software called a **database management system (DBMS)**. A DBMS has a number of advantages over the traditional, or 'flat' file system described in the hospital trust case study.

- ✪ Sharing of data
- ✪ Control of redundancy
- ✪ Data consistency
- ✪ Data independence
- ✪ Preserving integrity
- ✪ Privacy of data
- ✪ Evolutionary development
- ✪ Timely, accurate reporting
- ✪ Online enquiries

There are three basic types of DBMS: **hierarchical**, **network** and **relational**. They differ in the way that the links between different items of data are represented. Nowadays, the **relational database management system (RDBMS)**, in which the data is represented as tables, is by far the most popular, particularly on microcomputer systems. The RDBMS is the software package that controls the access to the database. User applications

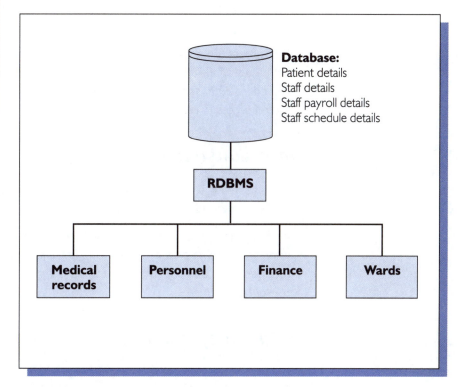

can only gain access to the database through the RDBMS. This is shown diagrammatically for the hospital trust case study in Figure 6.2.

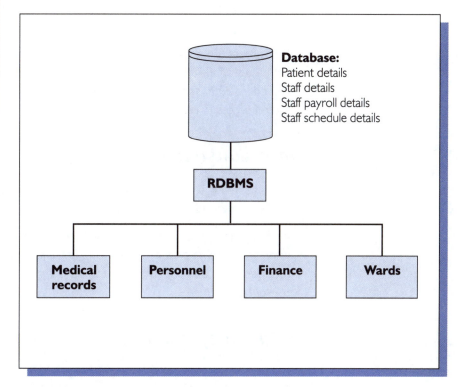

Figure 6.2 *Hospital trust RDBMS*

Sharing of data

Whereas a file of data on a single stand-alone computer can only be accessed by one user at a time, a database implemented on a network enables different users to share the data it contains, at the same time if necessary. If data is to be shared in this way, it is very important that the RDBMS implements **file** or **record locking** to prevent the possibility of two users attempting to update the same record at the same time.

In the hospital trust's staff scheduling system, the managers of wards A and B might access the staff schedules simultaneously to check the availability of a nurse. If the nurse were found to be available, both managers could update the nurse's record. The first update written to the database would allocate the nurse to ward A, but this would then be overwritten by the second update which would allocate the nurse to ward B. To avoid this, the system must lock the file or record, after it is accessed by the first manager, to ensure that it cannot be accessed by another manager until the update is completed. The manager of ward B would then find that the nurse had already been allocated to ward A.

Control of redundancy

In an unstructured system, the same data item is likely to appear in more than one file. This would make the overall system inefficient and could lead to inaccurate data being processed.

In the hospital trust system, the address of a staff member might appear in both the staff file and the staff payroll file. This is an example of duplicate or redundant data, since it is more efficient to hold this data once only and for shared access to be allowed.

Data consistency

Data contained in any system must be the same at all times, and any updates must be immediately implemented in all files.

Inconsistency of data is a problem with departmental filing methods, whereas, in the hospital trust database, any change of address need only be recorded once, and then the new address is immediately available to all relevant departments.

Data independence

In non-database systems the data and the programs that access the data must match exactly.

If a field is added to patient records to store the patients' blood group, then all programs accessing patient records would need to be altered, whether or not they make use of the blood group field.

This problem is overcome in a database management system where each program's **logical view** of the data is independent of the way the data is physically held. Each program may only need a subset of the data fields and may logically 'view' the fields in different orders. Information required by new programs can be added to the database and existing applications can continue to function without the need for reprogramming.

Preserving integrity

Without an integrated database, the Finance department of the hospital trust might continue to make salary payments to a member of staff who had left sometime earlier, even though the staff member's record had been deleted from the Personnel file. In an integrated database system, both the Finance and Personnel departments would be accessing the same physical data (although their logical 'views' of it would be different) so this problem could not occur.

Privacy of data (security)

The controlling software, the RDBMS, permits only selective access to the data on a database by users in a department. This is generally done by users being issued with identity numbers (IDs) and passwords, which are then recognised by the RDBMS. This helps to avoid the problem of unauthorised access to sensitive data. In a non-database system, control is not centralised, and so it is much harder to restrict access to sensitive data.

Evolutionary development

With central control, an IT specialist can be made responsible for the efficient functioning of the database. A **database administrator (DBA)** analyses the current and future data requirements of each department, and progressively amends the structure of the database so it evolves to meet those requirements.

Timely, accurate reporting

All transactions recorded on a database system update every user's view of the database instantly. As a result, routine reports needed by a hospital trust, such as daily bed occupancy rates, weekly statistics, and monthly staffing levels, are available to managers and supervisors with reliability and accuracy. More information is therefore produced which helps the efficient operation of an organisation and enables well-informed strategic decisions to be made.

Online enquiries

All users of a database can use a query language that is easy to learn rather than each department requiring their own IT experts to extract specific information.

The use of **Structured Query Languages (SQL)** *enables a nurse to find out which consultant a particular patient is under, or a personnel officer to look up which staff may be eligible for early retirement.*

Exercise 6.3

Discuss the risks involved in holding all of an organisation's data in one place. What could be done to minimise these risks?

Data types

Data recorded on a computer system is stored on a magnetic disk as a stream of bits. Software that is accessing this data must know what it represents, i.e. whether the bits represent numbers, characters, or perhaps a graphical image. When setting up a database therefore, the designer must indicate what type of data is being represented by a particular field.

ASCII

American Standard Code for Information Interchange.

GIF

Graphics Interchange Format

✪ Numeric data is stored as a number of bytes depending on the size of the largest number to be stored, e.g. 1 byte (8 bits) can store numbers between −128 and +127, 2 bytes can store numbers between −32768 and +32767.

✪ Characters are stored using a standard code, nowadays usually **ASCII**.

✪ Graphical images may be stored as bitmap files (BMP) or in a compressed format such as **GIF**.

Video Store

In the video store database, a video title is defined as a text field, whereas the number of rentals in a week numeric. Dates are stored as the number of days since 1 January 1980 to enable days overdue to be calculated by subtraction.

In practice, the range of different data types available depends on the software used. Microsoft Access supports a number of data types, see Table 6.3.

How data is stored affects how it can be processed and one result of having a wide range of data types available is that the software can perform more efficiently, e.g. by defining dates and monetary values with their own data types instead of being simply text and numbers. Also, a wider range of calculations can be performed. In addition, by defining **masks** or special field types, **validation** routines can be incorporated so there is less risk of incorrect data being entered when updating the database. If a date is stored as a text data type, a careless entry such as '23/16/97' may be accepted by the software as a valid entry, whereas if it had been defined as a date data type, all data entry for this field would have automatically been validated. The software would have compared the '16' in the month position with the range for an acceptable month number, i.e. 1 to 12, and reported it to the user as being invalid, i.e. out of range.

Table 6.3 *Data types in Microsoft Access*

Data type	Stores	Video store examples
Text	Alphanumeric characters	Video Title, Certificate, Supplier, Surname, Forename, Title, Address, Telephone
Memo	Alphanumeric characters (usually several sentences or paragraphs)	None, but often used for comments
Number	Numeric values (integers or fractional values)	Rentals, Week Number
Date/Time	Dates and times	Issue Date, Return Date
Currency	Monetary values	Daily Rate
Counter	A numeric value that is automatically incremented for each new record added to a table	Video ID, Member ID
Yes/No	Boolean values	Overdue?
OLE object	OLE objects, graphics or other binary data	None, but could be used to display a photo of a member on screen

Forms and reports may also contain calculated fields. A calculated field is not really a data type since a calculation is an event, not a data item.

A calculation of interest to the video store owner is the revenue earned by each video title in a given week. The data for this calculation is stored in the rentals and daily rate fields. By multiplying these values together, the owner can discover the earnings for each title, which appears as a calculated field in a form or a report.

Field properties

A field property determines how the data it contains is stored, handled and displayed. A data type is regarded as a property of a field, and a field can have a number of properties depending on its data type.

The lengths of text fields and numeric fields can be specified by the database developer.

The video store owner may find that no member has a surname longer than 20 characters. The developer can then set the member's surname field length to be 25, allowing a margin of safety.

The daily rate of a video rental is usually between £1 and £3, so the daily rate field length is set at three digits, giving a maximum of £9.99. If it is defined as a currency data type, the number of decimal places is fixed at two.

The format property specifies the display and printing of numbers, dates, times and text.

The format of the 'Issue date' field in the video store database can be set to appear as, say, 1/4/99 or 01-Apr-99.

The format of a numeric field can be set to display a preset number of digits. A week number can only be in the range 1 to 52, and so can be set as an integer up to two digits long.

Particular text fields can be assigned a format property if they have a standard appearance, e.g. a postcode.

As with defining data types, defining the properties of a field is done when the database is created, and the range of properties available depends on the RDBMS being used.

Activity 6.2

Find out what data type formats are available on your RDBMS.

Validation checks

▼▼▼▼▼▼▼▼▼

Validation
checks that data is reasonable, not necessarily correct.

Verification
involves comparing data to look for discrepancies

▲▲▲▲▲▲▲▲▲

Validation checks are built into the database as a part of the field properties and are defined by the database developer. A data value entered by a user is checked by the software to see if it conforms to these validation rules. If it does, the data is recorded in the appropriate table. If it does not, the user is prompted for the correct data value. A number of basic validation checks may be carried out, as shown in Table 6.4.

It is important to realise that validation will not guarantee that the data is correct, only that it is reasonable. Transcription errors often occur as data is entered and these can sometimes only be eliminated by re-entering the data and checking against the original. This process is called **verification.** Even this is no guarantee that the data is totally correct as there may have been errors in the original source documents from which the data was entered.

Table 6.4 *Validation checks*

Type of check	Description	Video shop example
Presence check	The user's data entry is checked for null values, i.e. whether the user has attempted to leave a field blank.	In adding a new video title, the user may not remember its certificate. An attempt to leave this field blank results in a prompt for the data to be entered, since every video title **must** have a certificate.
Length check	Fields with a predefined format property may have a fixed length.	A video title may be restricted to 30 characters. An attempt to key in more than 30 characters is prevented and the user must input an abbreviated title.
Format check	The user is prevented from making a data entry which does not correspond to the predefined format for that field.	The member ID could consist of the member's initials followed by an index number, e.g. Emma Stoddard might be given the ID number ES01, and Eric Smith ES02, etc. The format for this field is AA99. A format check detects an attempted incorrect input such as ESS1, or E551, and the software should prompt for a correct input.
Range check	Numeric values are checked to ensure they are between defined upper and lower limits.	Week number values can only be between 1 and 52. If this were predefined, the software would not accept entries such as 53 or 0.

Activity
6.3

Find out what validation checks are built into your RDBMS.

Logical data modelling

Logical data modelling is a top-down design method often used in developing a database application. This approach has three stages:

1   Identify the **entities** that make up the system.

2   Analyse the data to associate the data used by an organisation, with particular entities.

3   Identify the **relationships** between entities.

The systems analyst develops an **entity-relationship model (ERM)** which is shown graphically as an **entity-relationship diagram (ERD)**.

Information about an entity may exist in a database independently of any other entities, although entities may be related to one another. The types of entities held in a database depend on the organisation and its applications.

Leisure Centre

The database used by a leisure centre stores information concerning these entities:

★   Activity area, e.g. pool, gym

★   Activity, e.g. swimming lesson, aerobics session

★   Members

★   Instructors

Entities are represented graphically by the name of the entity in capitals in a box with round corners known as a **soft box** as shown in Figure 6.3.

Exercise 6.4

Think of a database being used by your school or college. What four entities could it contain?

Figure 6.3 *Representation of entities*

Library database

In the library database, three entities can be immediately identified:

★ Book

★ Borrower

★ Publisher

Borrowers can borrow whichever book or books they want, and a book can be borrowed by any borrower. The library may have a number of copies of a particular book but each book only has one publisher. Another way of saying this is:

A. '*one* book can be borrowed by *many* borrowers'

B. '*one* borrower can borrow *many* books'

C. '*one* book is published by only *one* publisher'

D. '*one* publisher publishes *many* books'

These four relationships link the entities 'book', 'borrower' and 'publisher', and are shown diagrammatically in Figure 6.4

A relationship is a link between two different entities, which describes the correspondence between them.

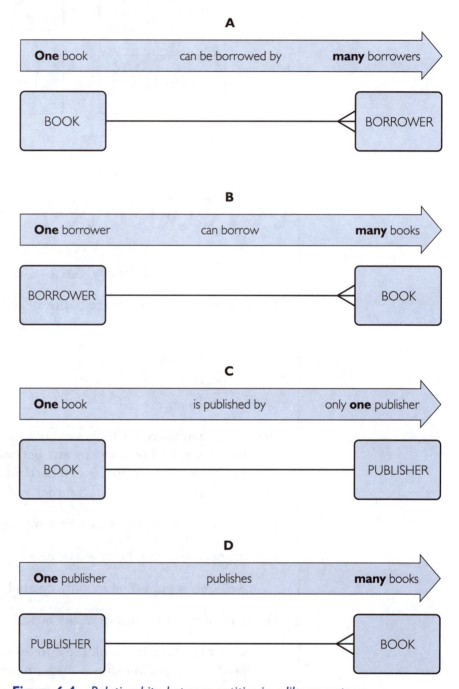

Figure 6.4 *Relationships between entities in a library system*

Figure 6.4 illustrates the two basic types of relationships between entities:

✪ one-to-one

✪ one-to-many (or many-to-one)

There are two ways of representing the one-to-many relationship as shown in Figure 6.5.

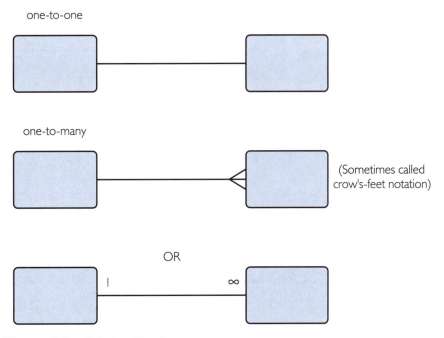

one-to-one

one-to-many

(Sometimes called crow's-feet notation)

OR

Figure 6.5 *Relationship diagrams*

Entity-relationship diagram (ERD)

The four diagrams A, B, C and D in Figure 6.4 can be condensed into the single ERD shown in Figure 6.6. Note that there are two relationships between book and borrower:

One borrower can borrow many books (one-to-many)

One book can be borrowed by many borrowers (many-to-one)

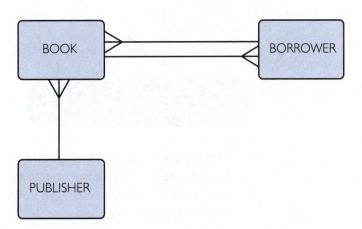

Figure 6.6 *Entity-relationship diagram for a library database*

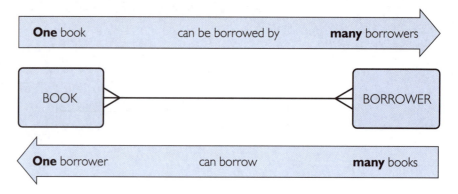

Figure 6.7   *Many-to-many relationship*

Taken together these relationships can be considered as many-to-many and shown diagrammatically as in Figure 6.7.

The many-to-many relationship cannot be directly handled in an RDBMS so, in cases such as this, the solution is to introduce an additional entity. In the library case study, the entity which can be used to link book and borrower is 'loan'.

One book may have many loans (one-to-many)

One borrower may make many loans (one-to-many)

This is shown in Figure 6.8.

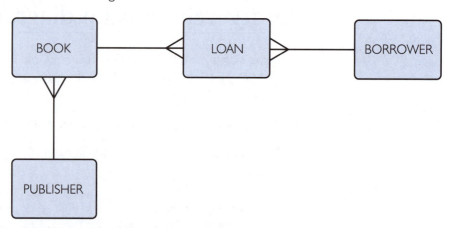

Figure 6.8   *Removal of many-to-many relationship*

Exercise 6.5

The leisure centre database contains four entities: Activity, Activity Area, Instructor and Member. Each instructor is a specialist, and takes only one activity, e.g. aerobics or basketball. However, each activity has a number of

continued

specialists who could take it. Also, each activity can only be done in one designated activity area, but each activity area can accommodate two or three different activities.

Complete these statements:

★   One instructor can lead one activity
★   One activity can be led by . . .
★   One activity can take place in . . .
★   One activity area can be used for . . .
★   One member may book . . .
★   One activity may be booked by . . .

Activity 6.4

Using the library example to help you, draw the ERD for the leisure centre database. Your finished diagram should *not* contain a many-to-many relationship.

Attributes

Each entity in a database has a set of **attributes.** These are simply the details that you want to hold for each entity.

The library entity 'Book' may have these attributes:

★   *Dewey classification number*
★   *ISBN*
★   *Title*
★   *Author*
★   *Publisher*
★   *Acquisition date*
★   *Acquisition number*

When designing the database, it is convenient to use the format of the entity name followed by the list of attributes enclosed in brackets.

The entity Book Title *could be written as*
    Book Title (Dewey Classification Number, ISBN, Title, Author, Publisher, Acquisition Date, Acquisition Number).

The entity Publisher *could be written as*
    Publisher (Name, Address, Telephone, Fax).

For the leisure centre example, complete these attribute lists:

★ Instructor (
★ Activity (
★ Activity Area (
★ Member (

When implementing a database, the entity is usually referred to as a **table**, or in some RDBMSs as a **form**. An attribute may be referred to as a **field**, or **column**. Each entry in a table is known as a **record**, a **row** or a **tuple**.

Key fields

In a relational database, it is essential that each record in a table contains a field that uniquely identifies that record. Such a field is called the **primary key**, and its purpose is to distinguish one, and only one, particular record from the others in that table, e.g. student number rather than student name.

Occasionally, there are tables where a single field used as a primary key is insufficient to ensure uniqueness of records. In these cases more than one field may be needed. The combination of fields needed to form the key is known as a **composite key**.

College Tracking System

The course co-ordinator of the Vocational A-level ICT needs to keep track of which student has achieved which unit (identified by the unit number), together with a note of how many assignments that element has. Each student has a tutor, and each unit taught has an assessor. The data can be presented in a Word document as shown in Table 6.5. At the beginning of the course, all students' details are recorded in the table and, as each unit is achieved, a new line is inserted into the table to record the details of the unit achieved.

Table 6.5 *Word table used to record students and their achievements*

STUDENT Surname	Forename	Student number	Sex	Tutor	Tutor code	Unit (Ass)	Assessor code	Assessor name	Date achieved
Rajabali	Batul	812865	F	Doash, M	MVD	1(4)	SMB	Bryant, S	7/10/98
						2(3)	JCB	Bentley, J	3/12/98
						3(2)	MVD	Doash, M	23/2/99
Boateng	Benjamin	823063	M	Bryant, S	SMB	1(4)	SMB	Bryant, J	25/10/98
						3(2)	MVD	Doash, M	6/3/99
Schoburg	Carlton	836651	M	Doash, M	MVD	2(3)	JCB	Bentley, J	9/12/98
						3(2)	MVD	Doash, M	15/3/99
Bell	Selisha	867340	F	Doash, M	MVD	1(4)	SMB	Bryant, S	27/10/98

With thousands of enrolments, it is very likely that there would be many students with the same surname, and so, when they enrol at the college, students are each allocated a number that is unique.

The original Word table shown in Table 6.5 can be represented in the form

Student(Surname, Forename, <u>Student Number,</u> Sex, Tutor, Tutor Code,

Unit ID(Assignments), Assessor Code, Assessor Name, Date Achieved)

The primary key field is indicated by underlining and the fields with the line above are those that are repeated for each unit achieved.

If there were only a small number of students in the college it might not be necessary to use student numbers. A composite key consisting of the student's forename, surname and date of birth would probably ensure uniqueness of the key, but in general it is better to allocate a key which is known to be unique.

In addition to identifying fields as primary keys, a database designer may also identify fields to be used as **secondary keys**, also known as **index keys**.

In the student table, the designer could define the tutor field as a secondary key. The RDBMS can then build an index of students in each tutor group. This enables a list of students in a particular tutor group to be produced very quickly by accessing the relevant student records directly rather than by reading every student record and checking the tutor field.

Although there is more processing involved when a new record is added, the speed of input is not seriously affected because it is limited anyway by the typing speed of the operator.

Unlike a primary key, the data in a secondary key need not be unique. Duplicate data can be held in each record of a secondary key. The need for such keys is identified by an analyst through consultation with the people who are using the data.

If an attribute in a table is the primary key of another table it is called a **foreign key**.

If there was a separate table of staff, then Tutor Code and Assessor Code would be foreign keys in the table 'Student'.

Data dictionary

A data dictionary is a list of the components that make up a database: the entity tables, the attributes/fields and the relationships between entities.

- ✪ For each table, an entry in the data dictionary contains its name and purpose.
- ✪ For each field, an entry contains its name, purpose, the tables in which it appears and other characteristics.
- ✪ For each relation, an entry contains its name, the tables and fields it links, and its type (one-to-one, one-to-many).
- ✪ The data dictionary can itself be held as a series of tables in the database.

Activity 6.5

Use a DBMS to set up a table containing information about the students in your group.

Figure 6.19 (on page 279) gives an example of how a table is set up using Microsoft Access.

Normalisation

Normalisation is the process by which a database designer refines the initial (or un-normalised) set of tables. This results in a database design which

- ✪ avoids duplication of data whenever possible
- ✪ structures the database to anticipate attributes and entities which may be needed in the future

✪ logically separates distinct entities so that later modifications to one will not adversely affect others.

Normalisation may be seen as a **bottom-up** process and often starts from the documents and files currently in use by the organisation. It may be an alternative to the **top-down** approach of the ERD which, if done correctly, should result in normalised tables. However, in reality, most database design consists of a combination of the top-down and bottom-up approaches with the normalisation process being used to check on the initial entity-relationship model. The result of normalisation is a database in which all possible entities have been identified and separated, each being represented by its own table.

Atomic attributes

All attributes in a table should be atomic; i.e. all fields in each record must contain only a single data value, not a group of values.

In the student table in the College Tracking System, all attributes are atomic except for the Unit ID (assignments) field. This field holds information on each student which shows both the unit achieved and how many assignments that unit has. These fields must be separated so that all the attributes contained in each record are atomic. Unit ID (assignments) becomes two fields Unit ID and Assignments:

Activity 6.6

Referring back to the video store case study, the store rents video titles on a daily basis. The owner wants a system to find out which video titles are the most popular, and which are the least popular. A data model for this situation could start as:

Video (<u>Video ID</u>, Title, Certificate, Supplier, Weekly Rentals)

Identify which attribute is non-atomic and rewrite this table showing a new field list, with all attributes atomic.

Normalisation process

The normalisation of an initial data model (in un-normalised form) into a final database consists of three stages:

1   Producing a first normal form (1NF) of the model.

2   Refining the 1NF into a second normal form (2NF).

3   Further refining the 2NF model into a third normal form (3NF).

First normal form – eliminate repeating groups of attributes

A table is said to be in first normal form (1NF) if it contains no repeating attributes or groups of attributes and all data items are atomic.

The problem with the initial model of the student table is that as students progress through the course, they will need to be credited with each unit they achieve. This means that for each student, a group of fields (Unit ID, Assignments, Assessor Code, Assessor Name) will need to be repeated as many times as the number of units achieved. Since each student is likely to progress at a different rate, it would be difficult to predict the length of each student record through the year. As indicated earlier, a repeating group is generally represented with a line drawn over the fields as:

> Student (<u>Student number</u>, Surname, Forename, Sex, Tutor, Tutor code,
>
> <u>Unit ID, Assignments, Assessor code, Assessor name, Date achieved)</u>

To remove the repeating groups, it is clear that two entities exist: Student and Unit. The fields can be separated into two tables:

> Student (<u>Student Number</u>, Surname, Forename, Sex, Tutor, Tutor Code, Unit ID, Date Archived)
>
> Unit (<u>Unit ID</u>, Assignments, Assessor Code, Assessor Name)

where Unit ID becomes the primary key for the new table Unit.

So that the Student table can hold the data of all units achieved by each student, Unit ID must now become part of the primary key for that table. The data in the tables can now show all students and all elements. This is shown in Table 6.6.

Activity 6.7

> The video store owner has decided that the database should also provide information about the amount of money taken each week for each video. The initial model is now:
>
> Video (<u>Video ID</u>, Title, Daily Rate, Certificate, Supplier ID, Supplier Address, Week Number, Rentals)
>
> **Identify the repeating groups and refine to 1NF.**

E. F. Codd also defined fourth normal form (4NF) and fifth normal form (5NF) but these are not normally needed except in the most complex databases.

Did You Know?

Table 6.6 *Student and unit tables in 1NF*

STUDENT

Surname	Forename	Student number	Sex	Tutor	Tutor code	Unit ID	Date achieved
Rajabali	Batul	812865	F	Doash, M	MVD	1	7/10/98
Rajabali	Batul	812865	F	Doash, M	MVD	2	3/12/98
Rajabali	Batul	812865	F	Doash, M	MVD	3	23/2/99
Boateng	Benjamin	823063	M	Bryant, S	SMB	1	25/10/98
Boateng	Benjamin	823063	M	Bryant, S	SMB	3	6/3/99
Schoburg	Carlton	836651	M	Doash, M	MVD	2	9/12/98
Schoburg	Carlton	836651	M	Doash, M	MVD	3	15/3/99
Bell	Selisha	867340	F	Doash, M	MVD	1	27/10/98

UNIT

Unit ID	Assignments	Assessor code	Assessor name
1	4	SMB	Bryant, S
2	3	JCB	Bentley, J
3	2	MVD	Doash, M
4	3	PMC	Castor, C
5	4	RPC	Clare, R
6	2	SBA	Ahmed, S

Second normal form – reducing duplicate data

Although the two entities are now separated, the data model as it now stands still has the problem of duplicate or redundant data.

A table is said to be in 2NF when it is in first normal form and no field that is not part of a composite primary key is dependent on only a portion of the primary key. In other words all the fields in a table *other than the primary key fields* must be entirely to do with the primary key. In the Student table, all the fields are to do with a student (Name, Sex, Tutor, etc.) except the Unit ID field. That is to do with the units, not the students. Therefore the Unit ID field is not dependent on the primary key, i.e. Student Number. This table is not in 2NF.

If the database were to be implemented on a computer system now, the large amounts of duplicated data would result in slower updating of data and the process of users extracting information from it would be more complicated and prone to errors. The data it contained would be more likely to be inconsistent between tables, which would result in unreliable reports being output.

To put the Student table into 2NF, list all the primary keys and their combinations:

> Student Number
> Unit ID
> Student Number, Unit ID

Next place each field with its appropriate primary key:

> Student Number, Surname, Forename, Sex, Tutor, Tutor Code
> Unit ID, Assignments, Assessor Code, Assessor Name
> Student Number, Unit ID, Date Achieved

Now give each table an appropriate name:

> Student (Student Number, Surname, Forename, Sex, Tutor, Tutor Code)
> Element (Element ID, PCs, Assessor Code, Assessor Name)
> Student Achievement (Student Number, Unit ID, Date Achieved)

The data model has now been refined to 2NF. The tables are now as shown in Table 6.7.

Activity 6.8

Having given further thought to how a computerised administration system could help the business, the video store owner has decided to include its members in the data model so that it can be known which member has which title at any time. The 1NF of the model is now:

Video (Video ID, Title, Daily Rate, Certificate, Supplier ID, Address, Week Number)

Weekly Rental (Week Number, Rentals)

Member (Member ID, Surname, Forename, Title, Address, Telephone, Video ID, Issue Date, Return Date, Overdue?)

Refine this data model to 2NF.

Table 6.7 *GTS Tables in 2NF*

STUDENT

Surname	Forename	Student Number	Sex	Tutor	Tutor Code
Rajabali	Batul	812865	F	Doash, M	MVD
Boateng	Benjamin	823063	M	Bryant, S	SMB
Schoburg	Carlton	836651	M	Doash, M	MVD
Bell	Selisha	867340	F	Doash, M	MVD

UNIT

Unit ID	Assignments	Assessor Code	Assessor Name
1	4	SMB	Bryant, S
2	3	SMB	Bryant, S
3	2	SMB	Bryant, S
4	3	SMB	Bryant, S
5	4	JCB	Bentley, J
6	2	JCB	Bentley, J

STUDENT ACHIEVEMENT

Student Number	Unit ID	Date Achieved
812865	1	7/10/98
812865	2	3/12/98
812865	3	23/2/99
823063	1	25/10/98
823063	3	6/3/99
836651	2	9/12/98
836651	3	15/3/99
867340	1	27/10/98

Third normal form

A table is in third normal form (3NF) when it is in 2NF and every field, which is not part of the primary key, is *wholly* dependent on that key. There are no non-key dependencies, i.e. the fields in a table belong only in that table, and should not be placed in any other table at all. The tables Student and Unit each contain information regarding the teaching staff. This may appear satisfactory at first glance, since each student has a tutor and each unit has an assessor. However, if a new member of staff joins the staff team, the new details cannot be recorded until a new tutor group or a new unit is entered on the database. Also, the tables in 2NF still contain much redundant data.

The 2NF of the College Tracking System is:

> Student (<u>Student Number</u>, Surname, Forename, Sex, Tutor, Tutor Code)
> Unit (<u>Element ID</u>, Assignments, Assessor Code, Assessor Name)
> Student Achievement (<u>Student Number, Unit ID</u>, Date Achieved)

A tutor and an assessor are simply members of staff. Therefore, in this example, the 3NF involves creating a separate table for staff:

> Student (<u>Student Number</u>, Surname, Forename, Sex, Tutor Code)
> Unit (<u>Unit ID</u>, Assignments, Assessor Code)
> Student Achievement (<u>Student Number, Unit ID</u>, Date Achieved)
> Staff (<u>Staff Code</u>, Staff Name)

Notice that the field names Tutor Code, Assessor Code and Staff Code are all **synonyms**, i.e. they all hold *exactly* the same data. We can describe any of them as having two **aliases**, e.g. Assessor Code alias Tutor Code, alias Staff Code. The data model is now in 3NF and can be implemented as a database. The tables are now as shown in Table 6.8.

Assuming one member of staff is the assessor for a number of units, the ER diagram for this system is then as shown in Figure 6.9.

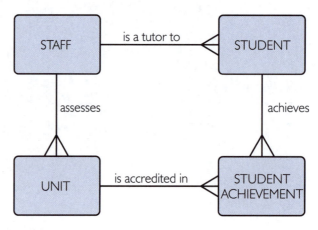

Figure 6.9 *Entity-relationship diagram*

Table 6.8 *GTS Table in 3NF*

STUDENT

Surname	Forename	Student Number	Sex	Tutor Code
Rajabali	Batul	812865	F	MVD
Boateng	Benjamin	823063	M	SMB
Schoburg	Carlton	836651	M	MVD
Bell	Selisha	867340	F	MVD

UNIT

Unit ID	Assignments	Assessor Code
1	4	SMB
2	3	SMB
3	4	SMB
4	3	SMB
5	4	JCB
6	2	JCB

STUDENT ACHIEVEMENT

Student Number	Unit ID	Date Achieved
812865	1.1	3-Oct-96
812865	1.2	3-Oct-96
812865	1.3	21-Oct-96
823063	2.1	25-Oct-96
823063	2.3	27-Oct-96
836651	1.2	10-Oct-96
836651	1.3	20-Oct-96
867340	3.1	25-Oct-96

STAFF

Staff Code	Staff Name
JCB	Bentley, J
MVD	Doash, M
SMB	Bryant, S
PMC	Caster, P
RPC	Clare, R
SBA	Ahmed, S

The 2NF of the video store data model is now:

Video (<u>Video ID</u>, Title, Daily Rate, Certificate, Supplier ID, Address)
Weekly Rental (<u>Week Number, Video ID</u>, Rentals)
Member (<u>Member ID</u>, Surname, Forename, Title, Address, Telephone)
Member Rental (<u>Member ID, Video ID</u>, Issue Date, Return Date, Overdue?)

Refine this data model to 3NF and produce the final ER diagram.

Relational database structures

DriveRite Driving School

The administrative assistant at DriveRite is studying database systems at evening classes. A requirement of the course is that he must implement a database solution for a real user. He has carried out an analysis of the current DriveRite system and has written a memo to his boss suggesting that he could now implement a computerised database system for DriveRite (see Figure 6.10). Attached to the memo is a copy of a systems analysis report (Figure 6.11), which includes the following appendices:

★ a list of the current data stores (Figure 6.12)

★ a sample of the lesson booking sheet (Figure 6.13)

★ a sample of the instructor schedule (Figure 6.14)

★ an ERD representing the initial data model (Figure 6.15)

MEMO

25th July 1999

To: Judith Woodcock, Proprietor, DriveRite Driving School

From: Jim Jones Administrative Assistant

Copy: file

Proposal for computerisation of Driving Lesson Booking System

Further to our conversation yesterday on the above topic, I enclose a copy of my systems analysis report including specimen booking sheets, instructor schedules and an initial data model.

Next Stage

If you approve the basic concepts I have outlined I shall be only too pleased to proceed with the complete design of the initial system for your approval.

This will comprise a more complete data analysis and complete refinement of the outline system identifying all inputs, outputs and keys involved.

The final part of this will be to carry out a process called normalisation to make sure that any unnecessary duplication of data is avoided and processing can be as efficient as possible. I can then proceed to implement the system using the Microsoft Access database management system.

Figure 6.10 *DriveRite system proposal*

DriveRite Driving School
Systems Analysis Report

An example of the documents used in the system are shown in Appendices 1 and 2.

A list of the current data stores is shown in Appendix 3.

An initial data model is shown in Appendix 4.

Description of the processes and data involved

1. Booking a lesson

Pupils ring up the school to book one or more lessons. The booking clerk fills in an appointment on the booking sheet. If it is a new pupil, their details are recorded onto a record card and placed in an index file. Current pupils may book by telephone, or alternatively at the end of a lesson, arrange their next lesson with the instructor. This will be entered in a diary held by the instructor.

At the end of the day, the instructors return to base, and transfer these entries on to the central booking sheet. Any clashes will be resolved by telephoning the pupils to change the appointments straight away.

A copy of the driving lesson booking sheet can be found in Appendix 1.

2. Scheduling the instructors

At the end of each day, the instructors are given a schedule of their lessons for the following day.

An example schedule form is shown in Appendix 2.

An entry is made at the end of each lesson, recording:

- fees paid
- attendance
- time of next lesson, if arranged

At the end of the day, the completed schedule is returned to the school.

3. Collecting fees

Fees must be paid for each lesson at the time of the lesson. A record of the fees paid is kept on the instructors' schedules.

4. Paying the instructors

Instructors work on a self-employed basis, and are paid a fixed rate per hour of instruction. The number of hours are calculated from the previous week's schedules, and paid weekly. If the pupil does not attend, the instructor does not get paid.

5. Requirements of the new system

  5.1   Instructor schedules can be produced automatically

  5.2   Instructors' wages can be calculated and wage slips produced

  5.3   Any daily booking form can be accessed on screen to check availability

  5.4   Facilities for the entry and storage of pupil data

  5.5   Facilities for the entry and storage of booking data

  5.6   Facilities for the entry and storage of instructor data

  5.7   Facilities for the entry and storage of completed schedule data

6. Constraints of the new system

Must run on currently owned hardware

Figure 6.11   *DriveRite systems analysis report*

Appendix 3
Current data stores

Pupil card index:

One card for each pupil. Each card contains:

Surname, First name, Title, Date of birth, Address, Telephone number, Weekly record of fees paid.

Instructor File:

For each instructor:

Surname, First name, Title, Date of birth, Address, Telephone number, Weekly record of wages paid.

Booking:

Each sheet of the booking form contains the bookings for one day of all the drivers.

Schedule:

Each schedule is one instructor's bookings (lessons) for the day.

Each schedule has the date, the driver's name and, for each time slot, the student's name, address, telephone number, attendance and details of the next lesson.

Figure 6.12 *DriveRite current data stores*

Date:	**Lesson Booking Sheet**				
Time/Instructor	Ali	Michael	Ruth	Ashvinder	James
0800					
0900					
1000					
1100					
1200					
1300					
1400					
1500					
1600					
1700					
1800					
1900					
2000					

Figure 6.13 *DriveRite lesson booking sheet*

Instructor Schedule

Instructor name ....

Date ....

Time	Pupil name	Address	Phone	Attended?	Next appt.	Comments
0800						
0900						
1000						
1100						
1200						
1300						
1400						
1500						
1600						
1700						
1800						
1900						
2000						

Figure 6.14 *DriveRite instructor schedule*

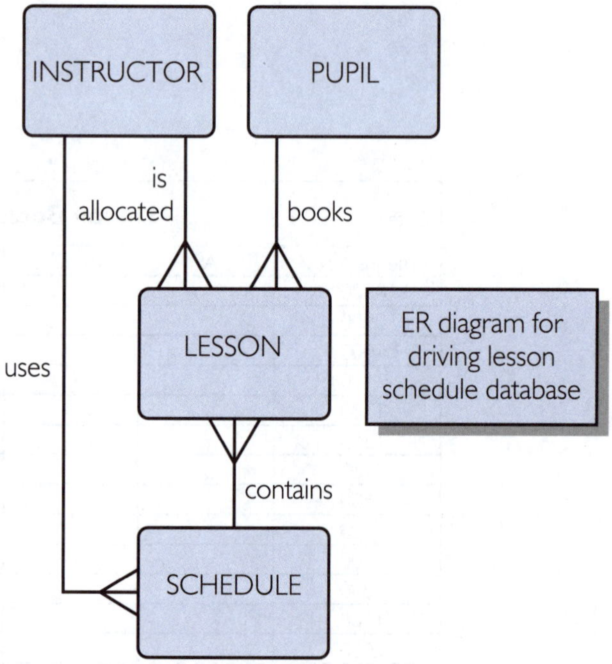
INSTRUCTOR
PUPIL
is allocated
books
uses
LESSON
ER diagram for driving lesson schedule database
contains
SCHEDULE

Figure 6.15 *DriveRite system initial data model*

The following sections show the steps taken to develop the final data model.

Step 1 Produce the field lists for each entity (table) in the preliminary ER diagram with the key fields identified

Instructor (<u>Ins ID</u>, Surname, Forename, Title, Dob, Address, Telephone, Weekly Wages)

Pupil (<u>Pupil ID</u>, Surname, Forename, Title, Dob, Address, Telephone, Weekly Payments)

Lesson (<u>Date</u>, <u>Time</u>, Pupil ID, Ins ID)

Schedule (<u>Ins ID</u>, <u>Date</u>, Time, Pupil ID, Surname, Forename, Address, Telephone, Attended?, Next Lesson, Comment)

Step 2 Remove non-atomic data and identify repeating groups

Instructor (<u>Ins ID</u>, Surname, Forename, Title, Dob, Address, Telephone, Week No, Wage Paid)

Pupil (<u>Pupil ID</u>, Surname, Forename, Title, Dob, Address, Telephone, Week No, Payment Made)

Lesson (<u>Date</u>, <u>Time</u>, Pupil ID, Ins ID)

Schedule (<u>Ins ID</u>, <u>Date</u>, Time, Pupil ID, Surname, Forename, Address, Telephone, Attended?, Next Lesson, Comment)

Step 3 Remove repeating groups to create the First Normal Form

Instructor (<u>Ins ID</u>, Surname, Forename, Title, Dob, Address, Telephone)

Instructor wages (<u>Ins ID</u>, <u>Week No</u>, Wages)

Pupil (<u>Pupil ID</u>, Surname, Forename, Title, Dob, Address, Telephone)

Pupil payments (<u>Pupil ID</u>, <u>Week No</u>, Payment)

Lesson (<u>Date</u>, <u>Time</u>, Pupil ID, Ins ID)

Schedule (<u>Ins ID</u>, <u>Date</u>)

Schedule Detail (<u>Time</u>, Pupil ID, Surname, Forename, Address, Telephone, Attended?, Comments)

The data model is now in 1NF. The use of the composite key date and time in the Lesson table may not be unique, as lessons could be booked for two different instructors at the same time. A new field, Lesson ID is required as the primary key.

Step 4 Remove redundant data to create the Second Normal Form

Instructor (Ins ID, Surname, Forename, Title, Dob, Address, Telephone)

Instructor wages (Ins ID, Week No, Wages)

Pupil (Pupil ID, Surname, Forename, Title, Dob, Address, Telephone)

Pupil payments (Pupil ID, Week No, Payment)

Lesson (Lesson ID, Date, Time, Pupil ID, Ins ID, Attended?, Comments)

The data model is now in 2NF. This is also 3NF since in each table every field, which is not part of the primary key, is *wholly* dependent on that key.

Notice that the refined data model now contains tables, which represent the entities of the system, i.e. the objects that perform the transactions of the business. Schedule has disappeared because that is simply a report issued to each instructor. It is not an entity, and so there is no table.

Step 5 Produce the final ER diagram

This is shown in Figure 6.16.

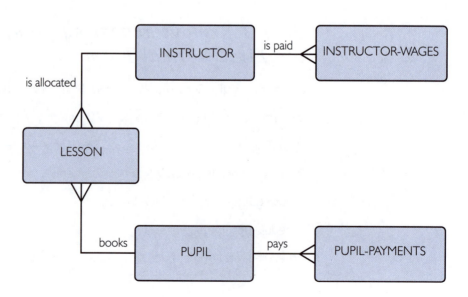

Figure 6.16   *DriveRite system final data model*

Relational database construction

The finished DriveRite database design can be implemented using a Relational Database Management System, or RDBMS. Any RDBMS should enable a database system to be implemented in a way which provides the end-user with a system that is robust, able to record transactions with minimal risk of errors being made, and produce analyses and reports that are reliable and precise. In addition, users should find the system easy to use without having to spend large sums of money on training. Also, an organisation that has a need for a computer-based system would already have been operating successfully for some time, and so a developer should be able to implement the new system with the least disruption to its business.

The process of constructing the database system can be broken down into five steps.

1   Construct tables, defining the entities
2   Define relationships between tables
3   Create data entry forms
4   Create queries
5   Create report forms

The following sections give examples of how Microsoft Access can be used to carry out each of these stages for the DriveRite database.

1 Construct tables, defining the entities

Start by establishing a new database and giving it a name using the screens shown in Figure 6.17.

Microsoft Access then shows a menu (Figure 6.18) from which New Table is selected.

Microsoft Access then shows a screen (Figure 6.19) on which the names and type of each field in the table can be defined. The definition of the fields for the Pupil table are shown. Notice that the field to be used as the key field can also be defined.

The same method is used to define the fields for the other four tables of the DriveRite database.

2 Define relationships between tables

Microsoft Access allows this to be done graphically and the result is shown in Figure 6.20. Notice that this diagram shows the same relationships that are defined in the ERD shown in Figure 6.16.

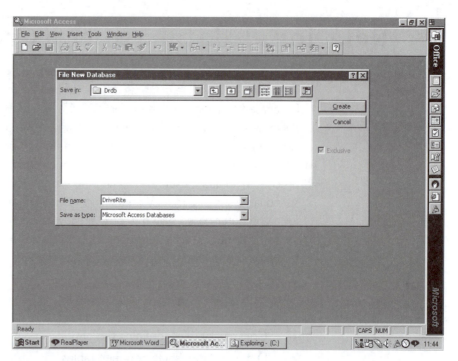

Figure 6.17 *New Database screen*

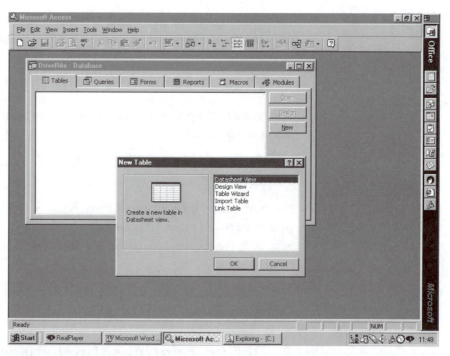

Figure 6.18 *Main Menu screen*

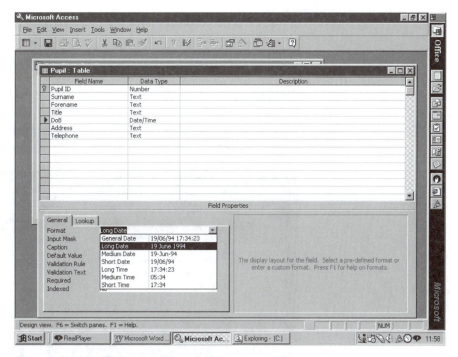

Figure 6.19 *Table Design screen*

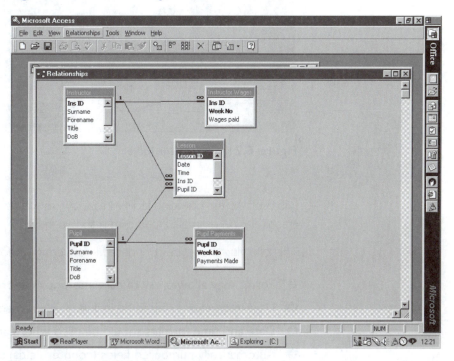

Figure 6.20 *Relationships screen*

Activity 6.10

Set up the normalised tables and relationships that you have defined for the video store system.

3 Create data entry forms

At this point, an empty database has been created. Data can be input into the tables directly by using a screen such as the one shown in Figure 6.21 for the Instructor table. However, more 'user friendly' input screens are required to enable transactions such as bookings or payments to be recorded by clerical staff with limited computer skills. The input screens are called **forms**; they are exactly like paper forms containing instructions and empty spaces to fill.

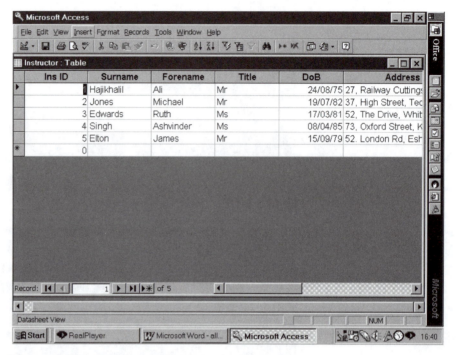

Figure 6.21 *Instructor table*

Microsoft Access has good facilities to allow you to design your input forms graphically. An example input form is shown in Figure 6.22.

The following should be considered in the design of forms:

- ✪ Forms may allow entry of data into one or more tables.
- ✪ User instructions should be included where necessary.
- ✪ Date and time formats should be used where appropriate.
- ✪ Automatically numbered fields (counter fields) should be used where appropriate.
- ✪ Calculated fields should be included where possible.
- ✪ Entry fields should be clearly labelled.
- ✪ Selection of data from built-in lists should be used where appropriate.
- ✪ Entry fields should be of appropriate length.

✪ Validation checks on entered data should be included wherever possible.

✪ Field names must comply with the data dictionary.

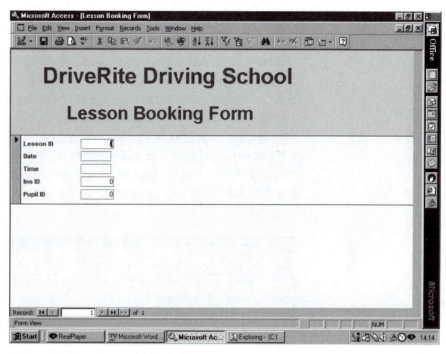

Figure 6.22 *Lesson booking form*

The design and usage of data input screens is part of the overall **human–computer interface (HCI)**. Screens should be accessed in a way that is familiar to the user. A user will typically have been using a number of documents for recording transactions before considering a computer system. The data entry screens should therefore be designed with these documents in mind. This makes the system seem less unfamiliar to the user, requiring them to make the same kind of entries as before but using a keyboard and a mouse rather than pen and paper.

4 Create queries

Once a database has been loaded with data, the user usually wants to interrogate it to extract information.

In the DriveRite system, these might be examples of such queries:

★ *List all pupils over the age of 25.*

★ *List pupils and instructors for all lessons in January.*

★ *List all students who have not attended booked lessons this week.*

Exercise 6.7

Suggest queries that might be needed in the video store system.

Queries can be defined by using a language called SQL (structured query language). Figure 6.23 shows an example of an SQL query used to list all pupils over 25. Notice that the pupil's age is not held as a field in the Pupil table but is calculated using a function **Datediff** which works out the difference in years between the pupil's date of birth and today's date. Today's date is returned by another function **Now**. There are a large number of functions supplied with Microsoft Access that can be used in calculations. The details of these functions and the parameters they require can be found by using the Microsoft Access help system.

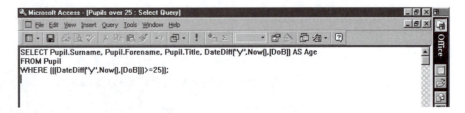

Figure 6.23 *SQL example*

Like any computer language, SQL has a set of rules (or **syntax**) which must be followed in formulating the query. However, Microsoft Access can make life easier by allowing queries to be input in a more user friendly format called **Query by example** or **QBE**, which automatically translates queries into SQL. You just define which fields of which tables to select and the criteria for selection. Figure 6.24 shows an example of a query on the DriveRite database that will select all lessons booked during January, with the names of the instructors and their pupils. In this query, three tables – Pupil, Instructor and Lesson – are used. The function Month is used to return the number of the month using the date as a parameter. The criterion '= 1' then selects only those lessons booked in January. Figure 6.24 also shows the results obtained from this query and the SQL statements generated.

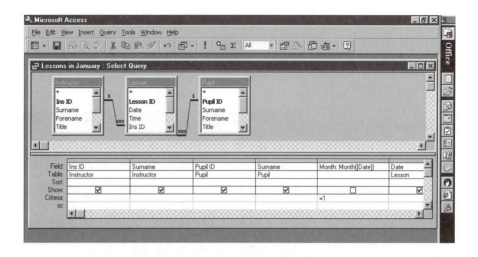

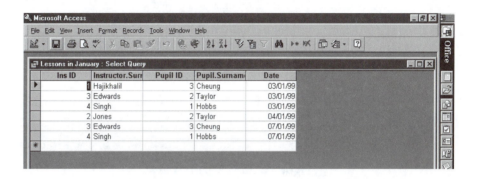

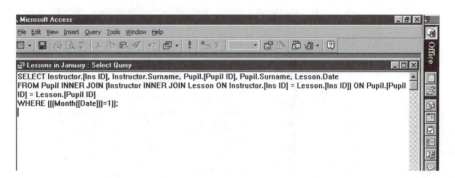

Figure 6.24 *QBE example*

5 Create report forms

Printed reports also need careful design. Microsoft Access, like other RDBMSs, has extensive facilities for producing reports. Although reports are quite straightforward to create, the developer must bear in mind who is going to see the printout. The format will probably differ between reports used within a company and those sent to customers. Reports should always conform to a company's standards and present a consistent and professional image.

An example of a report produced by DriveRite would be a monthly summary of lessons given by each instructor. Figure 6.25 shows how this report is defined in Microsoft Access and Figure 6.26 shows the finished report.

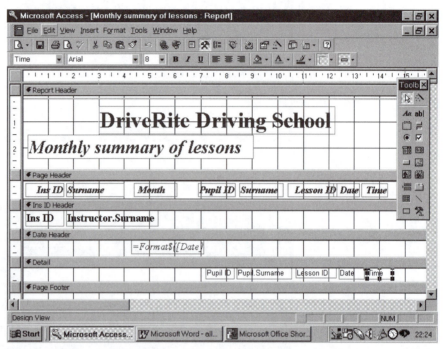

Figure 6.25 *Report example*

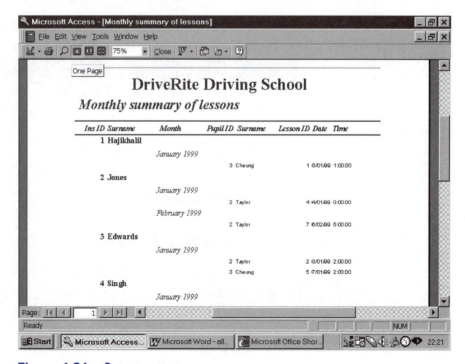

Figure 6.26 *Report output*

Produce a report from the video database showing
the number of videos rented by each customer during
each month of a particular year.

Wizards

Wizards are part of the Microsoft Access system, which automate some of
the design functions. When designing forms or reports using a wizard, the
designer is offered a choice of standard layouts and colour schemes. It is
often convenient to use a wizard to produce an initial report or form design
and then to modify this to meet the specific requirements of the application.
Wizards are certainly very useful in speeding up the process of building an
application, particularly for **prototyping**, i.e. building a basic system to test
design ideas.

Figure 6.27 shows the use of a wizard in designing a form to update the
Instructor table.

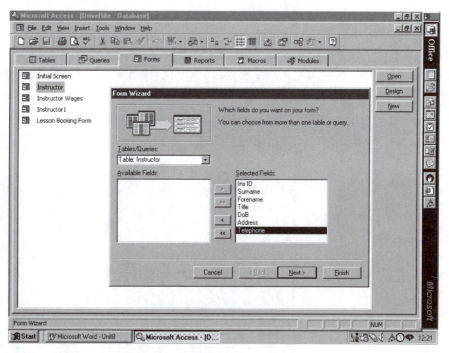

Figure 6.27 *Use of a form design wizard*

Use the forms design wizard to design a form to input details of a new video.

Menu screens

The user of a database application will generally be unfamiliar with the workings of the database package itself. It is therefore desirable to provide a menu system, which will enable the user to navigate between the various parts of the application simply by selecting from menus or clicking buttons with the mouse. Figure 6.28 shows the design of an initial screen giving the user the choice of a number of different functions in the DriveRite system. The buttons can be drawn on the screen using the command button tool from the toolbar shown on the right of the screen. A suitable label can then be typed straight onto the button. Every object on a screen has a set of **properties** associated with it, and the properties of the button can be viewed by double clicking with the mouse in design view. To cause some action to take place when the button is clicked, the On-Click event property must be set to run a macro (a stored set of instructions) to carry out the action. In Figure 6.29 the On-Click property is set to run the macro NewInstructor.

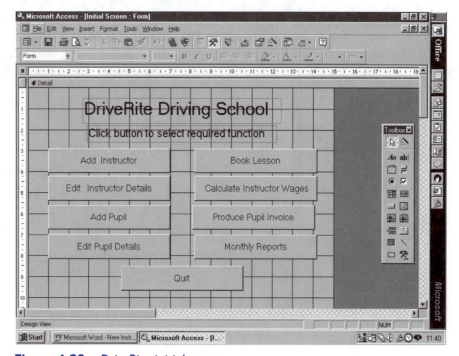

Figure 6.28 *DriveRite initial screen*

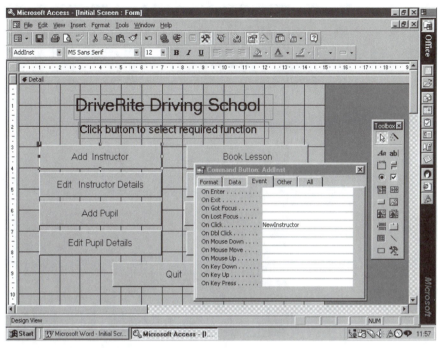

Figure 6.29 *Setting On-Click property*

Macros

The macro NewInstructor is a one-line macro that opens the Instructor form ready to accept input of a new instructor's details. This macro is set up using the macro screen shown in Figure 6.30. The macro actions available are shown in a drop-down menu and when the action is selected, the required arguments (or parameters) are shown at the bottom of the macro screen. In the example macro, the important arguments are the name of the form to be opened (Instructor) and the data mode (Add).

Linking between forms in this way is one of the most common uses of macros, but more complex multi-line macros can be used to customise an application, e.g. macros can be written to carry out more complex data validation checks than are available in the standard features of Microsoft Access.

Activity 6.13

Design a menu screen for the video store system. Use the OpenForm macro action to display the new video input screen when the appropriate menu button is clicked.

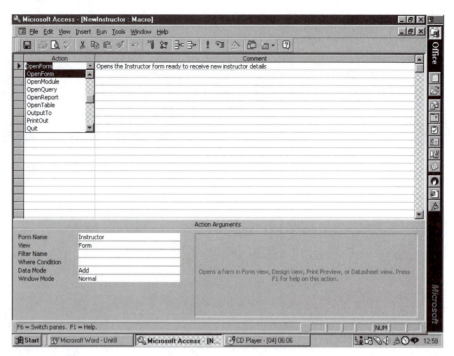

Figure 6.30   *New instructor macro*

Testing

Testing is perhaps the most important stage in the development of any database application. However stunning the design of the screens and however extensive and imaginative the facilities provided, users will very soon become disillusioned with an application that is full of errors or fails to fully meet their requirements. It is a fact of computing life that no matter how skilled the developers, it is very unlikely that an application of any complexity will be free of all errors. The function of the testing phase of development is to ensure that as many errors as possible are eliminated before the application 'goes live'. Many computer applications are critical to the success of an organisation and an application that fails can literally cause the failure of the organisation.

Phases of testing

Testing is often divided into two phases, alpha and beta testing.

Alpha testing

This is the phase in which the application is put through a stringent set of tests to try to ensure that the application meets the user requirements. It is, of course, essential that the user requirements are clearly specified in the first place. In this phase, testing should ideally be carried out by a group independent of the actual developers, as the developers are likely to make incorrect assumptions about what is working correctly. The testers should work from a test specification that should include a **test script** that ensures that all functionality is properly tested.

Beta testing

However extensive the alpha testing has been, it is often the case that the real users have their own ideas about how an application should work. It is therefore common practice for users to undertake a phase of testing called **beta testing**. Users are given access to a preliminary or pre-release version of the application which they can test in their own environment with their own data. The users then report any errors or missing functionality to the developers who should fix the problem before the final release. Beta testing also gives the users an opportunity to become familiar with the new application and to gain confidence that it meets their requirement. It is in this phase that any shortcomings in the original user requirements specifications become apparent, but any changes to the requirements should, where possible, be postponed to a future release of the application and testing should be strictly against the original requirements.

Testing methods

Testing of a database application generally consists of providing a wide range of input data and checking that the outputs of the system are correct. This type of testing is commonly known as **black box testing** because the testers should be treating the application as a black box the inner workings of which are unknown to them. **White box testing**, on the other hand, looks at the inner structure of the application and tries to ensure that all possible paths through the software are tested. White box testing is generally more applicable to control systems, particularly safety-critical systems such as those in aircraft or nuclear power stations.

In devising a set of black box tests, the following should be considered:

- ✪ A wide range of acceptable input data including maximum and minimum values should be included.
- ✪ A wide range of unacceptable input values should be included to check data validation.
- ✪ Inputs such as mouse clicks or key combinations that require a specific response should be checked.
- ✪ Unexpected mouse clicks and key combinations should be checked to ensure no undesirable effects.

- Database tables should be checked before and after a series of transactions to ensure they have been correctly updated.
- Reports should be carefully examined to ensure accuracy and correct formatting.

Activity 6.14

Create suitable test data for the video store system.

Documentation

Even when the database application has been tested and is fully working it cannot be considered complete until it is fully documented.

The documentation for any application falls into two major categories: maintenance documentation and user documentation.

Maintenance documentation

In the commercial world, it is estimated that at least 70 per cent of IT budgets are spent on the maintenance of existing applications rather than the development of new ones. Maintenance includes fixing errors caused by poor design or programming 'bugs' as well as enhancing the application to meet new or changed user requirements. Applications development is rarely a solitary activity, but is generally carried out by teams. The members of a team may change and, in a short space of time, it is quite possible that the maintenance of an application has to be carried out by staff who had no involvement with the original development. In fact, the original developers may no longer be working for the same organisation. It is therefore essential that any application includes documentation that will allow it to be maintained by new staff.

The following can be used as a checklist of maintenance documentation requirements:

- User specification documents
- Details of the minimum hardware needed to run the application and the versions of operating systems and other software with which it is required to run

- Entity-relationship diagrams
- Data dictionary
- Listings of macros and program code (Visual Basic for Applications) which should contain adequate comments to allow the logic to be easily understood
- Details of input data validation rules
- Copies of screen layouts and printed reports
- Copies of test specifications and test reports
- List of known problems and restrictions

User documentation

The users of an application are not necessarily IT literate and will almost certainly not be database experts. It is therefore important that ease of use is one of the main design criteria. Things that may be obvious to the developer need to be spelt out in detail to the user. A well-designed user interface should be intuitive (i.e. need little or no explanation) but should also include a simple to use online help system such as is found in most Windows-based software (including Microsoft Access). Online help in applications should be modelled on the Windows help systems.

A well-designed user interface with comprehensive online help documentation can greatly reduce the need for paper documentation but some users will still feel more comfortable with the traditional paper user manuals which should include at least details of the following:

- How to start the application
- How to add new records
- How to edit or delete existing records
- How to initiate queries and produce reports
- The meaning of all error messages

Activity 6.15

Review the online help and the user manuals for a commercial software package. What do you consider are its good and not-so-good features? Do you think paper manuals are still necessary or is online help alone sufficient?

Revision questions

1 What is the difference between data and information?

2 Name three different types of Database Management System (DBMS).

3 What is an entity and how is it represented in an entity-relationship diagram?

4 What is the name of the language used to define queries in a RDBMS?

5 What does Microsoft Access provide to simplify the process of defining a database query?

6 Name three types of validation check that could be applied to input data.

7 Name three different data types that might appear in a database table.

8 How is a one-to-many relationship represented in an entity-relationship diagram?

9 What type of relationship cannot be directly implemented in a RDBMS?

10 What is the name of the field that uniquely identifies a record in a RDBMS?

11 What is a composite key? What is a foreign key?

12 What is the purpose of an index key?

13 What is the name of the process by which a database designer refines the structure of database tables to avoid duplication of data and ensure accurate and efficient updating?

14 What is meant by stating that one attribute is an alias of another?

15 What is the difference between black box and white box testing?

Impact of ICT on Society

7

- The historical development of ICT
- The impact ICT has had on society
- Legislation relating to ICT

This chapter has a practical focus throughout, with many activities and case studies. You will look at different methods of production and see how they have affected, and are affecting, working practices. The chapter takes into account the social and economic implications that ICT is having, and you will consider current issues such as ICT and the environment. Case studies looking at different public service industries have been used to highlight the impact of ICT. Finally, the chapter looks at the progression of ICT and the implications for the future. You will need to do research on your own and in groups and make visits to places like libraries, science museums and universities.

This chapter looks in detail at seven topics.

- ✪ Development of ICT over the last two decades
- ✪ ICT in our society
- ✪ The impact of ICT on working practices
- ✪ The impact of ICT on methods of production
- ✪ The effects of ICT on the environment
- ✪ Legislation for ICT users
- ✪ The future use of ICT

Development of ICT over the last two decades

The development of ICT over the last two decades can be considered in a number of areas:

- ❂ Hardware and software development
- ❂ Communication development
- ❂ Information sources development
- ❂ Data capture development
- ❂ Resolution and sound development
- ❂ Speed

Activity 7.1

In small groups, brainstorm at least three examples for each of the areas listed above. Pool all your ideas together and take notes. For each development, identify at least one advantage and one disadvantage.

Hardware and software development

Charles Babbage, a nineteenth-century mathematician, invented the first computer. He had requested from the government a grant, to develop a difference engine but became more enterprising and, in the 1820s, created an analytical engine that could perform calculations to 20 digits of accuracy. This engine constituted four of the main components of the modern computer; input in the form of punched cards, output in the form of a printer for permanent record, storage in the form of a store and processing in the form of a mill for arithmetic operations.

Activity 7.2

Figure 7.1 is an extract taken from a student's essay. Read the extract and then research around the topic. Check the facts against other sources and establish the extract's accuracy and reliability.

Hardware development

The very first computers were extremely large. They were built around vacuum tubes, glass tubes that housed the switching circuitry. Historians named this era in the early 1950s as the <u>first generation</u> of computers. Only very large organisations could afford to buy these early computers; they needed to be housed in temperature-controlled centres and required experienced staff for programming and maintenance, all of which was very expensive.

Moving in to the <u>second generation</u> of computers in 1956, transistors began to be used. Computers using this technology were smaller and cheaper than those using the vacuum tube technology. With the development of more programming languages, these computers were also easier to program and hence were more widely used by organisations.

Progressing in to the <u>third generation</u> of computers in the mid 1960s advancements in technology enabled many transistors to be bunched together on to a single <u>integrated circuit</u> (IC) board on a silicon chip. Yet again this new technology meant that computers were less expensive, smaller, more reliable and efficient, and worked much faster.

In 1969, the first microprocessor was invented bringing along the <u>fourth generation</u> of computers. The microprocessor housed all the workings of a computer on one tiny computer chip. Silicon chips were soon produced cheaply on production lines.

By the mid 1970s, many computer companies were using the silicon chip technology and, instead of having computers which filled rooms, the size had decreased to that of computers which were similar in size to typewriters. These computers were called personal computers (PCs) and first appeared in 1974. Technology has continued to advance, computers have decreased in size and cost while their processing power, reliability and efficiency have increased. PCs enabled portability; personal computers were no longer static machines, they could be moved around the home or work place.

Therefore, over the last two decades, component miniaturisation has had the double impact of reducing costs and improving the quality of equipment. <u>Fifth generation</u> computers are still being experimented with, there is much more new technology on the way!

Figure 7.1 *Extract from a student's essay*

While hardware has been developing, so too has software.

Exercise 7.1

Find out as much as you can about the history of computers and their inventors, try to answer the following questions:

★ What is ENIAC?

★ What was the first adding machine?

★ What was the first automatic loom?

★ Who created the first digital computer?

★ What was Grace Hopper famous for?

Activity 7.3

Find out which computor languages were invented during the 1970s. Use the table below to help you.

Name of language	Type	Creator	Date
Ada			
BASIC			
C			
CAI (computer aided instruction)			
COBOL (common business oriented language)			
FORTRAN			
LOGO			
Pascal			

This table lists languages in alphabetical order. You might prefer to present your table in date order.

In groups of three or four, explore books and magazines for pictures of computers, date them and present a history of development timeline of hardware and software, including the most recent configurations.

Each student might like to take a particular period in time.

Communication development

Did You Know?

The United States launched the Satellite Echo 1 in 1960.

The early computers were deemed 'stand-alone' machines. They could not communicate directly with other computers. Instead, information was transferred from machine to machine using paper tape, punched card or magnetic tape.

Initial communications date from the early 1960s when some of the first communications satellites were launched.

Figure 7.2 shows an extract of an article in a students' newsletter about methods of communication.

★ Check the facts against other sources and establish the extract's accuracy and reliability.

★ Write up your futuristic ideas about modes of communication.

Did You Know?

Some IT professionals (e.g. BT's Head of Research) have predicted chips inserted under the skin with data allowing people to buy things by choosing them and leaving the shop. A scanner at the door will register your code and the goods.

The first satellites merely reflected signals rather than transmitting them, they were limited by the need for powerful transmitters and large ground antennae. Satellite communications currently make use of active systems, in which each satellite carries its own equipment for reception and transmission. Commercial satellites provide a wide range of communication services, television being one of the main users.

It is anticipated that by the year 2010 the days of sending messages via cables and computer lines will have disappeared. The problem at present is that the original networks for communication were designed to let several calls be made at random times, but the systems easily get jammed with voice, Internet and other data traffic. The problem will be solved by greater capacity with the use of high bandwidth connections and the freeing of more radio frequencies.

Methods of Communication

Cable is a form of communication that provides many people with television pictures and telephone services. It uses underground cables, coaxial or fibre optic. There are different types of cabling used for the purposes of communication:

Electric cable is composed of one or more electric conductors covered by insulation for transmitting electric power or the impulses of an electronic communications system.

Coaxial cable developed in 1963 consists of several copper tubes; each tube contains a wire conductor that extends along its centre. The copper tubes shield the transmitted signal from electrical interference and prevent energy loss by radiation. The entire cable is sheathed in lead and is generally filled with nitrogen under pressure to prevent corrosion. The coaxial cable has a broad band frequency range and is the current transmitter of telephone signals. A cable consisting of 22 coaxial tubes arranged in tight rings sheathed in polythene and lead can carry 132,000 messages simultaneously.

Fibre optic cables are replacing coaxial cables and are used for interference-free, secure data transmission; they ensure very fast data transfer.

Messages are digitally coded through pulses of light and transmitted over great distances. They transmit data as light through fibres or thin rods of glass or some other transparent material of high refractive index. Examples where fibre optics are used include dentistry, laser surgery, facsimile systems, phototypesetting and computer graphics. Fibre optics are being used in local area networks (LANs) connecting users to centralised computers and printers.

Wireless communication includes technologies such as infra-red communication; an example of this would be your television remote control. Satellites make use of this technology using a high directional narrow beam for two-way transmission. Microwave transmission is used in sailing; highly directional transmitters and receivers with dish aerials.

Different types of cable/communication and their main features

Type	Features
Twisted pair	A pair of insulated copper wires twisted together, surrounded by copper braid and insulation; most common application data transmission
Fibre optic cable	Very fine glass strand using modulated light beams; most common application interference free rapid data transmission
Infra-red	Direct uninterrupted line of sight between transmitter and receiver; most common application TV remote control
Coaxial	Has two conductors, one is a central wire which is insulated from the second which is made up of braided strands; most common application TV aerial to TV
Microwave	Highly directional transmitters and receivers with dish aerials; most common applications public telephone service
Satellite	Highly directional narrow beam two-way transmission; most common application international communications

Figure 7.2 *Extract from an article in a student newsletter*

The idea of being able to talk to someone in holographic format, may not be a distant dream!

Information sources development

The development of databases has provided new opportunities to solve problems, which would have previously not been contemplated.

The Welsh National Poisons Unit

This database speeds up diagnosis by replacing the traditional pen and paper based system used in the eight poison units in the UK and Ireland. Until the system was created, each of the eight units relied on their own recording and experience to help diagnosis. Centralising the information has given every local unit rapid access to the details of more than 11,000 poisons, from household bleach and painkillers such as paracetamol to the latest high-tech drugs. Calls are logged and experts continuously analyse information and update the database.

Activity 7.6

Research and then list ten organisations which make use of extensive databases. Where possible, use the Internet for your research.

Recent examples include the National Health Service, DVLC, Police and the Inland Revenue.

Police databases

The police have databases which help them to track down criminals such as serial killers. They acknowledge (in recent documentaries) that, had this type of technology been available during the early 1970s, some persistent criminals may have been tracked down earlier.

Electronic mail (e-mail) has allowed information to be transferred quickly and cheaply. With co-operation between networks, this has led to the Internet.

With the development of the World Wide Web in the 1990s, many people can use the Internet, with pictures, sounds and video easily accessible. The Internet enables you to communicate quickly and efficiently all over the world. It allows increased availability of thousands of information sources: explore vast amounts of information, ask specific questions to ascertain obscure facts, publish your own information, play games and participate in discussions.

Exercise 7.2

Think about the effects of e-mail on other industries, e.g. mail, couriers, postmen, envelope producers.

Activity 7.7

Look forward and suggest how a database may be used in the future to solve problems.

★ Think about the limitations of using a database.

★ Think about electronic voting. Although this may be quicker and more convenient than travelling to a polling station, would it make it possible to identify who voted for whom?

★ Think about the same issues regarding databases for organ donation. It is possible to match suitable recipients but there are security limitations of this, as file inversion may mean inappropriate tracking of donors – before they are ready to donate their organs!

Discuss your ideas with others in your group.

Data capture development

With advances in technology, methods of data capture have also changed.

Activity 7.8

Make notes on as many data capture devices as possible, ordering them by date of invention. Illustrate your notes with scanned pictures or images from the Internet.

You may refer to your work from Chapter 4: *Systems Installation and Configuration*.

People now use technology involving character readers, light readers and magnetic strip readers.

Activity 7.9

Figure 7.3 shows an extract of an information sheet produced by a Vocational A-level ICT student.

★ Read through the sheet and write an evaluation covering the article's accuracy, relevancy and content.

★ Scan in text using OCR – or rekey.

★ Revise the text by adding data – dates/makes/ pictures – to create an overview of data capture development.

Resolution and sound development

Improved **resolution** enables the user to see images on the computer terminal much clearer. A computer monitor is connected to the computer via a video graphics adapter (VGA). A computer holds an image in its video memory. The more video memory a computer has the clearer the image can be.

Images on the computer screen are made up of tiny dots, called **pixels**. The higher the resolution of the screen, the closer the dots, the clearer the image. Modern-day **CAD (computer-aided design)** requires very high resolution screens. If, for example, a screen is low resolution, the user may not see an accurate representation of the drawing.

Monitors are now able to show video. As with TVs, monitors refresh/update their images many times per second. Therefore, a monitor that has the capability to refresh its image more quickly will give a much clearer image.

A permanent output from a monitor is a printout – a **hardcopy** of the image. Printers cannot match all the colours that the monitor shows but good printers give a very good representation of what is seen on the screen.

Sound can also be added to the computer via a sound card, this is a built-in synthesiser. Combining sound, text, graphics and animation gives multimedia, which can be purely visual or interactive. With the development of multimedia, CD-ROMs have been mass produced, helping to increase information availability.

Information compression means reducing the amount of space, e.g. **zipping** files. When a file is compressed, it must be re-expanded before it can be read again. A simple example of data compression is where combinations of letters are replaced by a single number. In this sentence, the pair of letters 'th' appears five times, if 'th' is replaced by the number '1' five characters have been saved. If this is done with other combinations of letters such as 'it' and 'is', even more characters are saved, reducing the file size. The zipping of files makes archiving of files easy and means that less of the hard drive is used up. Many users zip files before they send them over the Internet or network as it makes file transmission quicker and more efficient. Software companies have created software to zip and unzip files. Some software uses drag and drop techniques to zip and unzip files, other software will automatically unzip files when re-opened. Users need to be careful about unzipping files on to systems as they could contain viruses.

> **Always scan files for viruses before unzipping them.**

Speed development

New technology has led to massive improvements in speed. The faster the **transmission** rate, the quicker the information is received and can be processed. It also has cost implications, as the shorter the call, the lower the connection charge.

Often **baud rate** is compared to one **bit per second**, but the latter is technically more accurate for high-speed transmissions such as modems. A

Transmission
is the passing of information between computers.

Baud rate
is the unit used to measure speed of serial data transmission.

Bits per second
(bps) is the measure of speed that data moves between various parts of the computer.

On the first generation of computers, papertape and punched card were used. This was where a machine punched holes in a piece of card or tape, this was then read and the data interpreted. Kimball tags are used on retail goods, the tag is a small punched card attached to the good, which provides the data, required to sell the good through a till.

Nowadays magnetic strip readers and bar code readers are more commonly used. One example where this type of technology is used is the back of a credit card.

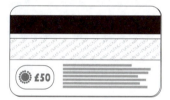

If you turn a credit card over there is a strip running along the card; this holds a magnetic pattern. When swiped by a magnetic strip reader, this pattern is read and then interpreted into the required format. A bar code reader uses similar technology; it is most commonly used in supermarkets to collect the product code. Using this method speeds up the time it takes to serve one person and, as a result, can shorten the queuing time.

Optical mark readers (OMR) are most commonly used in the reading of multiple choice examination papers. The document is scanned and the marks detected and then converted into a value.

Optical character recognition (OCR) is a method to get data into a computer system where a hard copy version already exists. It is a fast and cheap but poor in quality. The method scans text and builds up an image comprising a pixel image and then is compared to a stored character or set of characters.

Magnetic ink character recognition (MICR) is used mainly in the processing and production of bank's cheques. Special ink and characters are used, which can be magnetised for automatic reading. The reader recognises the magnetic field on the cheque and converts it to readable code.

Voice data capture is activated by spoken commands rather than by typing commands in to a keyboard, clicking with a mouse, or pushing buttons. This is commonly being used in offices for dictation and control systems where some form of voice activated input is required.

Figure 7.3 *Extract from an information sheet produced by a Vocational A-level ICT student*

baud rate actually measures the number of events, or signal changes that occur in one second.

A 9600 baud modem that encodes 4 bits per event, actually operates at 2400 baud but transmits 9600 bits per second.

Exercise 7.3

Find out the speed of your modem.

Hardware functions Different CPUs will process information at different speeds. The faster the computer's internal clock, the faster information will be processed. This is generally measured in terms of MHz.

Exercise 7.4

Find out the clock speed on your computer.

It is not solely the CPU that determines how fast data will be processed, but it is also the architecture of the computer. However, the quicker the CPU, the faster information will be processed. Many computers now have more than one processor so that each can perform different functions in parallel, to speed up the whole processing activity. This is called **parallel processing**.

Software functions are linked to the hardware. The computer's hardware configuration will depend upon how fast the software operates. There are also different types of computer software that will make varying demands on the computer system. The speed at which software will run also depends upon which operating system is being used.

In the past sound, video and data was transmitted using analogue wave, today this is increasingly becoming replaced with **digital technology**.

Digital techniques allow greater accuracy and transmit considerably more information over the same physical links. With the introduction of fibre optic cables where signals are transmitted using pulses of light to represent the on–off bit of information, digital transmission is becoming the standard. An example of digital techniques taking over from **analogue technology** is the ISDN telephone system. This uses digital techniques to transfer the sound instead of analogue methods currently used in most homes and, consequently, this has been of great benefit to users of the Internet.

With all the new technologies becoming available, constant retraining is necessary. Software has been created to help with this retraining. Multimedia software is used for interactive teaching which meets the needs of retraining.

Exercise 7.5

Think of examples where multimedia software is used for teaching in your school or college.

 Activity 7.10

Research the developments in speed in the new technologies, and answer these questions:

★ What effect has component miniaturisation had on the costs and quality of computer hardware?

★ What effect has the Internet had on the access to information and services?

★ What is an Internet café?

★ In what way have the technologies of telephone, fax, television, photography, electronic mail, Internet, on-line databases converged?

★ Apart from access to the Internet, how can information in the home be increased?

★ How has bandwidth and connection affected the functionality of communications equipment?

★ How have the changes in input methods helped a non-ICT literate user to access ICT?

★ In what ways has improved resolution affected video, film and multimedia?

★ Is there a need for users to be constantly retrained? Explain your answer.

★ How has the functionality of software increased?

★ How has the compatibility in software packages enabled the same platform to be used?

The information society

History shows the move from the agricultural society, through the industrialised society and now to the information society.

The increased availability of information has affected public services in many ways and it is important to decide whether society is better served as a result.

This section considers five areas:

- ✪ Information services
- ✪ Emergency services
- ✪ The National Health Service
- ✪ Education
- ✪ Public transport

Facilities are changing through the use of ICT

▼▼▼▼▼▼▼▼
Touch screen
is a special type of monitor that is able to detect a user's finger pointing at a particular area on the screen.
▲▲▲▲▲▲▲▲

Touch screens, may be found at Tourist Information Offices, train stations, airports and libraries. People can inform themselves, even when staffed offices are closed.

Activity 7.11

Identify at least one touch screen – copy the screen and explain how it is used.

▼▼▼▼▼▼▼▼
Automatic teller machines (ATMs)
use computer technology to transfer money, and provide customers with extra facilities such as a printed balance or details of recent transactions.
▲▲▲▲▲▲▲▲

Automatic teller machines (ATMs) provided by banks in a range of locations.

Exercise 7.6

What are the benefits of the ATMs for the user and for the bank. What facilities do ATM machines offer? What security checks exist with ATMs?

Information boards are provided in motorway service stations and railway stations.

On-screen help is available in different languages, for example in telephone boxes.

Activity 7.12

Visit a phone box, check how these facilities work, make notes on the language options.

Virtual reality (VR) systems can be used in training, education and entertainment. Using advanced graphics, users are transposed to a realistic, interactive environment. A headset, possibly incorporating sound, enables increased interaction.

A program might simulate the user walking through a house. As the user turns his/her head, s/he sees different parts of the room. Wearing a headset can make the image seem very real.

More recently, data gloves have also been introduced, the computer will sense movements from the user's hand and the computer will make a response.

Exercise 7.7

Think of another example where this type of VR would be useful.

Virtual reality is not just being used for entertainment; many industries are using VR in design and training.

Architects use VR to visualise new designs for buildings.

Aviation authorities use VR in their education of new trainees by simulating flights.

Marketing departments use VR as a means of advertising their product/organisation.

VR is also being used to treat sufferers of child abuse and people who are afraid of heights. Muscular dystrophy patients can learn to use a wheelchair through virtual reality.

The Fire Service

The Fire Service has launched its biggest training initiative where every fire brigade in Britain will evaluate a new VR training simulator that teaches officers to react to major incidents. One of the main benefits of VR training is that where it simulates danger, there is no immediate risk to the fire officers. It also reduces costs. It can take up to a dozen engines, 60 fire-fighters and £10,000 to stage an 'accident' that will usefully train just one of the 5500 incident commanding officers. The types of VR training involved in this project include severe road traffic accidents and massive fires, where the officers can walk around a 3D model. Simulated in the model would be real-life smoke, people running around, presence of other emergency services, etc. The VR models react to the decisions that the commanding officers make. If they make the wrong decisions, the situation can deteriorate.

Information services

The increased availability of information has meant that some organisations have had to revise their methods of operation. Table 7.1 shows how ICT has affected public services like directory enquiries.

Activity 7.13

Visit a library which has yet to be computerised and see how long it takes to locate a specific publication, timing yourself and noting down how easy it is.
Visit a library that has been computerised, and see how long locating a specific publication takes.
Compare the two libraries.

Emergency services

When a 999 call is made (or 112 which is now the international standard), the details are taken, patched through to the appropriate emergency service, a signal is sent and the appropriate action taken. At a fire station, a printout is received of the location of the call and the nature of the problem.

Table 7.1 *How ICT has affected public services*

Place	How?	Why?
Directory enquiries	Operators can trace telephone numbers, searching the database by a person's surname and location	Saves time and phone bill (waiting time reduced)
Mail order	If you give your postcode and house number, your full postal address will automatically be displayed for the operator	Saves the operator time in having to ask you questions and keying in the whole address, The more the operator has to key in, the increased chance of inaccuracies; typing errors are possible, for example 'Horley' or 'Hawley'
Museums	On line information about the exhibits	Enlivens visits and makes for a more interesting experience
Libraries	On line database system allowing user to run own searches on book title, author, how many copies out on loan and when they are due back	Saves time and staff

Exercise 7.8

How does the use of ICT in the emergency services affect you as an individual, and society as a whole?

Law enforcement organisations also use ICT as an information source.

The police have databases of criminal records. They can check to see if a person has had, for example, a previous speeding or petty theft offence.

The National Health Service

If you are admitted to the Accident and Emergency (A&E) department in a hospital, you will be asked for your name and postcode. From this information, the staff can search the NHS database and gain access to all your medical records, e.g. the name of your doctor, and your date of birth.

ICT has also helped in the field of data acquisition. For example, the use of monitors, scanners and analysers, which aid the medical profession in performing surgery. Expert systems have enabled diagnoses to be made.

Within the community, all infant records are entered into a central database. These records could be then transferred from one health authority to another. ICT also assists in compiling statistics within a health authority. Nationally, all statistics can be collated together to show, for example, levels of immunisation both locally and nationally. ICT has also helped statisticians to predict life expectancies.

Exercise 7.9

How does the use of ICT in the NHS affect you as an individual, and society as a whole?

Education

Within education, ICT is being used extensively not just as a part of the National Curriculum requirements but as a management, assessment, diagnostic, and statistical tool.

- ✪ For management, ICT can help run the administrative services by using student databases within schools which catalogue all the student's details, name, date of birth, etc. and their examination results.

- ✪ Through use of spreadsheet applications, statistical analysis can be performed and resultant performance indicators used to improve standards.

- ✪ Use of ICT in schools as a means of education is vital. As this chapter illustrates, ICT is the way ahead and those who are not computer literate will have difficulties in tomorrow's society!

- ✪ The use of ICT in the classroom can enhance the possibility of diversity – students may be allowed to proceed at their own pace.

- ✪ ICT can aid students in improving their own learning through multimedia applications and self-help packages.

- ✪ Virtual reality systems may be used too for educational stimuli: exploring artificial environments, imaginary or reality based.

- ✪ For those people who are unable to attend educational establishments, distance learning may be introduced.

Activity
7.14

For one week, log how much ICT-related work that you do in school and how much ICT-orientated equipment you used at home. Then write a report on how you would have performed the tasks you used with the ICT equipment – if it was not invented yet!

Public transport

One of the most common applications of ICT is the use of information boards displaying waiting times at bus stops, airports, train and tube stations. They give precise up-to-date information, whereas previously the only guidance to waiting times would have been a hardcopy timetable or possibly a public announcement in the larger stations. Drivers have also been given direct communication with the depot through the use of ICT. Roadside tracking devices are being used to determine the exact location of buses so these can be monitored by the depot.

Activity
7.15

Visit a bus/train/motorway service station or airport. Write down any useful information that the information boards display and explain why it is useful.

★ How would you have obtained this information if this technology had not been available?

★ Are the information boards an advantage?

You could work in small groups for this activity and share information.

In the aviation industry, ICT is being used in aeroplanes with their in-flight technology, autopilot, radio-tracking, etc. More commonly in the motor industry ICT is being used through new devices such as in-car traffic announcements. Mobile phone companies have homed in on this part of the industry and are offering phones that give information on the latest traffic situation when a number is keyed in.

Joe Bloggsheim from Germany

Joe is visiting the Lake District. He goes to a tourist information centre but it is shut – it is a Bank Holiday! He wants to find out about the local attractions, so he uses touch screens, which are located outside the tourist information centre. He finds out he needs a train to get to where he wants to go. He reads the information board at the train station to find out the train times. He needs to draw cash out of his bank but it too is shut, so he uses ATM which has an on-screen language help facility. He finally calls a friend to tell her about his holiday, using a telephone with on-screen help to dial the number.

Activity 7.16

Write a report on how Mr Bloggsheim would have managed before technology of touch screens, etc. Is he better informed from the ICT he has used?

The impact of ICT on working practices

Working practices have been affected by ICT. It is important to look at the ways in which they have been affected and to assess whether the consequences have been positive. This section consider three topics:

- ✪ Location and pattern
- ✪ Work skills and retraining
- ✪ The social aspect for employees and employers

Location and pattern

With advances in technology, working from home is a realistic goal, particularly with the cost of computers and communication continually falling.

Did You Know?

Futurist Alvin Toffler popularised the term 'electronic cottage' to describe a home where modern technology allows a person to work.

Did You Know?

Stress is thought to be caused, not by the amount of work you do, but by the lack of control you feel you have over the work you are doing.

There are advantages of employees working from home:

- ✪ Fewer people are commuting to work so fewer cars are on the road. This reduces **pollution** and **congestion**.

- ✪ There is an increased amount of **leisure time** – not commuting can save many hours a day. This, in turn, may have the knock-on effect of increasing motivation to work and increasing job satisfaction.

- ✪ Working from home gives people the option to work **flexi-time** and hence not have to fall in to the standard conventions of a nine-to-five routine. This allows greater interaction with the family, e.g. parents working during the school times, or when children are asleep. It also allows those with other responsibilities, e.g. aged parents, to meet both obligations (home and work). Individuals can also shop when it is not so busy, work when it rains, do the gardening when it's not – basically giving individuals more control over their own time.

- ✪ **Hotdesking** saves office space and hence costs. People share desk space, using any available desk when in the office. Generally, this desk has a network link and hotdesking employees all have laptops.

Organisations such as British Telecom use hotdesking in some departments. When in the office, BT staff use a password to log onto the ICT system, so the telephone system and computer network know where they are.

Digital Equipment Corporation (DEC)

DEC pioneered flexible working in the UK in the early 1990s with one hotdesk for every two employees. More recently that has changed to one department having eight hotdesks for over 100 people. It has been calculated that, through the flexible working practices that Digital promote, in the UK alone, £3.5 million have been saved.

With the changes that have occurred in working practices, society as a whole has more leisure time. This in itself has meant changes in the leisure industry. There are now many more ways to occupy leisure time: cinemas, bowling, leisure parks, and activity centres.

Working from home has also given parents the flexibility to keep working, or to work part time. Employees can work from home and look after their children at the same time. This has had a direct impact on childcare provision. Working from home, however, can cause problems at two ends of the continuum:

- ✪ Those who are not self-disciplined enough to work without supervision
- ✪ Those who become addicted to work – the workaholic

Some jobs require communication and contact with people overseas, so not all offices work on a nine-to-five basis.

Activity 7.17

★ Do you know anyone who works from home? If you do, ask them if you could interview them.

★ Give feedback from your interview to the rest of the group.

★ Would you want to work from home? If so why? If not, why not?

ICT has meant that 24-hour operation is possible. With robots and automated procedures, working throughout the night is common practice in many industries.

Activity 7.18

Find out the local industries which work on a 24-hour operational basis.

What are the limitations/advantages of operating such a system?

Work skills and retraining

With the information age, many people had to increase their knowledge and understanding of work skills. Humans began being replaced by automated machinery, such as robots. With the advances in automation, people who used to do jobs such as shorthand typing, operating lathes and tills became deskilled.

Exercise 7.10

Think of some more jobs that have been deskilled.

On the other hand, due to the information age, there are jobs requiring a great deal of new skill. Programming of computers is one good example, the very cause of the deskilling in the first place.

Exercise 7.11

Think of some more jobs that have been reskilled.

As a result of deskilling/reskilling, retraining on a large scale has had to be implemented. This has resulted in a whole new industry of people who are responsible for training.

Activity 7.19

Find out what courses are available for those wanting to retrain.

The social aspect for employees and employers

Although there are many benefits of working from home, there are also disadvantages:

✪ Some employees gain a great deal of satisfaction from having praise bestowed upon them when a job is done well. Using computer technology seems to depersonalise the whole process. Supervision disappears as employees may work at home.

✪ Those who find themselves in positions where they are not directly supervised can lose motivation and become bored. This may also be made worse by the lack of contact with colleagues.

- Quality may also suffer if employees take the attitude 'no one sees me doing the job, so it doesn't really matter'.

- There are fewer opportunities for brainstorming with colleagues, and so problems may take longer to solve. Many hands make light work! The idea-sharing process may be lost while, at the same time, '**team work**' is one of the latest buzzwords in industry.

- **Job security**: increased automation and computer technology puts jobs at risk. Robots take over jobs that were reserved for humans and are doing those jobs much more quickly and with fewer errors. As employers cannot predict the pace at which ICT may progress, in industries where ICT is fundamental, short-term contracts may be offered. Therefore, staff lose any sense of job security.

- Increased **stress** can be due to the pace of change, and changes in supervision, plus the lack of job security.

Activity 7.20

Hold a classroom debate putting forward arguments for/against introducing automation into the office environment and the introduction of a scheme for working from home.

Back all arguments with facts and case studies from organisations that have experienced similar changes.

Using ICT can also cause problems when errors occur. Who is to blame? Well, the computer!

ICT also has an effect on the employers and they too experience stress. There will be a need to change the way staff are supervised, especially when employees work from home. This may have a knock-on effect on rates of pay. There may not be a need for direct line supervisors and employees may be supervised by using a performance-related pay (PRP) scheme or fixed-price contracts.

With increased automation, the initial investment costs are high. Organisations need to do extensive research into the long-term effects that automation may have on their organisations. If the long-term prospects of automation are good, managers need to be very careful how they market the introduction of automating processes: they generally mean job losses which may well stimulate union opposition.

Activity

7.21

Automation doesn't cause unemployment, because more people are needed to make the new technology, in fact, it creates jobs!

List the arguments that support and those that contradict this statement. What evidence can you find for these arguments?

The impact of ICT on methods of production

Did You Know?

Just-in-time (JIT) manufacturing is a technique devised to hold in stock only the precise amount required, therefore reducing costs of stock on the shelf.

ICT has improved the processes of production and process control, including the introduction of robotics.

Computers can be used to control a variety of processes, e.g. logging employees' hours of work, paint spraying cars, advising the user that stock levels are too low and more parts need to be ordered.

Exercise 7.12

List five ways in which production has changed.

Activity

7.22

Figure 7.4 shows an extract produced by a student. Read the extract and then research around the topic, re-writing the notes in your own words, supplying more detail.

Production control; production needs to respond quickly to changes in demand and requires up-to-date information. Machine loading, material control, batch size calculations and machine utilisation are all ways in which the computer can help. Computers are able to handle more complex calculations and sort through large amounts of data quickly and accurately.

Process control is the direct control of physical processes. Process control has improved dramatically since digital techniques have been introduced. Process control focuses on the automatic monitoring of an industrial based activity. The use of computers has enabled accurate and quick responses saving time and money. Computer feedback information via sensors and the appropriate action will be taken.

Figure 7.4   *Extract from a student's notes on production and process control*

Activity 7.23

Write to companies about any computerised processes they have. Find out the company's reasons for computerisation/automation in terms of cost, employment implications, and the benefits and limitations since the introduction of ICT.

You may like to use relevant experiences from part-time jobs or work experience.

Looking at production and process control since ICT has been introduced, Table 7.2 lists the benefits and limitations.

Table 7.2 *Benefits and limitations of ICT in production*

Factor	Benefit/Limitation
Speed	Undoubtedly quicker, e.g. 24-hour car manufacture – robots do not suffer from fatigue, illness, boredom, attitude.
Decision-making process	Decisions can be made instantaneously, often without human intervention.
Cost	Initial outlay for machinery and equipment high, but long-term profits better due to processes being completed more quickly and with greater precision.
Safety	Eliminates need for humans to work in hazardous environments, such as having to deal with toxic substances.
Quality	Quality of product should be just as high as with manual methods. Computers are programmed to feed back information to ensure a consistently high service is given. For example, sensors are used to ensure that the correct amount of paint is being sprayed on cars; if the paint is not being sprayed within the defined tolerances, production will cease until the problem has been rectified.

Exercise 7.13

Suggest more factors for Table 7.2.

Automation through ICT has affected issues such as health and safety (H&S), employment levels and working practices.

With the introduction of more automation, H&S issues have been reviewed. Legislation is covered on pages 340–8 with specific reference to ICT. (Levels of employment and working practices were discussed on pages 312–17.)

The changes in working practices have not only affected the business world but, as can be seen from the examples given above, have affected society as a whole.

The effects of ICT on the environment

With the introduction of ICT, many things have been promised, including a **paperless office** and a global society.

Exercise 7.14

List the effects of ICT on the environment, and identify goals that ICT may help society to achieve.

Paper, paper and more paper!

Communications can be made without paper via e-mails, electronic files, verbal communication, etc.

★ *Before computers were used extensively, a facsimile (fax) was a much used item of office equipment. Nowadays, faxes are becoming rarer and office staff send and receive data between computers over telephone lines by e-mail. Video links allow staff within companies to talk and see each other, reducing other costs too, e.g. travel costs.*

★ *Designers can create drawings using graphics packages, therefore using paper hardly at all.*

Activity 7.24

Figure 7.5 shows an extract from a newspaper article. Read the article, research the topic further and then comment about what you have read.

The Paperless Society, FACT or FICTION?

Existing documents can be either typed or scanned on to the organisation's system. In some industries, for example, there are certain legal reasons for keeping paper copies of documents on site for a certain period of time. Some car manufacturers are required to keep original paper copies of all drawings relating to

specific models in archives for at least forty years. These do not necessarily need to be kept on site. In doing this, the amount of paper used will be reduced. Memos, agendas, minutes can all be sent by e-mail in electronic files. This does not just have to be an internal function, networks will allow

external transfer of information. This would lead to a paperless society surely? It has been argued that, in fact, computers generate more paperwork. The amount of mail that is delivered to our houses has increased with the computing age; mail merges and information databases have enabled more 'junk' mail to appear on the doormat.

Figure 7.5 *Extract from a newspaper article*

Activity 7.25

Find out about any local industries using computerised methods rather than paper methods for keeping documents. List any reasons why companies may have to keep paper copies of documents.

Global society

Improved travel and communication break down barriers of distance and time between countries:

✪ E-mail messages can be sent without regard for the recipient's office hours.

✪ Organisations can buy and sell anywhere in the world – not just within driving distance.

✪ International communication helps to increase understanding between people of different cultures and so reduces prejudice.

Positive and negative effects

It would be short-sighted to consider only the positive effects that ICT has on the environment. You must also look at the drawbacks (Table 7.3).

Table 7.3   *Negative effects of ICT on the environment*

Factor	Effect
Changes in transportation needs	More leisure time may increase amount of time spent on the road, driving to/from leisure.
Increased pollution	Pollution of air by particles of toner from the printer, noise pollution in closed environment, static electricity, electromagnetic radiation.
Computers are driven by electricity	Use of scarce resources.
Control of pollution	Computers respond to changes in the environment detected by sensors; if these sensors fail or incorrect data is transmitted, problems may occur. A simple example of this may be a computer-controlled greenhouse, where sensors detect the humidity, temperature, etc., in the greenhouse. If the sensors fail, and incorrect information is supplied to the computer, the plants may die.

Exercise 7.15

Suggest some more negative effects for Table 7.3.

Legislation for ICT users

Table 7.4 lists the most relevant legislation relating to ICT.

Table 7.4   *Legislation for ICT users*

Acts	Date	Description
Health and Safety at Work Act	1974	Outlines general duties which employers have to employees and members of the public, and employees have to themselves and to each other
Data Protection Act	1984	A safeguard to control personal data
Copyright, Designs and Patents Act	1988	Protects 'intellectual property' and establishes the rights of the author.
Electricity at Work Regulations	1989	Protects against the most common accidents caused by electrical faults
Computer Misuse Act	1990	Protects against misuse of both hardware and software
Obscene Publications Act	1990	Trys to prevent obscene material being published
Health and Safety Regulations	1992	Explains what employers must do and what equipment must be like
Data Protection Act	1998	Revised version of 1984 Act

Activity 7.26

A student was set a task of finding out about all the legislation relating to ICT. Figure 7.6 shows an extract from a report that the student has produced. In copying this extract, the last two sections were omitted: Obscene Publications Act of 1990 and the Data Protection Act 1998. Check that you agree with what has been written and fill in the gaps.

Legislation relating to ICT

Data Protection Act 12th July 1984: This sets out requirements for the control of personal data. The Act aims to safeguard integrity, privacy and security of personal data. It ensures that the registered holder of the data attends to matters such as the accuracy and the appropriateness of the data. Data users are required to be part of a public register supplying details about themselves and the nature, purpose and range of the data they hold. If an organisation plans to keep personal information about people on a computer other than names and addresses for more than 30 days, it must register with the Data Protection Registrar. If a data user holds personal data about an individual, that individual can require the data user to supply a copy of that data. At all times, organisations must obtain the data fairly, for example not tell people it wants the data for one purpose, when they really want it for something else.

Computer Misuse Act 1990: This Act is aimed at computer 'hackers'. It defines computer misuse as the unauthorised use of computer systems and relates both to hardware (using a particular computer without permission) and software (accessing parts of the system without authorisation). It introduced three new offences relating to unauthorised computer access and to unauthorised modification or deletion of data. It aims to prevent anti-social behaviour such as computer pornography.

Health and Safety at Work Act 1974: This Act provides a framework for governing the actions of employers and employees. The Act sets out general duties which employers have to employees and members of the public, and employees have to themselves and to each other. The Health & Safety Act is a large document but, to summarise, employers are required to: assess risks to health and safety of their employees and provide risk assessment, implement any health and safety measures as identified by the risk assessment, set up emergency procedure provisions and provide employees with clear instructions as well as training where necessary. The Act covers general issues such as eye strain, radiation from VDU screens, stress, ergonomics and hazards.

Electricity at Work Regulations 1989: As many accidents in the work place are related to electricity, the Electricity at Work Regulations are in place to prevent the most common accidents. For example, the Act states that electrical wires should be well covered and should not stretch across walkways.

Health and Safety Regulations 1992: These Regulations explain what employers must do and what the equipment must be like. The regulations appertain to normal use of a computer. The regulations are lengthy but cover aspects such as: work surfaces, breaks from using the computer, sight testing and training.

Copyright, Designs and Patents Act 1988: This Act protects 'intellectual property' and establishes the rights of the author. The unauthorised use of any software that has not been properly purchased with a software license is illegal. In-practice, this means that copying software bought by someone else is likely to be an offence. For example, you cannot copy your friend's software, even to try it out. Copyright relating to written material usually continues until 70 years after an author's death.

Obscene Publications Act 1990: ....

Data Protection Act 1998 ....

Figure 7.6 *Extract from a student's report on legislation for ICT users*

Imagine that you work in an office that uses ICT every day. Obtain a copy of the Health and Safety Act 1992 Regulations. Draw a picture of a person sitting at a computer and write a list of do's and don'ts for this person. Write a report to the managing director of your organisation, highlighting the main points of the Regulations and explaining your concerns.

Reasons for legislation

Each piece of legislation has been drawn up to protect the user in some way:

- ✪ To meet moral obligations to protect workers from harm and to minimise the effects of exposure to uncensored materials
- ✪ To provide legal backing so that it is possible to seek redress if rights are violated
- ✪ To protect the confidentiality of information kept about the individual
- ✪ To observe copyright for those who create original works

Computer crime is a large industry and many millions of pounds are lost each year due to computer misuse/fraud. Therefore, it is essential to have some form of legislation to protect companies and the individual.

It is not only the users that the legislation is there to protect, but the employers/company owners themselves.

Exercise 7.16

Suggest other legislation that might be introduced.

Threats to information

Any information that is kept on a system is subject to corruption, sabotage, industrial espionage and theft. This can be split further into large-scale organisational theft and personal theft.

Large-scale organisations must try to prevent industrial espionage, malicious interference and deliberate acts of destruction. Personal data must be protected

Did You Know?

In 1996 the FBI announced that 40% of corporate, university and government sites had been violated by, for example, changing data, stealing passwords and preventing legitimate users from gaining access to systems.

against blackmail and unauthorised disclosure. The two most common ways that this theft takes place are **bugging** and **hacking**. Being aware of the problems should make it easier to prevent the loss.

Exercise 7.17

Choose four measures from the list in Figure 7.7 and expand on these ideas further.

Measures that can be taken to prevent theft of data, software and hardware

- Using password protection, not the name of your favourite pets!
- Recording registration numbers of software licenses and of hardware components
- Introducing government legislation
- Shredding of all unwanted hardcopy documentation
- Installing keyboard locks
- Having secured areas in places where data is sensitive, for example only allow people with appropriate access into these areas
- Carrying out spot checks
- Using encryption software to scramble transmissions; cryptosystem
- Taking backups
- Avoiding inadvertently leaving yourself logged on to a networked system
- Restricting physical access
- Constructing firewalls to guard against unauthorised access to an internal network

Figure 7.7 *The results of a brainstorming session*

EU legislation

On joining the European Union (EU), consideration of their legislation also had to be taken into account. The EU also have regulations on the use of computers and the Internet Code of Practice.

**Activity
7.28**

Explore the EU legislation and write a report which
identifies the main factors on the use of computers and
the Internet Code of Practice.

The future use of ICT

ICT has changed dramatically over the past century. It will continue to have an
impact on society, although it is difficult to predict how it will develop in the
21st century. Here we will look at its potential impact in four areas:

- ✪ Financial transactions
- ✪ Shopping habits
- ✪ Personal safety and freedom
- ✪ Commercial security

Financial transactions

In the future, these will be fully computerised. Before long there should be no
reason to carry cash since all transactions can be done using a smart card.
Indeed, cash may soon become a commodity of the past.

IBM

IBM presented their version of the future at the IATA
Passenger Services Conference in Los Angeles. Their vision
includes booking an airline ticket without having to be
served by staff – by use of a touch screen and a smart card.
All the information is downloaded directly on to the card,
which is then placed into a machine at the airport. Options
are given about seat preference and the gate number is
printed. The smart card then acts as a boarding pass at the
gate. At no point is a ticket ever issued to the traveller, the
smart card contains all the information. American Airlines
is trialling this system.

Shopping habits

More and more people are now using the World Wide Web (WWW) to do their shopping. Many information sources such as the Yellow Pages have been computerised. Customers can request specific goods, the price of goods, and place orders through a computer.

Activity 7.29

Explore some Internet sites, e.g. Amazon.com, to see how shopping has become a reality on the Internet.

★ What does the purchaser need to do to be able to buy products on the net?

★ Are there any risks?

★ What may be the effect on 'normal' shops in the high street?

★ What may be the effect on individual shoppers?

★ What may be the effect on society?

Visa Cash

Visa Cash is a new type of payment card, called an electronic purse. It contains a microchip used for purchasing low-cost items. Using a cash loader, you put the card in the machine and transfer up to £50 from your Visa credit or debit card. To make a purchase you simply put the card into a Visa Cash terminal, key in the correct amount and the card is debited. There is no need to sign anything. To check the amount remaining on the card, you just put it into a card reader, it will shown the amount left and detail the last five transactions made.

Personal safety and freedom

Global Positioning Systems (GPS) can be used to track individuals, these ideas have already been introduced with the electronic tagging of criminals. How far are we actually away from the technology that can be seen in *Men in Black*?

Activity 7.30

Watch the film, *Men In Black*.

★ Write a report on the futuristic technology that is used in the film.

★ How close are we to some of the concepts?

★ Which ones do you think will become a reality in this century?

GPS is also being used with trains!

GPS and trains

A computer system on board trains determines the motion of the train against its position pinpointed by GPS satellites. This measures the smoothness of the journey, in an effort to locate parts of the track that are worn out. The information is fed to the headquarters where it is seen on a computer screen, it is overlaid on an Ordinance Survey map and problem areas on the network are identified.

Geographic Information Systems (GIS) is making crime scenes easier to find, and is allowing police to keep tabs on incidents and resources.

The Metropolitan Police

The Metropolitan Police are using GIS to display maps and then zoom in to any street or location and overlay details of crime incidents, traffic accidents and street patrols.

Surrey Police

Surrey Police are using a system which relies on a series of filmed scenarios depicting a crime scene, which is projected onto a screen set up within a firing range. The latest in interactive response techniques allows shots to be fired at a screen with hits logged on the central computer. Trainees interact with the scenarios shouting at them to stand still, drop weapons, etc., making the situations as 'real' as possible, preparing them for real life experience.

Smart card system at Aston University

At Aston University in Birmingham, a Smart card is essential to students' movements around the campus. It acts as a library card, an identification card, a card with which to purchase food and a card which permits access to certain parts of the campus. A machine not dissimilar to hole-in-the-wall machines loads it and when credit is low, students reload their cards with denominations from £5 to £100.

Swipe cards in a school in Birmingham

A school in Birmingham uses this technology to make the school a safer environment. On each of the doors of the school, there is a card reader which students must swipe to gain entry to the building. This prohibits anyone without a card entering the school.

The card is multifunctional as it also operates a cash-less canteen system where students must load money on their card for brunch and lunch each day. No money is taken at the till, the card is simply swiped and the money debited.

The card also operates printing and photocopying within the school and has the student's picture on it for ease of identification.

Activity 7.31

Think about how the technology is used at Aston University and the school in Birmingham, and write a report on how you think this type of technology may benefit your school/college.

Commercial security

Systems are being developed to improve detection of theft.

Activity 7.32

★ Working in small groups research the most recent developments in ICT.

★ Suggest another example of each of the entries for Table 7.5 and state how far on the technology has progressed, and then copy and complete Table 7.5.

Table 7.5 *Recent innovations that are still in the development/research stage*

Innovation	Description
Automatic speech recognition	Helping the disabled to communicate via computer technology
Virtual reality	Network VR simulations could enable people in many different locations to participate in teleconferences, virtual surgical operations, or simulated military training exercises
Intelligent agents	
Cyberspace facilities	
Microtechnology	
Nanotechnology	
Artificial intelligence and artificial life	

Activity 7.33

Watch a film set in the future (e.g. *Men in Black*). Write a report on the futuristic technology used in the film.

★ How close are we to some of the concepts?

★ Which ones do you think will become a reality in this century?

Have a look at older science fiction films or TV shows for an idea of how people's perceptions of the future have changed!

Revision questions

1 List three measures that can be taken to prevent theft of data, software and hardware.

2 What is virtual reality?

3 What are the dates of these Acts?
   Health and Safety at Work Act
   Copyright, Designs and Patents Act
   Electricity at Work Regulations.
   Computer Misuse Act
   Obscene Publications Act
   Health and Safety Regulations

4 What is the Data Protection Act (1998)?

5 What do the letters COBOL stand for?

6 What type of language is Pascal?

7 Explain how a touch screen works.

8 From the table, fill in the missing gaps:

9 What is an information board and where could you find one?

10 What is information compression?

11 What is a pixel?

12 What is hotdesking?

13 If a person has been deskilled, what has happened to them?

14 What does the term 'paperless office' mean?

15 What is meant by the term 'global society'?

16 How can the Internet have an impact upon shopping habits?

17 What is GPS?

Different types of cable / communication and their main features	
Type	**Features**
	A pair of insulated copper wires twisted together, surrounded by copper braid and insulation, most common application, data transmission
Fibre optic cable	
	Highly directional transmitters and receivers with dish aerials, most common applications public telephone service
Satellite	

Good Working Practice Guide

The type of information kept on an ICT system, and possibly transmitted to other users, is subject to laws. Computers make the spread of information easy and the detection of abuse is quite difficult.

Among the laws introduced to combat computer-based crime are:

✪ Computer Misuse Act (1990)

✪ Copyright, Designs and Patents Act (1998)

✪ Obscene Publications Act (1990)

Although you do not need to learn about all these laws for the compulsory units in your Vocational A-level course, you can learn more about them if you choose the unit linked to Chapter 7: *Impact of ICT on Society*.

Whichever units you decide to take, you should be aware of two important pieces of legislation:

✪ Health and safety issues (see page 340).

✪ The Data Protection Act (see page 343)

and other good working practices expected of you during your practical work.

For your work to progress smoothly, you can help yourself by adopting standard ways of working. This can also help you to work well with others.

In several units, standard ways of working are listed, e.g. in Unit 1: *Presenting Information*. You must apply these techniques to *all* of your ICT work.

Standard ways of working

There are many reasons for having standard ways of working in ICT. The most important is that information in ICT systems can be easily lost or misused.

- ✪ Unauthorised persons may gain access to confidential information.
- ✪ People may copy original work and present it as their own.
- ✪ Data files may be lost, corrupted by a virus or damaged in other ways.
- ✪ Computers may be damaged so that data stored in them cannot be recovered.
- ✪ Information presented professionally may be believed, even though it may be inaccurate.

Standard ways of working help you to overcome these problems. In your work with ICT you must ensure that you manage your work effectively, keep information secure and work safely.

Managing your work

- ✪ Plan your work to produce what is required to given deadlines.
- ✪ Use standard formats.
- ✪ Enter information so that you can easily make changes, e.g. using spaces, tabs and indents correctly to ensure consistent layout.
- ✪ Edit and save work regularly.
- ✪ Use file names that are sensible and remind you of the contents.
- ✪ Store files where you can easily find them in the directory/folder structure.
- ✪ Make dated backup copies of your work giving an idea of sequence.
- ✪ When you are using any information that has been collected using secondary research, check it for validity and cross reference with other books to ensure that it is correct.
- ✪ Keep a log of your work, especially any ICT problems you meet and how you solve them.

Preventing errors

Errors can happen easily:

- ✪ The operator miskeys while keying.
- ✪ The wrong disk or tape is used.
- ✪ The hardware malfunctions.
- ✪ The power fails.

Equipment faults can happen with the hardware, e.g. the screen, disk or tape. It is important to keep equipment and surfaces free of dust, and to store tapes and disks in sleeves or covers.

Loss of information can be damaging for the user. They can be embarrassed and might lose customers. At worst, a business may fail.

It is important to store consumables in a cool, dry and dust-free environment, and to replace them correctly. A paper jam when your deadline is fast approaching will not help!

Keeping information secure

You must learn to keep information secure (e.g. from theft, loss, viruses and fire), protecting confidentiality, and respecting copyright.

Security of data

Having data on an ICT system rather than in paper files has advantages and disadvantages.

- ✪ Lots of data can be stored on a single floppy disk.
- ✪ The data is more easily moved and removed (e.g. stolen).
- ✪ If linked via networks, access is quite easy.

To improve security, two types of control can be used:

1 **Physical control** includes locking doors, storing data in safes and issuing ID cards to users.

2 **Logical control** includes using a password system and setting different access levels for different members of staff.

Protection from viruses

Viruses can damage the files on an ICT system. To avoid introducing viruses, some simple precautions can be taken:

- **Install virus checking software on the system which checks all files as they are opened.**
- **Do not open files from sources that are unknown to you, e.g. sent over the Internet as attached files.**

Protection from fire

Fires can start from cables and connectors that are not electrically sound. It is also unwise to overload sockets.

Protecting confidentiality

People or companies may wish to keep information confidential so that others do not know about it. You must learn to keep this type of information secure and not pass it on to others (e.g. preventing illegal access to medical or criminal records).

Password systems aim to restrict access to data, and these systems are fine, so long as you keep your password secret. Surveys on choices of passwords show that most people choose obvious ones, which are easy for friends to guess: the name of their pet, or a favourite place.

With more and more people using Internet cafés, it is quite easy to watch someone entering a password, and then use this to gain access to files and information which is private to that person.

One way to avoid this problem is to change your password regularly. Then you have to remember what the current one is!

Respecting copyright laws

A computer program, words, pictures and graphic images may belong to other people. The people who created or own this material have copyright and you must not use their work without their permission. If you do, you are breaking the law. You must understand and respect copyright law. Where you do use information created by others, and have obtained their permission, it is important that you acknowledge the source, by using an appropriate reference or listing it in a bibliography.

Security procedures

If work stored on an ICT system is lost, it is important that there is another file that can be used in its place. You will need to understand and use suitable security procedures when using ICT systems:

- Making backup copies of your work
- Keeping dated backup copies of files on another disk and in another location
- Saving work regularly, and using different filenames

Backing-up data should be done regularly, e.g. daily. To avoid loss by fire or theft, backup copies are usually stored away from the ICT system, e.g. in a fire-proof safe or in another building.

Working safely

The ICT working environment is relatively safe. However, there are risks that should be minimised and hazards that should be avoided:

- Bad posture and physical stress
- Eye strain
- Hazards resulting from equipment or workplace layout

In Unit 4: *System Installation and Configuration*, you may experience the most risk, because you will be putting together the hardware for an ICT system. Chapter 4 offers specific advice on safety and security – see page 187.

The user, i.e. the operator, must be protected from potential danger. Seating is very important. Poor seating can result in poor posture and cause back problems, and many more working hours are lost due to illnesses such as RSI (repetitive strain injury). RSI is a painful complaint which usually attacks the wrist or arm of people who have used a keyboard or mouse for a long time.

Your environment should provide:

- Comfortable seating
- A suitable desk and VDU position
- A suitable keyboard position
- Provision for brief rest periods to avoid continuous VDU work
- A surrounding area that includes near and distant objects the eyes may focus on

Ergonomics studies the relationship between people and their environment. Many different things can be adjusted to make the operator as comfortable as possible.

- ✪ Seat height
- ✪ Table height
- ✪ Keyboard position
- ✪ Screen position

Most computers are powered by mains electricity, which introduces more potential hazards.

- ✪ Tripping over cables
- ✪ Static electricity build up
- ✪ Screen glare

Health and Safety at Work Act (1974)

The basis of health and safety law in Britain is covered by the Health and Safety at Work Act (1974). The Act sets out the general duties which employers have towards employees and members of the public. It also explains the duties that employees have to themselves and to each other.

These duties are qualified in the Act by the principle of 'so far as is reasonably practicable'. In other words, the degree of risk in a particular job or workplace needs to be balanced against the time, trouble, cost and physical difficulty of taking measures to avoid or reduce the risk.

What the law requires here is what good management and common sense would lead employers to do anyway: that is, to look at what the risks are and take sensible measures to tackle them.

Risk assessment

The main requirement on employers is to carry out a risk assessment. Employers with five or more employees have to record the significant findings of the risk assessment. Risk assessment should be straightforward in a simple workplace such as a typical office. It should only be complicated if it deals with serious hazards such as those in a nuclear power station, a chemical plant, laboratory or oil rig.

Besides carrying out a risk assessment, employers have other responsibilities:

- ✪ To make arrangements for implementing the health and safety measures identified as necessary by the risk assessment
- ✪ To appoint competent people (often themselves or company colleagues) to help them to implement the arrangements
- ✪ To set up emergency procedures
- ✪ To provide clear information and training to employees
- ✪ To work together with other employers sharing the same workplace

Guidance, ACOPs and regulations

The Health and Safety Commission (HSC) recently conducted a review of health and safety regulation. It found that people are confused about the differences between guidance, Approved Codes of Practice (ACOPs), and regulations and how they relate to each other. This section explains the differences between these terms.

There are three main reasons why the HSE publishes guidance on a range of subjects, specific to the H&S problems of an industry or of a particular process used in a number of industries.

- ✪ To help people interpret what the law says, including for example how requirements based on EU Directives fit with those under the Health and Safety at Work Act
- ✪ To help people comply with the law
- ✪ To give technical advice

Following guidance is not compulsory and employers are free to take other action. However, if they do follow guidance, they will normally be doing enough to comply with the law.

HSC/E aim to keep guidance up-to-date, because as technologies change, risks (and the measures needed to address them) change too.

ACOPs offer practical examples of good practice. They give advice on how to comply with the law by, for example, providing a guide to what is 'reasonably practicable'. If regulations use words like 'suitable and sufficient', an ACOP can illustrate what this requires in particular circumstances.

ACOPs have a special legal status. If employers are prosecuted for a breach of H&S law, and it is proved that they have not followed the relevant provisions of the ACOP, a court can find them at fault unless they can show that they have complied with the law in some other way.

Regulations are law, approved by Parliament. These are usually made under the Health and Safety at Work Act, following proposals from HSC. This applies to regulations based on EU Directives as well as 'home-grown' ones.

The Health and Safety at Work Act, and general duties in the Management Regulations, are goal-setting and leave employers freedom to decide how to control risks which they identify. Guidance and ACOPs give advice, but employers are free to take other measures provided they do what is reasonably practicable. However, some risks are so great, or the proper control measures so costly, that it would not be appropriate to leave employers discretion in deciding what to do about them. Regulations identify these risks and set out specific action that must be taken. Often these requirements are absolute – to do something without qualification by whether it is reasonably practicable.

Some regulations apply across *all* companies:

✪ **The Manual Handling Regulations apply wherever things are moved by hand or bodily force.**

✪ **The Display Screen Equipment Regulations apply wherever VDUs are used.**

Other regulations apply to hazards unique to specific industries, such as mining or nuclear safety law.

Besides the Health and Safety at Work Act itself, these regulations apply across the full range of workplaces.

✪ **The *Management of Health and Safety at Work Regulations 1992* require employers to carry out risk assessments, make arrangements to implement necessary measures, appoint competent people and arrange for appropriate information and training.**

✪ **The *Workplace (Health, Safety and Welfare) Regulations 1992* cover a wide range of basic health, safety and welfare issues such as ventilation, heating, lighting, workstations, seating and welfare facilities.**

✪ **The *Health and Safety (Display Screen Equipment) Regulations 1992* set out requirements for work with VDUs.**

✪ **The *Health and Safety (First Aid) Regulations 1981* cover requirements for first aid.**

✪ **The *Health and Safety Information for Employees Regulations 1989* require employers to display a poster telling employees what they need to know about health and safety.**

✪ **The *Employers' Liability (Compulsory Insurance) Regulations 1969* require employers to take out insurance against accidents and ill health to their employees.**

✪ The *Reporting of Injuries, Diseases and Dangerous Occurrences Regulations 1985 (RIDDOR)* require employers to notify certain occupational injuries, diseases and dangerous events.

For your own safety, and that of others around you, you should make sure you follow all safety procedures adopted by your employer, your college or school. Most of the material from this section came from a booklet entitled *Health and Safety Regulation – A Short Guide*, published by HSE (HSC13, 11/96, C1000) which was current as at April 1995. To obtain an up-to-date copy, telephone the HSE InfoLine (01541 545500) or write to HSE Information Centre, Broad Lane, Sheffield S3 7HQ.

You may also be interested to obtain copies of other relevant publications:

✪ 5 steps to risk assessment. IND (G) 163 (L) (free leaflet)

✪ Essentials of health and safety at work. ISBN 0 7176 0716 X

✪ First aid at work: general guidance for inclusion in first aid boxes IND (G) 4 (L) ISBN 0 7176 0440 3 (leaflet, priced packs of 25)

✪ Health and Safety law. What you should know (poster). ISBN 0 11 701424 9

✪ VDUs: an easy guide to the Regulations. HS (G) 90 ISBN 0 7176 0735 6

✪ Working with VDUs. IND (G) 36 (L) ISBN 0 7176 0814 X (single free copies, priced packs of ten)

✪ Workplace health, safety and welfare (leaflet, priced packs of ten). ISBN 0 7176 0890 5

These publications (whether free or priced) are available from HSE Books, PO Box 1999, Sudbury, Suffolk CO10 6FS (Tel: 01787 881165; Fax: 01787 313995). Priced publications are also available from all good book shops. Or you could visit the HSE website: http://www.hse.gov.uk. Many documents are available for downloading as Adobe Acrobat files.

Data Protection Act (DPA)

Much of the information stored on computers is about living people (personal data). The DPA places obligations on those who record and use personal data (data users). They must be open about the use (through the data protection register) and follow sound and proper practices (the Data Protection Principles). The DPA was revised in 1998 and the new regulations came into effect in March 1999.

The DPA also gives rights to individuals about whom information is recorded (data subjects). They may find out information about themselves, challenge it, have it corrected or erased if appropriate, and claim compensation in certain circumstances. When it was first passed in 1984, the DPA also allowed the UK to ratify the Council of Europe Convention on Data Protection, allowing information to flow freely between the UK and other European countries with similar laws.

The Data Protection Registrar

The Registrar, an independent officer appointed by Her Majesty the Queen and reporting directly to Parliament, has many duties:

✪ **Establishing and maintaining a register of data users and computer bureaux and making it publicly available**

✪ **Promoting compliance with the Data Protection Principles**

✪ **Encouraging, where appropriate, the development of Codes of Practice to help data users comply with the Principles**

✪ **Considering complaints about breaches of the Principles of the Act and, where appropriate, prosecuting offenders or serving notices**

What the DPA covers

The DPA only applies to automatically processed information. It does not cover information which is held and processed manually – for example, in ordinary paper files. Not all computerised information is covered by the DPA, only that which relates to living individuals. So, for example, it does not cover information which relates only to a company or an organisation.

Registration

The term 'computer' is never used in the DPA. Instead, it uses the terms data and data user. Anyone who holds personal information about living individuals on computer must register unless covered by one of the exemptions provided by the DPA. People or organisations who have personal data processed by a computer bureau, are still data users even if they do not have their own computer.

A computer bureau, in broad terms, means anyone processing personal data on someone else's behalf. To register as a data user, information has to be supplied for inclusion in the register:

✪ **The name and address of the data user**

✪ **A description of the purposes for which personal data are used**

- ✪ The type of personal data held
- ✪ Where the personal data are obtained
- ✪ To whom they will be disclosed
- ✪ A list of any countries outside the UK to which they may be transferred

The term computer bureau applies to anyone who carries out processing for someone else, even if it is not a commercial service. A register entry for a computer bureau will contain only its name and address.

Once a data user has registered, he or she must only act within the terms of his register entry. Not to do so is an offence. A data user can apply to the Registrar to alter his or her register entry at any time. It is an offence to fail to register or to provide false information to the Registrar.

The Data Protection Principles

Once registered, data users must comply with the principles in relation to the personal data held:

- ✪ Personal data shall be collected and processed fairly and lawfully.
- ✪ Personal data shall be held only for specified and lawful purposes.
- ✪ Personal data shall be used only for those purposes and only disclosed to those people described in the register entry.
- ✪ Personal data shall be adequate, relevant and not excessive in relation to the purposes for which they are held.
- ✪ Personal data shall be accurate and, where necessary, kept up to date.
- ✪ Personal data shall be held no longer than is necessary for the registered purpose.
- ✪ Personal data shall be protected by proper security.

However, the Registrar cannot enforce the principles against unregistered data users.

The principles also provide for individuals to have access to data held about themselves and, where appropriate, to have the data corrected or deleted.

Enforcing the DPA

The Registrar ensures that the Data Protection Principles are observed.

- The Registrar can serve an Enforcement Notice directing a registered person to take specific steps to comply with a principle.
- The Registrar can issue a De-registration Notice cancelling from the register the whole or part of any register entry.
- The Registrar can also issue a Transfer Prohibition Notice to prevent the transfer of personal data overseas.

Someone receiving one of these notices can appeal to the independent Data Protection Tribunal. The Tribunal has the power to substitute its own decision in place of the Registrar's. Breach of an Enforcement or Transfer Prohibition Notice is an offence.

If the Registrar considers that an offence has been committed under the DPA, he/she may prosecute the offender and a fine may be imposed. Prosecutions may also be brought by or with the consent of the Director of Public Prosecutions. Where the Registrar has reasonable grounds for suspecting a criminal offence or a breach of principle an application may be made to a circuit judge for a search warrant to enter and search any premises.

The Data Protection Tribunal

The Data Protection Tribunal consists of a legally qualified Chairman together with lay members. The lay members are appointed to represent the interests of data users and data subjects.

The Tribunal's task is to consider appeals by data users or computer bureaux against the Registrar's decisions. Appeals may relate to the refusal of a registration application or the service of an enforcement, de-registration or transfer prohibition notice.

The Tribunal can overturn the Registrar's decision and substitute whatever decision it thinks fit. On questions of law, there is a further appeal from the Tribunal to the High Court.

The rights of the individual

An individual is entitled to be supplied by a data user with a copy of any personal data held about him or her – the 'subject access' right. Individuals may write direct to the user for their data, or they may consult the register to obtain more details about the user.

Data users may charge up to £10 for meeting each request but some may decide to charge less, or nothing at all. They have up to 40 days in which to provide the data from the date of receiving adequate information to help them locate the data or identify the individual making the request. If the data are not provided within the 40 days, the individual concerned can complain to the Registrar or apply to the courts for an order that the data user should provide access.

A person who has suffered damage and any associated distress caused by the loss, unauthorised destruction or unauthorised disclosure of information about themselves, or through that information being inaccurate, can seek compensation through the High Court or County Court in England or Wales. If personal data are inaccurate, the individual may complain to the Registrar or apply to the High Court or County Court in England or Wales for correction or deletion of the inaccurate information.

Anyone who considers there has been a breach of one of the Principles, or any other provision of the Act, is entitled to complain to the Data Protection Registrar. When the Registrar has considered the complaint, he/she must notify the complainant of any action which he/she proposes to take.

Exemptions from the DPA

There are several exemptions. Manually held information, e.g. in card indexes or paper files, is not covered by the DPA. Otherwise the exemptions from the need to register are extremely narrow. They cover only the simplest tasks in the following areas: calculating pay and pensions, keeping accounts or records of purchases or sales, distributing articles or information (mailing lists), and preparing text documents. Most businesses find it difficult to meet and stay within the limits imposed by these exemptions and find it safer to register.

So, people and organisations who hold personal information about living individuals on computer or have such information processed on a computer by others (e.g. by a computer bureau or an accountant) probably need to register under the DPA. No matter how unimportant this information may appear (and it may be as little as a name and address), the fact that it is on computer almost certainly makes the data user liable for registration.

Where personal data are exempt from the whole of the DPA, those data need not be registered, there is no right of subject access and the Registrar and courts have no powers regarding this personal data. Some exemptions are unconditional, for example where national security is involved, or where an individual holds personal data for recreational purposes or for managing his own personal, family or household affairs. Other exemptions have conditions which must be complied with before the data can be deemed exempt: for example, where data are held for payroll, pensions and accounts, they are exempt unless they are also held for other purposes. Other conditional exemptions exist for unincorporated members' clubs and mailing lists. In the case of all the conditional exemptions, the data may not be disclosed without the consent of the individual to whom the data relates. Limited disclosures are permitted for the payroll, pensions and accounts exemptions without the consent of the individual.

There are also a number of exemptions from the need to provide information under the subject access provisions of the DPA. Some examples of where personal information may be withheld are where this would be likely to prejudice the prevention or detection of crime; the apprehension or prosecution of offenders; or the assessment or collection of any tax or duty.

Decisions to withhold information under these exemptions can be challenged by the Registrar on receipt of a complaint from a member of the public.

More detailed information on all aspects of the Data Protection Act is contained within 'The Guidelines' – a free publication available from the Registrar's Office. For more details visit the website http://www.hmso.gov.uk

Dos and don'ts

- ✪ *Do* plan your work to produce what is required to given deadlines.
- ✪ *Do* take a backup of your work.
- ✪ *Do* keep backup copies of files on another disk and in another location.
- ✪ *Do* keep a log to provide a record of what has happened, especially what has gone wrong.
- ✪ *Do* proof-read your database and spreadsheet information to ensure accuracy.
- ✪ *Do* save work regularly using different filenames.
- ✪ *Do* proof-read all documents before printing out the final copy.
- ✪ *Do* evaluate your work and suggest how it might be improved.
- ✪ *Do* keep information free from viruses.
- ✪ *Do* respect confidentiality.
- ✪ *Do* respect copyright.
- ✪ *Don't* disconnect or connect equipment without first isolating the power source.
- ✪ *Don't* eat or drink while working at a PC. A spilt drink can ruin a keyboard.

Portfolio Guide

Your portfolio should contain all the evidence collected as you work through the units. For some units, assessment is by external testing, but material in your portfolio may well be needed to show your achievement in Key Skills. It therefore makes sense to keep a portfolio of *all* your work for *all* your units, even those which are not portfolio assessed.

To decide what material you need to produce and put in your portfolio, you need to look at the assessment grid at the end of each unit specification. Your portfolio must contain at least the minimum stated in the first column of the Assessment Evidence section of each unit.

The assessment evidence section tells you exactly what type of evidence you need to produce – like list, notes, records and summary – to show what depth of work is needed, and you need to check you have met this level of presentation.

- ✪ **Lists** are simply a series of brief comments on the main points.

- ✪ **Notes** are more than just a list. For each item, you may write a paragraph of information. You may write notes when preparing for a task. They may include draft ideas, initial plans and drawings, and so on.

- ✪ A **record** is an account of the activity which is being assessed. It could be a written record, including tables of data, a checklist of activities and so on. You decide exactly what to include, after discussion with your teacher.

- ✪ A **report** is a finished piece of work which brings together lots of ideas and information.

✪ A **summary** is a short account, similar to a record but should not include all your working papers.

For some activities your teacher will watch you working, and then write an assessment of your performance. In some situations, another person, e.g. your supervisor in a work placement, may observe you.

With a presentation, you will present your finished work to an audience (maybe only to your teacher), but your portfolio evidence might include a taped recording or a video together with the material (e.g. OHTs or slides) that you used. Your teacher will be responsible for agreeing that you used a good standard of English during your presentation, and that your manner and tone were suitable for your audience.

Some units ask for a special form of evidence to be produced by you:

✪ Unit 1 asks for a collection of original documents.

✪ Unit 3 asks for a spreadsheet solution, and user and technical documentation.

✪ Unit 4 asks for a specification of a complete ICT system.

✪ Unit 6 asks for a relational database including design and analysis notes, a user guide and technical documentation.

For the tested units (Units 2 and 5), the assessment grid does say what you have to produce, but your awarding body will specify the precise requirement in pre-release material given to you some time before the examination. See the *Examination Guide* on page 361.

Performance when doing assignments

When you prepare for a task and are identifying sources of information, your teacher may consider these questions:

✪ Were you usually told what tasks needed to be done and then have to be guided through them?

✪ Were you able to decide what steps you needed to take, and did you arrange the tasks into a sensible order, setting your own timescale?

✪ Did you use sources of information suggested by your teacher, and were you able to select and use the relevant information from these sources?

✪ Were you able to understand what the task involved without any guidance from your teacher?

- Did you understand what information was required and did you look for extra sources of information, as well as investigating those suggested by your teacher?

The more independent you are, the higher your grade should be.

Similarly, the more care you take over planning and monitoring your work, the more likely you are to be successful, and the higher your grade should be. Sometimes, through no fault of your own, the plan does not work:

- Computers crash
- Books and other sources may not be available
- People that you have arranged to meet may fall ill and have to postpone your appointment

Even if things do not go wrong, you should be able to demonstrate that you have regularly checked progress against the original plan.

The quality of your work is also very important.

- If you are a grade E student, you will be able to demonstrate a basic understanding of the knowledge and skills required, but you may not be able to make connections between different aspects of your work. You should be able to use the normal ICT terminology but may need some help from your teacher.

- If you are a grade C student, you should be able to make connections between different aspects of your work and demonstrate a clear understanding. Your use of ICT terminology should be accurate, and your written work should show confidence in the expression of your ideas.

- If you are a grade A student, you will have a clear understanding of the knowledge, skills and understanding required. You will draw on your personal experience to draw conclusions or suggest alternative courses of action.

Evaluating your work is an important part of improving your own performance – it is one of the six Key Skills.

- Higher grade students are able to learn from what they have done to date. They learn from any mistakes and build on success.
- Lower grade students will be saying – oh, that went wrong last time!

What are the general 'rules' that allow your teacher to decide whether your work is at level E, C or A? This depends on the unit – and is detailed in the section called Assessment Strategies. Although this section is written for your teacher, you should read it carefully. Then you'll know how your work will be viewed by your teacher. These are the qualities that your teacher will be looking for:

- ✪ Increasing depth and breadth of understanding
- ✪ Increasing coherence, evaluation and analysis
- ✪ Increasing independence and originality
- ✪ Increasing objectivity and critical understanding

Presenting information

It will help your teacher – and give extra information about your performance overall – if your portfolio is presented well. Chapter 1 covers Unit 1: Presenting Information. As a student on the Vocational A-level course in ICT, you must be able to demonstrate that you can do this well!

If you use a word processor, apart from showing IT Key Skills, you will be able to:

- ✪ edit your work until you are happy with it;
- ✪ choose a style which reflects your own personality and a point size and a font that you like;
- ✪ include clip art or other graphics, e.g. using WordArt, to improve the appearance of your portfolio material.

The structure of your portfolio

There are a number of sections that your portfolio should include. This will demonstrate that you can structure material and present it in a sensible way.

The main sections are listed here, but you can choose your own sections if you prefer.

- ✪ Front cover
- ✪ Contents list
- ✪ Assignment material
- ✪ Appendices

You may also have checklist sheets supplied by your teacher. These may be used to refer to where Key Skills are demonstrated. In addition, you may have material which confirms that your teacher saw you present some information, or has discussed your material with you.

Your name (and centre details) should appear at least once on the portfolio. For safety reasons, it is good practice to include this information on every page. If you are using software, this is easily achieved by using a header or footer.

It will be important that your contents list matches whatever you have included in the rest of your portfolio. Although it appears at the very start of your portfolio, it is one of the last pages you can complete. However, if you produce it using a word processor, you can prepare a contents page at the very beginning and update it every time you add some material to your portfolio. Then it will be one less job to do when you are rushing to meet the final deadline.

In this book, the pages run from 1 to 368, and the Contents page (on page v) shows the starting page numbers for each chapter. For your portfolio, it may be easier to number the sections and then, within each section, number the pages by section. This numbering method is often used in manuals and means that extra sections can be added at any time, without it upsetting the page numbering too much.

For the material produced when doing assignments, plus any material produced when doing activities, it probably makes sense to present the material in the same order as you completed the work. For each assignment, make sure you show clearly what the assignment is called, and what it covers. It may be possible to use material produced in another course as evidence of your ICT skills. It will help your teacher if you write clearly on each assignment, which unit (and course) the assignment refers to.

Sometimes it makes sense to move some material to an appendix. This shortens a section, and yet the material is available if the reader wants to look at it. So, for example, lengthy tables or diagrams or copies of original source materials may be put into an appendix.

You can also list your references within an appendix. It is important to include all your references: the books, magazines, websites and CD-ROMs you used to find information for your assignments.

While building your portfolio, leave yourself messages about things you still have to include. You could write these notes on your plan (which will provide evidence that you have been reviewing and monitoring your plan), or put Post-it notes on pages that still have work to be done, or write yourself a checklist, which you can then tick off as you complete the work.

Moderation and internal assessment

Your portfolio material is first marked by a teacher and marking is then internally standardised by other specially trained staff at your school or college. The teacher who marks your portfolio and the staff who carry out internal assessment of all the portfolio material use the unit assessment grids in accordance with the procedures of their awarding body.

The teachers must be able to verify that the work submitted by you is your own work. This does not prevent groups of students working together in the initial stages, but it is important to ensure your individual contribution is clearly identified separately from that of any group in which you work.

When all portfolios have been internally standardised, data about your portfolio – and all the other students on your course – is then submitted to the awarding body by a specified date, after which postal moderation takes place in accordance with the awarding body's procedures and the Code of Practice.

Detailed arrangements for moderation is forwarded to all schools and colleges before the start of the course, so your teacher should be able to tell you when your deadlines will be.

Key Skills Guide

Job skills fall into two types: vocational skills and key skills.

Vocational skills are the skills that are linked to the actual job:

- The ability to use a keyboard or mouse
- The experience of using a word processing package
- The experience of using a DTP (desktop publishing) package
- The ability to install software and to customise application programs

You will learn vocational skills while following this course, and in doing so will need to use key skills.

Key skills are not specific to a subject like ICT. Instead they are useful for most jobs and include these abilities.

- To think for yourself
- To work without supervision
- To work in a team
- To work with numbers
- To solve problems
- To communicate your ideas to others
- To remember names and other important facts
- To work to a deadline

So, key skills can help you to improve your own learning and performance in education and training, work and life in general.

- *In your learning*, key skills help you to focus on what and how you are learning. In this way, while reviewing your progress, you can get better results.

- *In your career*, key skills enable you to be flexible in whatever kind of work you do. Employers look for key skills when recruiting and promoting people. In particular, your ability to work well in a team, and your motivation to learn, will be of interest to your interviewer. These skills are relevant to all levels of an organisation, including self-employment.

- *In your personal life*, key skills can help you to organise yourself, manage your money, handle information and get on with others.

Key Skills qualifications are available in three main areas:

- Communication
- Application of number
- Information technology

The broad aim of these three Key Skills units is to develop and recognise these skills:

- to obtain and interpret different types of information: written, numerical and electronic;
- to use, develop and communicate different types of information;
- to present the results of your work effectively so as to meet the purpose of your studies, work or other activities.

There are three other 'wider' Key Skills:

- Working with others
- Improving own learning and performance
- Problem solving

These three Key Skills will become essential for success in your course. Many activities are based on teamwork, and employers are particularly interested in your ability to work well within a team. Note that the 'Working with others' Key Skills specification also includes working on your own! Employers are also looking for staff who can work unsupervised and who are motivated – not only to get a job, but to improve their own learning by attending courses and learning as much as possible while working.

Key Skills awards are available in each of these six areas at levels 1, 2, 3 and 4. At level 5, a single unit combines communication skills with the skills of working with others, improving own learning and performance, and problem solving.

As you move up the levels, you are expected to take more responsibility for decisions on how you use your skills to suit different tasks, problems and situations. Students working at levels 1 and 2 work with straightforward subjects and materials, in routine situations. Students at higher levels deal with complex subjects and activities that are more demanding. At the higher levels, planning is very important. Students at levels 3 and 4 need to think about how to tackle tasks, what resources they will need and how to check their own work.

To achieve this qualification, you must demonstrate your skills through a portfolio of evidence. This evidence should not involve you in a lot of extra work. Instead, you should be able to collect evidence from your day-to-day studies, work or other activities and an appropriate form of independent assessment. As well as producing a portfolio of evidence, you also have to pass an externally set test.

Key Skills signposting

Within the Vocational A-level course, you have the opportunity to learn, practice and gather evidence of all six Key Skills.

Within each unit of the specification for the Vocational A-level in ICT, there is a section called *Guidance on Key Skills*. This highlights the most relevant Key Skills opportunities available for that particular unit. The Key Skills guidance has been designed to support the teaching, learning and assessment of the vocational content, as well as the teaching, learning and assessment of the Key Skills.

Key Skills and vocational achievement are interdependent and the guidance section shows how vocational and Key Skills achievement can be combined.

Guidance is referenced in two ways: keys to attainment and signposts. The two sections should be used together – they are intended to complement each other.

Keys to attainment are Key Skills (or aspects of Key Skills) which you should achieve at the same time as you meet the vocational requirements of the unit. They are considered to be central to your vocational achievement.

Signposting shows opportunities for the development of Key Skills during teaching, learning and assessment.

The compulsory units should provide you with all the opportunities you need to demonstrate Key Skills, but there are also opportunities within the optional units. In choosing your mix of units, you will need to ensure that Key Skills evidence can be produced without having to do lots of extra work.

To help you, the three awarding bodies include grids in their respective specifications, showing which Key Skills match which of their units. In this book, each activity includes an indication of which Key Skills may be useful, and this may also help you to decide where your evidence of Key Skills will naturally arise.

 Communication

 Application of number

 Working with others

 Problem solving

 Improving own learning and performance

It is possible that you may need to develop additional evidence elsewhere – even on another course – to meet fully the requirements of the Key Skills specifications.

Note that Information Technology Key Skills (level 3) are automatically included in the units covered for Vocational A-level ICT. So you do not need anything extra to achieve Key Skills in IT, unless you are aiming for Key Skills at level 4 or higher.

Key Skills terms

The Key Skills specifications use terms in a specific way:

Evidence is what you produce to prove you have the key skills required. Examples may include things you have made, written work, artwork and diagrams, photos, audio/video recordings, print-outs, together with records from your assessor and others who have seen your work.

Portfolio is where you collect and organise evidence for assessment: in a file or a folder large enough to carry everything you have produced. Your portfolio should include a contents page to show where evidence for each part of the unit(s) can be found. For more details on how to prepare your portfolio, see the *Portfolio Guide* on page 349.

It is possible – and it makes sense – to use some evidence for more than one Key Skill, e.g. a print-out of text and images, such as graphs and charts may provide evidence of written Communication skills as well as presenting findings in Application of Number.

The subject content and the material you use and produce are described either as straightforward or as complex.

Straightforward subjects and materials are the ones that you meet most often in your work, studies or other activities. Content is presented in a direct way so that it easy to identify the main points. The sentence structures are simple and the vocabulary will be familiar to you.

Complex subjects and materials present a number of ideas: some abstract ideas, some very detailed concepts and some requiring you to deal with sensitive issues. The relationship between ideas and any lines of reasoning may not be immediately clear. You may need to understand specialised vocabulary, and complicated sentence structures may be used.

During your Vocational A-level course, you will use and prepare **extended documents.** These include text books like this one, newspaper reports, articles on the Internet and essays that you write – anything that has more than three pages. Such documents may relate to straightforward or complex subjects. They may include images such as diagrams, pictures and charts.

Any activity that includes a number of related tasks, where the results of one task then affects how you carry out the remaining tasks is called a **substantial activity**. For the Key Skill Application of Number, a substantial activity may involve obtaining and interpreting information, using this information to carry out calculations and then explaining how the results of your calculations meet the purpose of the activity.

How to read a Key Skills unit

Each Key Skills specification document is four sides of A4, presented as a folded sheet of A3 paper. It covers one level of one Key Skill area, e.g. Application of Number, level 2.

It is important to read the whole specification because all four pages present a different view of the Key Skill.

What is this unit about?

On the front cover, the first section gives an outline of the unit. Check that you have the correct Key Skills specification, at the right level. The specification documents look very similar, so it is easy to be looking at the wrong level.

How do I use the information in this unit?

A second section on the front cover shows the other three pages: parts A, B and C of the specification, and explains the purpose of each section.

Part A: What you need to know

This lists what you need to learn and practise to feel confident about applying the Key Skill in your studies, work or other aspects of your life. You should check whether you know how to do these things and think about the opportunities you might have for showing these skills. Some topics may be familiar to you, and you may feel confident you can produce evidence to prove this. For other topics, you may have some learning to do and you may need to practise before you are ready for assessment.

Part B: What you must do

This has a numbered list of the Key Skills you must show. The numbers used are then used as signposts in other examination specifications. For each numbered item, there is then a bullet list of evidence that you must produce. All your work for this section has to be assessed. You must have evidence that you can do *all* the things listed in the bullet points.

Part C: Guidance

This describes some activities you might like to use to develop and show your Key Skill and some ideas on the sort of activities that could be suitable. It also contains examples of the sort of evidence you could produce to prove you have the skills required.

Examination of Key Skills

External moderation will be used to check how well you demonstrate your Key Skills within your portfolio material. More details on how to present your portfolio are given in the *Portfolio Guide* on page 349.

Tests for Key Skills are being developed while this book is being written, so it is not possible to say exactly what form the examinations will take. Material will be made available later this year (2000) and teachers and students will then be able to access this information from the Internet.

Examination Guide

For the Vocational A-level in Information and Communication Technology, there are six **compulsory units:**

1 Presenting Information
2 ICT Serving Organisations
3 Spreadsheet Design
4 Systems Installation and Configuration
5 Systems Analysis
6 Database Design

There are three different awards available:

- ✪ For the 3-unit award – the Advanced Subsidiary Vocational Certificate of Education (ASVCE) award – you study only the first three compulsory units.

- ✪ For the 6-unit award – the Advanced Vocational Certificate of Education (AVCE) – you study six units: the first three compulsory units plus any three others chosen from the remaining mandatory units and the full range of optional units.

- ✪ For the 12-unit award – the Advanced Vocational Certificate of Education (AVCE, double award) – you study twelve units: the six compulsory units, plus another six units selected from the full range of optional units.

For some of the units, you will demonstrate your understanding by your portfolio material; for other units, you will externally assessed. However, the balance of portfolio to externally assessed units means that most of your work will be assessed as you work through the course (continuous assessment).

Each unit, whether assessed by portfolio or external assessment, is individually graded on a scale A to E. Points for each unit will be awarded on a scale of 0–24:

0–6	below pass
7–9	E
10–12	D
13–15	C
16–18	B
19–24	A

For tested units, your grade will reflect how many marks you earned in the test. For portfolio assessed material, the mark awarded will take into account the extent to which the evidence matches both the unit pass standards, represented by the set of criteria in the grade E column of the grid, and the grading standards, represented progressively by the criteria in the grade C and grade A columns.

Then, a single grade of A to E is decided on a points basis, to reflect your performance over all your units; this single grade is then your 'final' grade for the AVCE award (as with GCE A/AS-levels) and can be used for entry to higher education on the usual points basis. Note that for the 12-unit award, you will get two grades.

When you have completed the work for a single unit, you should be ready to sit the external test. Tests and assignments are scheduled to take place at set times of the year, after you have worked on a particular unit. It does not matter in which order you take the external tests, because each unit is available for assessment in both testing sessions: January and June. The important thing is to make sure you are confident that you have covered all the material for the unit, *before* you sit the test.

According to the unit, and your awarding body, you may be expected to do an assignment, or perhaps some preparatory work before sitting the written test.

Although your choice of units may result in more externally tested units, there is a minimum number of externally assessed units for Information and Communication Technology:

- ✪ 1 unit for the 3-unit ASVCE award
- ✪ 1 unit for the 6-unit AVCE award
- ✪ 3 units for the 12-unit AVCE (double) award

The written tests – one per tested unit – last two hours each, in which you write your answers within a booklet in the spaces provided.

Sample papers which you can use as 'mock' examinations for the tests are available on the web. The revision questions given at the end of each chapter, and particularly the externally assessed chapters (2, 5 and 7) will also provide you with some practice.

Which units are externally tested?

This grid shows, for each chapter, the unit numbers for those that are externally assessed by the three awarding bodies: OCR, AQA and EdExcel.

Chapter	Title	OCR	AQA	EdExcel
1	Presenting Information			
2	IT Serving Organisations	2	2	2
3	Spreadsheet Design			
4	Systems Installation and Configuration			
5	Systems Analysis	5	5	5
6	Database Design			
7	Impact of ICT on Society	9	9	19

As well as the *Impact of ICT on Society*, OCR and Edexcel also offer tested units within their other optional units.

Title	OCR	EdExcel
The Internet: systems and services		12
Structured program design methods	14	
Mathematics for ICT	22	
Investigating communications and networks	23	
Operating systems and systems architecture		23

Other books in this series provide material for these units, and the units which are assessed by portfolio only.

Abbreviations

AOB	any other business
ATM	automatic teller machine
AVCE	Advanced Vocational Certificate of Education
BACS	bankers automated clearing services
BIOS	basic input/output system
bps	bits per second
CAD	computer aided design
CMOSRAM	complementary metal oxide semiconductor random access memory
CPU	central processing unit
CV	curriculum vitae
DB	databus (connector)
DBA	database administrator
DBMS	database management system
DEC	Digital Equipment Corporation
DFD	data flow diagrams
DIL	dual-in-line (switches)
DIP	dual-in-line package (switch)
dpi	dots per inch

DTP	desktop publishing
DVD	digital versatile disk
EDO	extended data out
EFT	electronic funds transfer
EFTPOS	electronic funds transfer at point of sale
ERD	entity-relationship diagram
ERM	entity-relationship model
EU	European Union
fax	facsimile
GCSE	General Certificate of Secondary Education
GIGO	garbage in, garbage out
GIS	geographical information systems
GNVQ	General National Vocational Qualification
GPS	global positioning systems
GUI	graphical user interface
HCI	human computer interface
HR	human resources
ID	identity
ICT	Information and Communication Technology
ISA	industry standard architecture
ISO	International Standards Organisation
IT	information technology
JANET	Joint Academic Network
JIT	just in time
LAN	local area network
LCD	liquid crystal display
MHz	megahertz
MIS	management information systems
NI	National Insurance
NLQ	near letter quality
NRA	National Record of Achievement

PAYE	pay as you earn
PC	performance criteria
PCI	peripheral component interconnect
R&D	research and development
RAM	random access memory
RDBMS	relational database management system
ROM	read only memory
RJ	registered jack (connector)
RS	recommended standard
RSA	Royal Society of Arts
SEU	Shoot-Em-Up Games Ltd
SOP	sales order processing
SCSI	small computer standard interface
tab	tabulation
UK	United Kingdom
URL	uniform resource locator
VAT	value added tax
VDU	visual display unit
VR	virtual reality
WAN	wide area network
WWW	world wide web

Index

GPS (global positioning systems) 329
grading xviii
grammar 37–8, 42
graphic design packages 82
graphic images 161, 250
graphical user interface (GUI) 180, 184
graphs 30, 119–22
gutter margins 32

hacking 325
hand-held scanners 160
handwritten note 3
hanging indents 27
hard copy 302
hard disk 156
hard spaces 27
hardware 146–74
    hardware development 294–7
    hardware functions 304
hazards 339
HCI (human–computer interface) 280
headers 32, 119
headings 25, 31
health and safety 173, 188, 319
    audit 189
    regulations 342–3
Health and Safety at Work Act (1974) 323, 327, 340–3
Health and Safety Regulations (1992) 323, 325
help 122, 307
hiding cells 122
hierarchical DBMS 246
hierarchical organisational structure 67, 70
high-level DFDs 210–13
highlights, bold 26, 117
histograms 122
home page 85
hot desking 313
hot links 15
house style 5, 24, 25, 65
human resources (HR) 63

icon(s) 158, 184
ICT
    effects on the environment 320–2
    ICT services 66
    ICT serving organisations 55–100
ICT systems components
    hardware 146–74
    software 174–87
IDE interface 156, 171

IF function 110
impact of ICT on methods of production 317–19
impact of ICT on society 293–334
impact of ICT on working practices 312–17
in-car traffic announcements 311
income and expenditure statements 80
increments 111
indents 27, 336
independence xvii
index 23
index keys 261
indexed structure 78
informal note 3
informal style 5
information 242–3
    accuracy 35–44
    combining 30, 51
    communicating 58
    confidential 189, 336
    gathering 206–9
    GIS 329
    in the home 305
    information boards 307, 311
    information compression 156, 302
    information flow 91–7
    information providers 59
    information services 308
    information society 306–12
    information systems, features of 77–90
    loss of 337
    presenting 1–54, 352
    threats to 325–6
    types of 59
    use of 75–97
    see also data
information sources development 298–300
initialisation files 178
ink 172
input
    data input 131
    input devices 157–61
    input mask 237, 250
    input specification 233–7
installing an application 115
installing an operating system 176
INT function 112
integrity, preserving 248
intelligent agents 332
interface
    command 179
    HCI 280
    GUI 180, 184

IDE 156, 171
    SCSI 156, 171
    user interface 174, 177, 179–81
interlace mode 162
internal bus 149
internal documents 5
Internet 84–6, 91, 305, 338
interrupt request (IRQ) 149
interviews 206, 207
Intranet 84–6
inventory control systems 82
investigation 197, 204–9
invoice 7, 9, 10
ISA (industry-standard architecture) 150
ISBN 82
ISDN router 171
IsNumeric function 114
italics 25
itinerary 10, 11

JIT (just in time) 87, 317
job functions and departments 61–6
job security 316
job skills 335
jumpers 170
justification 26, 27, 117
keys
    composite key 260
    foreign key(s) 219, 262
    key fields 260–2
    primary key 218, 260
    secondary keys 261
    short-cut keys 127
Key Skills 355–60
keyboards 157
    concept keyboard 157–8
    keyboard locks 326
    keyboard position 340
kilobyte 151
knowledge xvii

LAN (local area network) 66, 84, 91
landscape orientation 31, 34
layout 180, 181, 336
learning 310, 356
left alignment 27
legislation 323–7
leisure time 313
length check 237, 253
letters, business 5
licences, software 326
limitations of development 199
lists 10, 29, 280, 349
location 312–14